"In this careful presentation of the evidence for early Christian attitudes and practices surrounding war and military service, George Kalantzis questions the notions that objections to military service were narrowly religious in a modern sense, or that nonviolence was the minority opinion of the church's intellectual elite. . . . Kalantzis makes no claims about the relevance of the ancient Christian understanding for modern believers, but the challenge to the contemporary church should be obvious."

—L. EDWARD PHILLIPS

Associate Professor of Worship and Liturgical Theology, Emory University

CAESAR
AND THE LAMB

CAESAR
AND THE LAMB

Early Christian Attitudes
on War and Military Service

GEORGE KALANTZIS

CASCADE *Books* · Eugene, Oregon

CAESAR AND THE LAMB
Early Christian Attitudes on War and Military Service

Cascade Books
An Imprint of Wipf and Stock Publishers
199 W. 8th Ave., Suite 3
Eugene, OR 97401

www.wipfandstock.com

ISBN 13: 978-1-60899-253-9

Portions of Tertullian, *The Crown* and *To Scapula* from Maurice Wiles and Mark Santer (eds.), *Documents in Early Christian Thought* (Cambridge: Cambridge University Press, 1975). Reprinted with the permission of Cambridge University Press.

The Acts of the Christian Martyrs. Translated by Herbert Musurillo (2000) pp. 241, 243, 254, 247, 249, 251, 253, 255, 261, 263, 265, 277, & 279. By permission of Oxford University Press.

Cataloging-in-Publication data:

Kalantzis, George

    Caesar and the lamb : early christian attitudes on war and military service. / George Kalantzis

    xviii + 230 p. ; 23 cm. —Includes bibliographical references and indexes.

    ISBN 13: 978-1-60899-253-9

    1. War—Religious aspects—Early church, ca. 30–600 2. War—Religious aspects—Christianity—History. I. Title.

BR195 W3 K25 2012

Manufactured in the U.S.A.

To

Apostolos and Kendall, Joy, and Polly

Μακάριοι οἱ εἰρηνοποιοί,

ὅτι αὐτοὶ υἱοὶ Θεοῦ κληθήσονται

Contents

Acknowledgments

THIS BOOK CAME INTO being with the help of many friends, colleagues, and students who insisted it needs to be written. Throughout our many years together, D. Stephen Long, L. Edward Phillips, and Brent Waters have forced me to think carefully about the concepts of Christian involvement in the military and in the affairs of the State that had formed my understanding of the Church growing up in Greece. They have been my foremost teachers in peace and reconciliation, and I thank the "horsemen of the Apocalypse" deeply.

It was during an annual meeting of the *Ekklesia Project* that Jim Tedrick invited me to write this book with Wipf & Stock. With Chris Spinks, Jim has provided continuous encouragement and careful editorial work, and I am grateful for their support.

Even before I started teaching at Wheaton College, a small group of bright and curious students drove up to Evanston, where I was teaching at the time, and invited me to start meeting with them every week for breakfast so that we might explore together the concept of intentional community. I owe a debt of gratitude to all the remarkable undergraduate students who came to the "Breakfast Group" at the ungodly hour of 7:45am every week for the past five years. They are not shy about asking hard questions—and they do not accept easy answers. But most of all, they yearn to live out the life of Christ. Elizabeth Dias, Adam Joyce, Tiffany Thomson, Carrie Díaz-Littauer, and Hayley Darden, started it all.

Wheaton College has been an encouraging community where honest and profitable dialogue has been at the center of our life together. Paul Robinson and the Human Needs and Global Resources (HNGR) community welcomed me from the very beginning. As did Sharron Coolidge and Norm Ewert who, for over thirty years, have borne faithful witness through the "Mennonite meals" at their home every Thursday evening. Countless students have received hope, encouragement, and a vision for peace and reconciliation through these two ministries.

Wheaton College also supported me with a sabbatical leave during which the bulk of this book was written. Elizabeth Eichling and Annika Turner provided invaluable assistance by collecting and organizing primary sources. Mark Lattimore read carefully over early stages of the manuscript and Laura Gerlicher Manzer labored over the index. C. S. Lewis insisted that friendship is born at the moment when one person says to another: "What! You too? I thought I was the only one." My colleagues, Keith Johnson, Matthew Milliner, Meredith Riedel, John Walford, and Jeff Greenman remind me of the joy of teaching. Becky Eggimann, Larycia Hawkins, and Heather Whitney invited me to a writing group where we read each other's work in a multidisciplinary fashion. This book would not have been the same without their careful input—they also did not allow me (with one exception) to have Latin in the titles of the chapters.

My wife, Irene, has suffered through countless iterations of the arguments in this book with patience and grace. She has been a constant companion in our journey together. It is to our children, Apostolos, Joy, and Polly, and our daughter-in-law, Kendall, who are truly living the way of peace-making every day of their lives, that this book is dedicated.

Soli Deo Gloria
G. K.
Feast of the Ascension 2012

Abbreviations

Acts of the Christian Martyrs

M. Agape	*Martyrdom of Agape, Irene, Chione, and Companions*
M. Carpus	*Martyrdom of Carpus*
M. Conon	*Martyrdom of Conon*
M. Crispina	*Martyrdom of Crispina*
M. Das.	*Martyrdom of Dasius*
M. Fel.	*Martyrdom of Felix the Bishop*
M. Fruc.	*Martyrdom of Fructuosus*
M. Irenaeus	*Martyrdom of Irenaeus, Bishop of Sirmium*
M. Jul.	*Martyrdom of Julius*
M. Justin	*Martyrdom of Justin*
M. Marc.	*Martyrdom of Marcellus*
M. Marinus	*Martyrdom of Marinus*
M. Max.	*Martyrdom of Maximilian*
M. Perp.	*Martyrdom of Perpetua and Felicitas*
M. Phileas	*Martyrdom of Phileas*
M. Polycarp	*Martyrdom of Polycarp*
Pass. Scil.	*Passio Sanctorum Scillitanorum*

ANF　　　*Ante-Nicene Fathers: The Writings of the Fathers down to A.D. 325. 10 vols. Edited by Alexander Roberts, James Donaldson, A. Cleveland Cox, and Allan Menzies. Buffalo: Christian Literature, 1885–96. Reprint, Peabody, MA: Hendrickson, 1994.*

Aristotle

Eth. nic.	*Ethica nichomachea (Nichmachean Ethics)*

Arnobius of Sicca

Nat.   *Adversus nationes libri VII (Seven Books against the Pagans)*

Athenagoras

Leg.   *Legatio pro Christianis (Plea on behalf of the Christians)*

Augustine

Civ.   *De civitate Dei (The City of God)*

Aulus Gellius

Noct. att.   *Noctes atticae (Attic Nights)*
1–2 Clem.   *1–2 Clement*

CIL   *Corpus inscriptionum latinarum*

Clement of Alexandria

Paed.   *Paedagogus (Christ the Educator)*
Protr.   *Protrepticus (Exhortation to the Greeks)*
Strom.   *Stromata (Miscellanies)*

Cyprian

Demetr.   *Ad Demetrianum*
Don.   *Ad Donatum (To Donatus)*
Laps.   *De lapsis (The Lapsed)*
Mort.   *De mortalitate (Mortality)*
Pat.   *De bono patientiae (The Advantage of Patience)*
Test.   *Ad Quirinium testimonia adversus Judaeos (To Quirinius: Testimonies against the Jews)*

Dio Cassius

Hist. Rom.   *Historia Romana (Roman History)*

Diogn.   *Epistle to Diognetus*

Eusebius

Hist. eccl.   *Historia ecclesiastica (Ecclesiastical History)*

Hippolytus

Comm. Dan.   *Commentarium in Danielum*

Ignatius

| Ign. *Pol.* | Ignatius, *To Polycarp* |
| Ign. *Rom.* | Ignatius, *To the Romans* |

ILS   *Inscriptiones Latinae selectae*

Irenaeus

| *Haer.* | *Adversus haereses (Against Heresies)* |

Jerome

Chron.	*Chronicon Eusebii a Graeco Latine redditum et continuatum*
Ep.	*Epistulae*
Vir. ill.	*De viris illustribus*

Justin

| *1 Apol.* | *Apologia i (First Apology)* |
| *Dial.* | *Dialogus cum Tryphone (Dialogue with Trypho)* |

Lactantius

Epit.	*Epitome divinarum institutionum (Epitome of the Divine Institutes)*
Inst.	*Divinarum institutionum libri VII (The Divine Institutes)*
Mort.	*De mortibus persecutorum (The Death of Persecutors)*

LCL   Loeb Classical Library

Minucius Felix

| *Oct.* | *Octavius* |

Origen

Cels.	*Contra Celsum (Against Celsus)*
Comm. Matt.	*Commentarium in evangelium Matthaei*
Comm. ser. Matt.	*Commentarium series in evangelium Matthaei*
Hom. Jos.	*Homilies on Joshua*
Mart.	*Exhortatio ad martyrium (Exhortation to Martyrdom)*

Philo

| *Spec.* | *De specialibus legibus (On the Special Laws)* |

Pliny the Younger

Ep.	*Epistulae*

Seneca

Ep.	*Epistulae morales*

Suetonius

Aug.	*Divus Augustus*
Dom.	*Domitianus*
Jul.	*Divus Julius*

Tacitus

Agr.	*Agricola*
Ann.	*Annales*

Tatian

Or.	*Oratio ad Graecos (Address to the Greeks)*

Tertullian

Adv. Jud.	*Adversus Judaeos (Against the Jews)*
Apol.	*Apologeticus (Apology)*
Bapt.	*De baptismo (Baptism)*
Carn. Chr.	*De carne Christi (The Flesh of Christ)*
Cor.	*De corona militis (The Crown)*
Fug.	*De fuga in persecutione (Flight in Persecution)*
Idol.	*De idolatria (Idolatry)*
Marc.	*Adversus Marcionem (Against Marcion)*
Pall.	*De pallio (The Pallium)*
Pat.	*De patientia (Patience)*
Praescr.	*De praescriptione haerticorum (Prescription against Heretics)*
Prax.	*Adversus Praxean (Against Praxeas)*
Res.	*De resurrectione carnis (The Resurrection of the Flesh)*
Scap.	*Ad Scapulam (To Scapula)*
Spect.	*De spectaculis (The Shows)*

ONE

A Witness to the Nations: The Power of Narratives

Christianity is not one of the great things of history; it is history which is one of the great things of Christianity.

—Henri de Lubac, *Paradoxes of Faith*

Good history is irreducibly a moral affair.

—Rowan Williams, *Why Study the Past?*

WHY THIS BOOK?

History is the stories we tell of our common past. Through stories we make sense of the world and gain a better understanding of who we are. As such, narratives are character formative: they help us define ourselves. The hearing and telling of stories, therefore, "is itself a way of answering questions about what we're really talking about."[1]

The idea behind this book is to focus on the attitudes of the earliest Christians on war and military service and tell the story of the struggle of the earliest Church, the communities of Christ at the margins of power and society, to bear witness to the nations that enveloped them as they transformed the dominant narratives of citizenship and loyalty, freedom, power, and control.

Even though this book examines the available patristic writings on war and military service in the first three centuries of the Christian

---

1. Williams, *Why Study the Past?*, 30.

1

Church in an organized manner, the ways earliest Christians thought of themselves and the state are not presented here through the lens of antiquarian curiosity. Following Rowan Williams's advice, my aim is to see if we can recognize in their worries concerns that are still worth worrying about. For I am convinced that "if we do find such recognition, we shall have found something of a common identity."[2] Together with the reader, then, I want to think our way into the world into which Christianity arose and ask questions of the past that may help us understand the genotype of the Christian faith with the hope that such an enterprise will also help us evaluate its expression in our own time.

We must expect to be surprised by the past; but we must also expect to be questioned by it, for it is *our* past. As Christians we claim that because of Jesus Christ, the familiar world has been broken apart and made new. We claim to stand in historical continuity with the work of God through time and space; we claim that the reality of the earliest Christians is both different from us *and* part of us. Rowan Williams insists that, "good history is irreducibly a moral affair . . . At the very least in persuading us to put some distance between ourselves and ourselves, between our imagination and what we habitually take for granted."[3] Williams concludes:

> For the Christian involved in church history, the sense of recognition, of anxieties in common, becomes a reinforcement of belief in the Church itself as a society whose roots are in something more than historical process as usually understood . . . As Christian students, . . . we shall always be haunted by [the question]: to what call is all this a response—faithful, unfaithful, uncomprehending, transfiguring? Can we acknowledge it as our call too? And more to the point, can we see that our immersion in the ways in which *they* responded becomes part of the way we actually hear the call ourselves in more and more diverse and more and more complete ways.[4]

My goal, therefore, is as much theological as it is historical. I aim to read the history of the earliest Church in a way that is theologically sensitive while still doing good history at the same time: for good theology does not come from bad history.

2. Ibid., 30.

3. Ibid., 24–25.

4. Ibid., 30–31.

So, how do we do good history? How are we to engage the arguments, lives, passions, questions, practices, and witness of people who are so different than us? In answering these questions we are bound to make judgments. David Bentley Hart tells us how not to do it. Hart begins his essay, "The Mirror of the Infinite: Gregory of Nyssa on the *Vestigia Trinitatis*," by reminding us that for the most part, "in our weaker moments, [we] prefer synopsis to precision [and] find in it a convenient implement for arranging our accounts of . . . history into simple taxonomies, under tidily discrete divisions."[5] That is not history at its best.

Doing history well means that we pay particular attention to differences between what Justo González calls the "innocent readings" of history and "responsible remembrance."[6] Innocent readings of history are a selective forgetfulness, a heuristic devise for our own agendas and power struggles. Responsible remembrance, on the other hand, sets us free from "the crippling imprisonment of what we can grasp and take for granted, the ultimate trivialising of our identity."[7] Responsible remembrance leads to responsible action.

Doing history well means that we are willing to engage the strangeness of the past, its language and customs that are unfamiliar to us, and neither see in it the present in fancy dress nor dismiss it as a wholly "foreign country," incomprehensible and distant, shrouded in savagery or ignorance. To do history well we have to find a balance between difference and continuity. As we look at the world of the Christians of the first three centuries we recognize that that world is not obvious to us, their concerns do not seem native to the world we think we inhabit. For the most part, we do not face the beasts of the arena, or the magistrate's knock at the door of our churches demanding the surrender of our sacred books and objects, on penalty of death. Can their concerns be ours?

A SCHOLARLY CONSENSUS?

The literature on the topic of early Christian attitudes on war and military service is vast and scholarly discussions have undergone polyvalent shifts

---

5. Hart, "The Mirror of the Infinite," 541.

6. González, *Mañana*, 79.

7. Williams, *Why Study the Past?*, 24.

in the span of the last century.[8] A decade apart, David Hunter[9] and Alan Kreider[10] have provided excellent summaries of these shifts in the scholarly consensus and have shown that for the most part of the twentieth century, beginning with Adolf Harnack's *Militia Christi*, first published in German in 1905 (an English translation was published in 1981),[11] Cecil John Cadoux's *Early Christian Attitudes to War* (1919),[12] and Jean-Michel Hornus's *It is Not Lawful for Me to Fight* (first published in French in 1960),[13] a broad consensus was formed around a tripartite agreement. The first part was that the earliest Christians renounced war and military service out of an aversion to bloodshed; second, by the end of the second century (and certainly by the end of the third), the increased militarism of the Roman state, the numerous inducements for enlistment, and active recruitment from the more Christianized eastern frontiers, meant that some Christians began to find military service an acceptable option, despite the teaching of Christian writers. The third point of consensus was that by the end of the fourth century, in the Constantinian era, "'a just war ethic' had developed (largely the work of Ambrose and Augustine), which met the need for a Christian accommodation to a changed political and social situation."[14] Harnack's *Militia Christi* has been at the core of this consensus. In his work Harnack suggests that the church of the first three centuries objected to the military profession because of

8. In 1988, Peter Brock produced a somewhat comprehensive bibliography, listing 111 books, articles, and chapters in books (Brock, *The Military Question in the Early Church*). Since then there have been numerous more essays and quite a few books on the topic.

9. Hunter, "A Decade of Research," 87–94; idem, "The Christian Church and the Roman Army in the First Three Centuries," 161–81.

10. Kreider, "Military Service in the Church Orders," 415–17.

11. Harnack, *Militia Christi*.

12. Cadoux, *Early Christian Attitudes to War*.

13. Hornus, *It Is Not Lawful for Me to Fight*. To these, one has to add MacGregor, *The New Testament Basis of Pacifism*; Harnack, *Die Mission und Ausbreitung des Christentums in den ersten drei Jahrhunderten*; Minn, "Tertullian and War"; Ryan, "The Rejection of Military Service by the Early Christians"; van Campenhausen, "Der Kriegsdienst der Christen in der Kirche des Altertums"; idem, *Tradition and Life in the Church*; Karpp, "Die Stellung der Alten Kirche zu Kriegsdienst und Krieg"; Bainton, "The Early Church and War"; idem, *Christian Attitudes Toward War and Peace*; and Daly, "The New Testament: Pacifism and Non-Violence." As well see the voluminous work of John Howard Yoder, including, the posthumous *Christian Attitudes to War, Peace, and Revolution*; *The War of the Lamb*; and *The Politics of Jesus*.

14. Hunter, "Decade of Research," 87.

an inherent rejection of war and killing, the idolatrous practices of the army (including the worship of the emperor, the cult of the military standards, and the religious character of the military oath, the *sacramentum*), and a weariness of the moral behavior of soldiers.[15] Among the other writers, some argue that the Church abandoned its pacifist roots in the fourth century during the detrimental and long-lasting compromise of the "Constantinian shift" (e.g., Bainton, Cadoux, Hornus, Yoder), while others saw this as a necessary, even positive, adaptation to the developing conditions of an expanding Church: an ecclesiastical realism of short (e.g., Moffatt, Campenhausen).

The most serious challenge to the first point of this consensus has come from the work of John Helgeland, who, in a series of publications, argues that the true locus of the Christian objections to military service were the religious nature and idolatrous practices of the Roman army and not ethical concerns or repudiation of killing.[16] Helgeland challenges what he calls the "pacifist domination of English-speaking scholarship on the subject" and warns against "overly broad and uncritical pacifist assumptions" that "often serve, ironically, to discredit pacifism and nonviolence and weaken the cause of peace." Helgeland insists that his ultimate goal is "to serve the cause of peace by freeing the Christian ideal of pacifism and nonviolence from the weight of misread history and faulty reasoning that, in the long run, will only serve to discredit it."[17]

James Turner Johnson, on the other hand, argues for the contingent effect of the imminent eschatology and millennial theology of the primitive Church as the dominant causes for its pacifist stance during its earliest period.[18] As the apocalyptic outlook of the passing generations of Christians matured, however, what Johnson calls "the sectarian relationship with the word" changed with it, resulting in a synthesis and a "positive moral acceptance of participation in affairs of the state, including military service and war."[19] The work of Louis J. Swift must

---

15. See especially chapter 2, "The Christian Religion and the Military Profession."

16. Helgeland, "Christians and the Roman Army A.D. 173–337"; idem, "Roman Army Religion"; idem, "Christians and the Roman Army from Marcus Aurelius to Constantine"; idem, "The Early Church and War." Also, Helgeland, Daly, and Burns, *Christians and the Military*.

17. Helgeland, Daly, and Burns, *Christians and the Military*, 1–2.

18. Johnson, *The Quest for Peace*.

19. Ibid., 17.

be noted as providing a *via media* in what must seem to many to be a discussion in unrelenting flux between the so-called pacifist and non-pacifist readings of the evidence.[20] Swift argues that "in the period before Constantine . . . both pacifist and non-pacifist positions existed side by side and . . . neither was able to supplant the other."[21] Swift concludes that that situation did not change in the fourth century. Rather than a reversal, the change that occurred with Constantine was "a major shift" made possible by the ambiguities Swift sees in the earlier evidence, on the one hand, and "the altered political circumstances in which Christians now found themselves," on the other.[22]

David Hunter has suggested that a "new consensus" emerges from the evidence that takes into account both the pacifist and non-pacifist positions. First, because early Christians were as repelled by the idolatry of the Roman State as much as they were by killing, if not more so, the most vocal early Christian opponents of military service based their objections as much upon their "abhorrence of Roman army religion" as their rejection of shedding blood. Second, by the end of the second century there is evidence that the practices of some Christians diverged from the theological principles of the writers of the Church (a trend that grew throughout the third century). The third point of consensus Hunter identifies is that, "the efforts of Christians to justify participation in warfare for a 'just' cause (most notably that of Augustine) stand in fundamental continuity with at least one strand of pre-Constantinian tradition."[23] To these, Alan Kreider added a fourth assertion, namely, regional variation: "attitudes and practices probably varied according to geographical location. Antimilitarist sentiment was strongest among Christians in the imperial heartlands and weakest on the borders."[24]

NOT A TIDY AND EDIFYING STORY

In this book I do not argue that these narratives are completely false or wrong. Rather, I argue that if history is the stories we tell of our

20. Swift, "St. Ambrose on Violence and War"; idem, "Augustine on War and Killing"; idem, "War and the Christian Conscience I"; idem, *Early Fathers*; idem, "Search the Scriptures"; and idem, "Early Christian Views."

21. Swift, *Early Fathers*, 79.

22. Ibid., 29.

23. Hunter, "Decade of Research," 93.

24. Kreider, "Military Service," 417.

common past, *how* we tell the stories is equally as important as *what* stories we choose to tell. I am grateful for the work of all those who have written and clarified many of the ideas about which we try to find consensus. However, even though some recent scholarship accepts as axiomatic that there was ambivalence among the earliest Christians, as we will see in chapter 3—usually pointing to the discrepancies between Christian theology and practice—I do not believe that such a conclusion is borne by the literary evidence. The discussions on the topic at hand cannot be indefinitely negotiable. Against certain aspects of the so-called "new consensus," I argue that the literary evidence confirms the very strong internal coherence of the Church's non-violent stance for the first three centuries.

I have tried to show that in order to understand the fullness of the arguments of the earliest Christians against war and service in the legions of the empire we need to understand their socioreligious context, as well as the power narratives of their time. To do so, we have to begin at the beginning: to place the Church within the narratives of Rome, the omnipresence of the gods, the power of Caesar, the cultic structures that arranged the cosmos, the public religion that demanded obeisance and sacrifice. We need to speak of the theater and performativity, so as to understand the power of martyrdom—the new world order that turned centuries-old social locutions upside down and coopted the power of the powerful on the scarred and mutilated bodies of the socially powerless. What emerges is a new call to non-violence, unrecognizable by the culture around them, for it took the form of civil disobedience as the mark of a transnational community bound together with the bonds of baptism. A community that honored Caesar by disobeying his commands and receiving upon their bodies the only response a state based on the power of the powerful could met—in imitation of Christ.

Only then are we able to evaluate the oppositions of the earliest Christians to war, and killing, and of serving in the armies of Caesar from within their own social location and ask questions of theology and practice. When we do that, we see that there is no polyglossia among the Christian writers. With remarkable univocity they speak of participation in the Christian mysteries as antithetical to killing, and the practices of the army, whether in wartime or peacetime. The dominical command to love one's enemies and pray for one's persecutors is a common thread woven throughout these documents. Greek and Latin writers alike speak of this uniqueness of the Christian communities.

What then of those we know to have served in the Roman army? The historical record is quite clear that when the antithesis between what Christians said they believed and what they practiced was pointed out—usually by the state—when a choice between loyalty to emperor and Christ was demanded, when the state did not turn a coopting blind eye to Christians among its ranks, the consequences for the Christians were grave.

I have written this book with the general reader in mind, and though much of what I say will be familiar to scholars in the field, I hope students of Christian history and theology will also benefit from a fresh look at the evidence. In this book I have steered way from making connections to our own times, for this book is not an exercise in retrieval and appropriation. Rather, I invite the reader to listen to the story; to engage the narratives of the earliest Christians first within their own cultural context, resisting the temptation of trying to make a tidy and edifying story that excises the complexities of lives lived in space and time. These are not the stories of naïve and idealistic bishops and academic philosophers blind to the affairs of the world. Every one of the writers we encounter in the documents collected at the end of the book had experienced the cruelty of war and persecution. Justin's sobriquet is *Martyr*. Origen and Tertullian had witnessed the cruelty of the Septimian persecutions, the imprisonment, torture, and execution of family members and fellow Christians. Irenaeus was a presbyter of the church in Lyon when members of his own congregation were condemned *ad bestias*. Cyprian was beheaded. They understood that wars were inevitable and that social order may necessitate violence on the part of the magistracy, but they also understood that what is asked of soldiers is to kill, and even though the camp may not turn (young) men into killers, "it removes the societal restrains on the savage part of us."[25] That was not an option for the Christian.

At the core of the Christian message is love. This is not an ordinary kind of love, as one has for one's kin. It is God's love for God's enemies. It is this love of God for the world, expressed in the divine self-giving through the incarnation of the Son that reconciles God's enemies with the Triune God, Father, Son, and Holy Spirit.[26]

25. Marlantes, *What It Is Like to Go To War*, 12.
26. Cf. John 3:16; John 1:14; Rom 5:10.

The result of that reconciliation is peace: God's peace. A peace unlike any other. A peace, the world cannot recognize. A peace not based simply on the absence of conflict, but on the proactive love of one's enemies as a first principle for the community that claims to have been born of this Gospel of Peace.[27]

Christians in every generation yearn to be found faithful to Christ's call to discipleship; to bear witness to the life-giving grace of God; to speak of God faithfully and truthfully through worship and practice as much as through all they think and write, through life, that is, as well as intellection. Throughout the writings of early Christians, the twin commandments to not kill and to love one's enemies were not simple gnomic sayings but formed a commanding moral topography.[28]

Early in the third century, Tertullian, presented this Christian distinctive of love of enemy and persecutor as unique among all peoples and as a sign of divine grace: "Here lies the perfection and distinctiveness of Christian goodness," Tertullian declared, "ordinary goodness is different; for all men love their friends but only Christians love their enemies" (*To Scapula* 1.4).

---

27. Cf. John 14:27; Matt 5:43–44; Eph 6:15.
28. Exod 20:13; Mark 10:19.

TWO

Ab Urbe Condita:
Narratives of Power

Be with me, as I found my City,
Jupiter, Father Mavors, and Mother Vesta:
And all you gods, whom piety summons, take note.
Let my work be done beneath your auspices.
May it last long, and rule a conquered world,
All subject, from the rising to the setting day.[1]

—Romulus

The temple of Vesta was at the center of Rome. It was the rhetorical center of the world and, unlike the temples of the other deities, the *Aedes Vestae* was round and domed because "Vesta is the same as earth; perpetual fire constitutes them both; earth and the hearth both stand for her dwelling place."[2] This link between heaven and earth, private and public, was at the core of *Romanitas*, Roman identity, and religion was intimately connected to the idea of "sacred space."

It is for this reason that our account of the relationship between this nascent community of the Way, the *Ekklesia*, and the empire within which it grew has to begin with an exploration of the dominant religio-political themes of *sacrifice*, *power*, and *social order* that saturated the

---

1. Ovid, *Fasti* 4.826–31. The English translation of Ovid's *Fasti* is by A. S. Kline and it is found on the website, *Poetry in Translation*, 2004 (http://www.poetryintranslation .com/PITBR/Latin/OvidFastiBkOne.htm). The Latin text is on the website, *The Latin Library* (http://www.thelatinlibrary.com/ovid/ovid.fasti1.shtml).

2. Ovid, *Fasti* 6.267.

very air it breathed and the soil in which it set roots. In doing so, we will be able to have a more fully-orbed understanding of the early Christian prescriptions against war and military service. For early Christians, the twin commandments to not kill (Exod 20:13; Mark 10:19) and to love one's enemies (Matt 5:43–44) were often treated within the very context of prescriptions against idolatry and the relationship between Caesar and Christ. Most often, Christian writers began with the demands of the gods of the Empire for obedience, sacrifice, and blood, and showed how and why Christians could not participate in such models of being and worship. Christians were to act out of the abiding conviction of the power and hope of the resurrection of Jesus. Canonical and extra-canonical writers alike insisted that Christianity was not simply a matter of ritual or ethical behavior, but as Averil Cameron puts it, Christianity "was always a matter of teaching, of interpretation, of definition. As Christ 'was' the Word, so Christianity *was* its discourse or discourses."[3] Christianity's relationship with the Roman culture that enveloped it was, at the end, such a competing discourse, one that arises from the everyday lives of peoples and their traditions.

It is in our perception of the sacred character of space and time, these most fundamental elements of everyday life, that the disjoint between our time and that of the early Church puts us at a disadvantage. We scarcely question why one should not desecrate cemeteries, or temples, or churches, or not pillage monasteries or libraries, or fight on Good Friday. In the words of John Howard Yoder: "The notion of the holy being represented within our world by certain days, places, and people, exempt from the ravages of violence even in a violent world is far from us. We have trouble understanding holiness in place or time. We lack the training in cultural anthropology and the imagination to grasp how minds work when certain places and certain days are so holy that people will not fight there or then. For [ancient and] medieval culture this holiness was important and effective."[4]

Engaging in this cultural anthropology of imagination opens up for us the force of the argument of the early Christian writers on the relationship of the Church to the State and its instruments of domination, namely war and the armies, and allows us to recognize that the

3. Cameron, *Christianity and the Rhetoric of Empire*, 32, emphasis original. Also, Robert Louis Wilken, *Spirit of Early Christian Thought*.

4. Yoder, *Christian Attitudes to War*, 120.

conflict between Rome and the Church was ultimately a collision of sacrificial discourses. The Scriptures, especially the New Testament, abound with these competing discourses and the very sacraments by which one is united with the Church and is identified with it (expressed even in the earliest forms of baptism and the Eucharist) were from the beginning imbued with a rhetoric of sacrifice that competed with that of Rome.[5] The Christian idea of the βασιλεία τοῦ θεοῦ (basileia tou theou), the "kingdom of God," inaugurated in Luke 4:19 and given structure in the Sermon on the Mount (Matt 4:23—7:20; especially 6:9–13) could not but be seen as a threat to the "kingdom of Caesar," and the peace which Christ bequeathed the disciples (John 14:27) threatened the *pax deorum* that guaranteed Rome's eternal place. It is for this reason that the weight early Christian writers such as Tertullian and Origen placed on the prohibitions against idolatry cannot be reduced to the anachronistic category of private piety, or to personal acts of worship, or even to the periphery of proper religious behavior and be dismissed simply under the heading of "warnings against idolatry."[6] On the contrary, all these prescriptions against idolatry carry within them the full force of the "public transcript" of sacrifice as formative of both communal and personal identity. Otherwise, one might conceive early Christian understandings of its relationship to the State and its wars and military as a paradox of extremes, oscillating between submission to Caesar and a rejection of all temporal authorities.

ETERNAL ROME AND THE PEACE OF THE GODS

The Roman world was a bloody world. Unforgiving.[7] After two centuries of expansionism and civil strife, the celebrated *pax Romana* was achieved

5. Among numerous reference in the New Testament see, for example, Matt 20:28; 26:22–25; Luke 22:17–20; John 3:16–18; Rom 6:3–5; 1 Cor 10:16; 11:23–26; Heb 9:11–14; 1 John 2:2; Rev 13:8.

6. As John Helgeland (with Daly and Burns) does in *Christians and the Military*, and again in "The Early Church and War," 34–47. Though paying a more nuanced attention to the role and influence of sacrifice, Peter J. Leithart comes to a similar conclusion in *Defending Constantine*. We are going to address both these writers and their conclusions in the next chapter.

7. Dio Cassius recounts that 9,000 wild animals were slaughtered during the one hundred days of inaugural festivities for the Colosseum in 81 CE and, on average, 5,000 gladiators died there each year. To celebrate his victories in Dacia in 107 CE, emperor Trajan funded contests involving 11,000 animals and 10,000 gladiators over the course

at the point of the *gladius* and was protected by Rome's twenty-eight legions and the gods who superintended it.[8] By the time of Constantine, in the fourth century, the massive military apparatus had greatly surpassed the Augustan ideals of the early Empire and expanded to over half-a-million troops (and almost an equal number of auxiliaries).[9]

Unlike us who accept too easily the secularity of the State, in the religious demography of the Roman world into which the early Church was birthed, such a concept did not exist. The concerns of ancient peoples were differently ordered, and as with all others, for the Romans, too, "political order was not a question, as it has become for us following the

---

of 123 days reenacting the glories of the campaigns. As most major cities of the vast empire wanted to emulate the entertainment of Rome, the sands of the arenas became the new altars of civic sacrifices. One need not limit one's imagination to the bloodthirsty spectacles of the arena and tales of literary imagination, though neither was peripheral to the Roman psyche, for the ordinary elements of life were also bounded by the same realities of death. Christian Laes, in *Children in the Roman Empire* shows clearly that: "Between 30–35% of newborns did not survive past the first month and less than 50% reached age 15. As such, parents had to grapple with death regularly. Even amid high infant mortality, Rome remained a society that bustled with children and teens. The average woman had between four and six children. Thus siblings were common, especially since remarriage was a regular occurrence. In regard to the familial unit, few knew their grandparents, and by age 20, fewer than half had a father. Mothers were a more long-lasting figure in children's lives, as they were often many years younger than their spouses. In terms of housing, most lived in the countryside amid relative poverty, and without the modern idea of the 'privacy of the nuclear family' (34). In the city of Rome, children would have dealt with overpopulation, violence, and malnutrition. All these factors had an effect on children's psyches, though it is often difficult to decipher the true experiences of non-elite Roman children due to the complete lack of child narratives and a literary bias towards the elite" (Bond, review of *Children in the Roman Empire*).

8. Dio Cassius, *Hist. Rom.* 55.23–24. Tacitus, *Annals* 4.5, notes that of the approximately 300,000 standing army of the imperial period, about half of them were legionaries and half auxiliaries, most recruited voluntarily and all serving for 20–25 years. Soon after the Roman civil war of the first century BCE and the Augustan reorganization, the Roman army was professionalized and established as a permanent force, unlike the citizen armies of the Republic. Soldiers received a stable salary (through the *aerarium militare*, the military treasury) and, those who served the length of their 25 year commitment, received a cash bonus on discharge equivalent to 13 years' pay. Whether auxiliaries also received such a retirement bonus is uncertain, but from the time of Claudius (41–54 CE) they received Roman citizenship upon discharge.

9. Born Gaius Octavius Thurinus (63 BCE–14 CE), the first emperor of Rome changed his name to Gaius Julius Caesar after the assassination of his great-uncle Gaius Julius Caesar, who adopted him as a son in 44 BCE. In 27 BCE, when Octavian (a variant of Octavius) consolidated his power following a brutal civil war, the Senate bestowed upon him the honorific *Augustus* ("revered one," or *Sebastos*, in Greek) on 16 January 27 BCE. Since then, he was known as Gaius Julius Caesar Augustus.

Eighteenth-century Enlightenment, of the functioning of a depersonalized machinery of government from which any final divine purpose or end is excluded. Rather, political order consisted in the exercise of legitimate authority within a space that had been sacralized, and therefore under the control of the gods, who willed order and therefore peace (*pax*)."[10] During the Augustan reforms and the years that followed, the *imperial cult* became the locus of expression for that political order.

Rome's first emperor ascended to power at the conclusion of the civil wars of the 40s BCE.[11] Throughout his reign, Octavius was careful to keep the appearance of the coveted Republican ideals of virtue and simplicity, expressed in personal and political humility, and adherence to the common good. He knew full well that the future of the empire rested on the emperor's ability to maintain the delicate balance between the (decreasing) influence of the Senate and the ever increasing might of the Roman military he alone commanded. Since early in his reign, Octavius embraced the title of *Augustus* and surrounded his reign with symbols of rebirth and renewal, cultivating an intensely religiopolitical identity that conformed to the deep religious sentiments of the Roman people.[12] The

10. Brent, *Cyprian and Roman Carthage*, 29.

11. The history of ancient Rome, as the Romans told it, can be roughly divided into three periods: the first, the period of the Kings, lasted from the legendary founding of the City (*ab urbe condita*) by Romulus on 21 April 753 BCE (the date from which the Roman calendar calculated time) until the overthrow of King Lucius Tarquinius Superbus ca. 509/8 BCE. The period of the Kings was followed by the Republican period during which Rome was governed by two consuls who were elected annually by the senate. This period stood in the minds of Romans as the golden age of Roman democracy, and the standard to which most subsequent generations paid homage—at least rhetorically. The Republican period transitioned into the Empire during a period of about forty years that begun with the turbulent civic strife of the early first century BCE, the appointment of Julius Caesar as sole *dictator* in 49 BCE, his assassination in 44 BCE, followed by another decade of civil war that eventuated in the victory of Octavius over Mark Antony in 31 BCE and Octavius's consolidation of power in 27 BCE. The period of the Roman Empire lasted well into Late Antiquity. The last Roman emperor, Romulus Augustus was deposed by the Goths in 476 CE. History is not without a sense of irony.

12. In *The Life of Augustus*, the Roman historian Suetonius notes how deeply Augustus drank from the well of religious piety and advanced his special relationship with the gods as their anointed. Augustus's horoscope, Suetonius tells us, predicted his glorious career and his favored relationship with the gods: "During his stay in Apollonia, he [Augustus] climbed up to the observatory of the astrologer Theogenes in the company of Agrippa. When a great and nearly unbelievable future was predicated to Agrippa, who asked first, Augustus persisted in not telling the hour of his birth and not wishing

family of Augustus's adoptive father, Julius Caesar, claimed descent from the goddess Venus and Caesar himself was thought to have ascended to the heavens upon his assassination in 44 BCE. Declared a *diuus* ("a god") by the Roman people, Caesar's *apotheosis* meant that Augustus too, a scion of the same Julian heritage, would not only receive equal honor upon his death, but that, even though he declined to be worshiped as a god during his lifetime, he could claim title of *diui filius*, "son of the divine one," a title he used often in his ubiquitous imperial iconography.[13]

A deeply religious and traditional people, the Romans turned to Augustus to restore the *mores maiorum*, the customs and ideals of the ancestors, the unwritten code from which the Romans derived their societal norms and which were seen to have been jeopardized during the years of civil strife. On 30 January 9 BCE, the *Ara Pacis Augustae* ("Altar of Augustan Peace") was consecrated by the Senate and the people of Rome to celebrate the peace Augustus had restored: the *Pax Augusta* was the civil manifestation of the *Pax Deorum*, the "Peace of the gods." With the help of the gods and the Senate, Augustus exceeded everyone's dreams. During his rule Rome became the greatest empire the world had ever seen.

Roman religiosity and cultic identity was neither a novelty of the first century BCE nor an innovation of the Julio-Claudians.[14] Even from

---

to disclose it, out of fear and shame that it might be found to be less significant. When, after much encouragement, he had just about hesitantly disclosed it, Theogenes jumped up and threw himself at his feet. As a result, Augustus had such trust in his fate that he published his horoscope and struck a silver coin with the sign of the constellation Capricorn, under which he was born (Suetonius, *Aug.* 94.12; also, Dio Cassius, *Hist. Rom.* 56.25.5; in Volk, *Manilius*, 132). If the stars revealed the will of the gods, and if the gods had ordained him to rule the universe, Augustus was simply fulfilling an unalterable fate, opposition to which would be futile from the start.

13. The Romans understood various gradations of "divinity" and made a somewhat consistent distinction between *diuus* (divine) and *deus* (god), that is lost in English translation. While the emperor was recognized as *diuus* (a/the "divine one") and their sons as *diui filii* ("sons of the divine"), their divine status was conferred upon them by the Senate by means of the proper offering of sacrifice and correct ritual—it was not an ontological category. *Deus* ("god"), on the other hand, was a title reserved primarily for the Olympians and their equals. Latin-speaking Christians used the title *Dei Filius* ("Son of God") for Jesus. For more details see Beard, North, and Price, *Religions of Rome*.

14. This was the family name of Julius Caesar and Augustus and indicates collectively his successors who belonged to his family. They included Tiberius (14–37 CE), Gaius, better known by his sobriquet *Caligula* (37–41 CE), Claudius (41–54 CE), and Nero (54–68 CE).

its founding narrative, death, sacrifice, and the *cultus*—religion—marked the sacred identity of Rome and sacralized the state, establishing both its physical space and its place in history. Having received a favorable omen from Jupiter, Romulus set out to mark the limits of the city and decreed the penalty of death on anyone who transgressed the *pomerium,* its sacred boundaries. His own brother was the first victim, for, not having received the prescript of the King, in an act of mocking defiance at what seemed to be inadequate defenses, Remus jumped over the newly erected walls. He was killed on the spot. Romulus's response to his brother's action and fate was far more than a proleptic political statement: it defined the very identity of the City he founded down through the ages—"*So dies the enemy who shall cross my walls!*"

Rome was not just a city on the Tiber. Rome was the *maxima rerum,* as Virgil declared, the greatest city in the world; and even in the fifth century, well into the Christian era, the poet Rutilius lauded Rome as the *generis hominum generixque deorum,* the parent of people and gods. Rome was the *axis mundi* and, for the Romans, the very space itself was set apart and confirmed by the gods who rendered it sacred.[15]

LORD AND GOD

Religione est cultu deorum, "religion is a way of honoring the gods," wrote Cicero, referring to the traditional honors paid to the gods by the state.[16] It may seem paradoxical that even though the ancient Romans had such a keen sense of sacred space and sacrifice and built massive temples to the gods, Roman religion was not concerned with distinguishing true from false beliefs: it was simply the proper *behavior* that characterized the life of the Roman citizen. Since Romans did not separate "religion from politics," or localize the gods to their allotted spheres, the ubiquity of local shrines and temples, festivals and sacrifices, votive offerings and oracles created for the world of the empire a narrative discourse in which the sacred and the secular, the political and the religious were infinitely intertwined. Whether domestic or public, religion in Rome "was more correctly understood as an existential category, discerning the proper actions that would ensure the success of the people and the state."[17] And the imperial cult became the paradigmatic expression of that *religio.*

15. Heyman, *Power of Sacrifice,* 2.

16. Cicero, *De natura deorum* 2.8.

17. Heyman, *Power of Sacrifice,* 12.

During the period of Christianity's early existence, the imperial cult was reinterpreted as an overarching symbol of everything that was connected with Roman religion, including the very notion of the State. Sacrifices were performed on behalf of the emperor, not necessarily offered *to* him. The imperial cult functioned as a political identity marker for an expansive empire and focused on the person of the emperor as the vicar of the gods on earth and as the people's representative to the gods, in the locus of the *paterfamilias*. The emperor's very titles of *Augustus Soter Eleutherius* ("Revered, Savior, Liberator") and the subsequent addition of *pater patriae* ("Father of the State") brought together this very Roman idea. The additional claim to the priestly office of *pontifex maximus* ("High Priest") and *augur* ("Interpreter/Diviner") in 12 BCE and the transformation of the concept of imperium itself during the first century BCE "as legitimate power exercised within sacred space, and the ritual means by which it was made sacred"[18] meant that *in his very office* the emperor was responsible for universal order under the auspices of the gods.[19] Struck on coins that advanced the imperial propaganda to the ends of the empire and beyond and engraved on countless monuments that adorned urban centers and small towns, the ubiquity of such imperial titles conferred an undeniable religious identity to the very person of the emperor. By the end of the first century, emperor Domitian (81–96 CE) assumed upon himself not simply the cognomen of *diui filius*, but that of a living god, a *Dominus et deus* ("Lord and god").[20]

Roman rhetoric presented participation in the imperial cult within the framework of civic obligation and the patriotic duty of Roman citizens. The official supplication was interpreted as apotropaic in nature, fulfilling the emperor's religious obligation as *pontifex maximus*, with the expressed aim of securing the *pax deorum* against the impending cosmic crisis, a peace whose reality he alone would have to determine in his capacity also as augur. By the time of Diocletian (284–305 CE) and the dawn of the fourth century, Rome had been transformed from

---

18. Brent, *Cyprian and Roman Carthage*, 55.

19. Oliver, *Morals and Law*, 160–63.

20. Suetonius, *Dom.* 13.1–2: "After he became emperor, . . . with equal arrogance, when he dictated the form of a letter to be used by his procurators, he began it thus: 'Our lord and god commands so and so;' whence it became a rule that no one should style him otherwise either in writing or speaking" (translated by N. S. Gill, available at http://ancienthistory.about.com/od/afemperors/a/102410-Suetonius-The-Life-Of-Domitian.htm).

the Augustan ideal of a *Principate* to a *Dominate*—the absolute rule of a *Dominus*, a god on earth.[21]

DO UT DES: SACRIFICE AS "PUBLIC TRANSCRIPT"

The relationship between the Romans and the gods who had given Rome her expanse in the centuries that followed her mythical founding was always at the core of Roman identity, and sacrifice was at the center of that identity. "Polyvalent at its core, *sacrifice* is so deeply rooted in the human religious consciousness that its association with specific social behaviors as well as a rhetorically constituted history has produced a sense of identity and stability for peoples throughout the ages."[22] Sacrifice was the primary means by which Romans communicated with the gods, discerned their will, established order and balance between the people and the state and between the state and the gods—a balance that would also secure Rome's privileged position. The worship of the gods and the sacrifices offered to them were essential for all aspects of life. The secrets of the future would be read in the entrails of the slaughtered animals. Contracts, decrees, and laws were sealed with sacrifice. Marriages would be blessed and households would become prosperous. Disease and illness would be averted and the daily meal would be rendered safe and a welcomed gift from the gods to whom a sacrificial libation was offered in return. Armies never marched without a favorable divine omen and a reading of the entrails of animals. Nor would the cohorts of the legions neglect to honor their divine guardians before battle or give them thanks afterwards. By the time of the Church, the *pax Romana* could not be separated from the *pax deorum*; and that peace was based on and sustained by sacrifice.

"If the Gods cannot and will not help us," mused Cicero, "if there is nothing on their side that touches our life, what reason have we to devote

---

21. David S. Potter describes this transition from the *Principate* to a *Dominate* in this way: "The style of Government so memorably described by Marcus [Aurelius], whereby the emperor sought to show himself as a model of correct aristocratic deportment, had given way to a style in which the emperor was seen to be distinct from all other mortals" (*Roman Empire at Bay*, 290).

22. Heyman, *Power of Sacrifice*, xv. Heyman provides an excellent treatment of the relationship between the concept of sacrifice and power and the dialectic between the competing sacrificial systems of Christians and Romans. See also Hedley, *Sacrifice Imagined*.

worship [*cultus*], honors [*honores*], and prayers [*preces*] to them?"[23] This was an attitude towards the gods the Romans had inherited from the Greeks and on which they based the *cultus*. For the most part, Greeks and Romans understood three reasons for sacrificing to the gods: (1) to honor them, (2) to express gratitude to them, and (3) to obtain some benefit: "We honor the gods," Theophrastus noted in his work *On Piety*, "either because we try to avert evil things and vouchsafe good things or we have been treated well or just to honor their good disposition."[24] This relationship of *do ut des* ("I give that you may give"), a perpetual cycle of reciprocal exchanges in the form of sacrifices and blessings, underscored the mutual obligations of gods and humans and characterized not only the contractual nature of Roman religion but extended to all forms of life, including social interactions.

The Romans engaged in many and varied forms of sacrifice that infused everyday life with a sense of religiosity and created a connection with the pantheon of deities that framed their identity. The irreducible locus of *Romanitas* was the *gens*, the family, organized around the *paterfamilias* and the *Lares*, the household gods whom the family honored with offerings of incense and grain at the *lararium*, the shrine inside the home. The Roman state itself was dedicated to the Capitoline triad of Jupiter, Mars, and Minerva, and defined the sacred boundaries of Rome by mirroring the familial relationship as a macrocosmic representation of that *gens* with the emperor as its *pater* and high priest, its *pontifex maximus*.[25]

The many and varied forms of both domestic and public sacrifice were also key forms of social discourse. Like most ancient peoples, the Romans used such social discourse to maintain not only their identity but also political and social power. Deriving from *facere* ("to make") and *sacer* ("sacred"), to *sacrifice* is to make an object sacred, to separate it from the category of the ordinary and place it in the family of the valuable, even if by the very act of sacrifice the object may seem to be wasted. In this way, sacrifice confers meaning. The first fruits, the choice calf, the firstborn of the womb are all to be set apart (and often burned),

---

23. Cicero, *De natura deorum* 1.3–4.

24. Porphyry, *De abstinentia* 2.24.1, in Drosdek, *Greek Philosophers as Theologians*, 197–98. Theophrastus of Eresus was Aristotle's successor as head of the Peripatetic School in Athens.

25. Cicero, *De domo sua* 1.1; *De legibus* 2.19–20.

offered to the divine in an act of gratuitous waste.[26] This act of "paradoxical negation," as Heyman calls it, is inherently self-descriptive because it is a "public transcript," that is, a societally agreed upon and recognizable public statement concerning how those in dominant positions of authority wish to be perceived.[27]

Throughout cultures, rituals of sacrifice function as performative identifiers of difference and community demarcations for the initiated and, at the same time, also mark those outside the community. Roman social institutions were also created and sustained by such political and religious public transcripts that formed social understandings of power, obligation, expectations, honor, dishonor, and set the boundaries that identify the community first to itself and then to those outside.[28] The very patron/client relationships that defined Roman social interactions, mirrored the divine/human relationship with the *humiliores*, those in the lower social strata, devoted to the comfort of the *honestiores*, those of status and property.

Even though mutually beneficial, the relationship between the gods and the state was always somewhat tenuous and Romans, like all ancient peoples, were convinced that the fragile balance of the cosmos and the empire was dependent on the proper exercise of religious rites. Domestic and public expressions of religion in Rome were not a matter of belief, but of proper action due the gods. "Proper religion, properly done was necessary in [the Roman] vision so that the gods would be placated. Discerning the will of the gods was intimately connected to both religious and political life."[29] The historian Livy described in detail the precision that was required for a sacrifice, otherwise the efficacy of the ritual might be invalidated under certain circumstances.[30] Rituals fail when not performed correctly, and the consequences are dire for the one who engages the gods in an unfitting manner.

26. See, for example, Exodus 13, 22, 34; Leviticus 27; Numbers 3, 8; Deuteronomy 15. For excellent description of the sacrificial system in the Old Testament, see Averbeck, "Sacrifices and Offerings," 706–33; and Boda, *A Severe Mercy*.

27. Heyman, *Power of Sacrifice*, xiii–xvi. Here Heyman uses "public transcript" as defined by James Scott in his development of the relationship of domination and resistance in *Domination and the Arts of Resistance*, 5ff.

28. See Douglas, *Purity and Danger*; and Bell, *Ritual Theory, Ritual Practice*.

29. Heyman, *Power of Sacrifice*, 29.

30. Levene, *Religion in Livy*, esp. 1–34.

Whether expiatory, propitiatory, or salutary, sacrifice was central to the Roman world as *Roman*, and the disposition of the gods marked the political and religious standing of Rome from its foundation. "Sacrifice was an integral element in the matrix of Roman religio-political power relations. To be Roman was to be religious. To be religious was to sacrifice in a variety of specified and ritually controlled ways." [31] As a "social transcript," personal and corporate sacrifice was at the heart of *Romanitas*; it evoked a sentiment of loyalty, of belonging both to the Roman family and to the state. The Christian refusal to participate in the sacrificial system was not simply a rejection of Roman religion: it was a fundamental challenge to Roman identity and that carefully crafted balance between the Roman state and the gods. The conflict between Rome and the Church was thus inevitable.

MARTYRDOM: THE NEW SACRIFICE

The first mention of the Christian movement by a Roman writer is found in the correspondence of Pliny the Younger (ca. 61–113 CE). Pliny was appointed governor of the province of Bithynia (modern Turkey) at the beginning of the second century and wrote a number of letters to the emperor Trajan seeking advice on various matters, including how to engage this new group of whom he had never heard before: the Christians. This correspondence reveals how religious cults whose identity was focused on the individual believer apart from one's relationship to the family and the public expressions of ritual piety raised suspicion and anxiety and offended Roman sensitivities. "Whatever the nature of their [confession]," wrote Pliny, "I am convinced that their stubbornness and unshakeable obstinacy ought not to go unpunished" (*Letters* 10.96.3).

Pliny identified Christianity as another fanatical group, a *superstitio*, a cult—and a foreign one at that. For the Romans, *superstitio* was the opposite of *religio*; it was the improper, or even excessive, forms of behavior that could threaten the fine balance of divine favor to the state. The piety of the Romans was civic, and communal, and public, which is why Roman society grew increasingly suspicious of religious practices that advocated the role of personal belief, private piety, and secret rituals.[32] "Christianity

---

31. Heyman, *Power of Sacrifice*, 43.

32. The suspicion of *private* piety should not be confused with *personal* piety, which was the expected norm.

brought something new that fit uncomfortably into settled assumptions of ancient society," says Robert Louis Wilken, "the Christian ideals had a different motivation and a different core."[33] For almost a century, small Christian communities arose primarily within a few urban centers around the Mediterranean basin and went unnoticed by most women and men in the Roman Empire. By the beginning of the second century, the earliest Christian writings, "highly theological and directed at Christian readers, present the life of Jesus and the beginning of the church as the turning point in history, whereas non-Christians see the Christian community as a tiny, peculiar, antisocial, irreligious sect, drawing its adherents from the lower strata of society."[34] As a non-dominant subgroup within the empire, the nascent Christian movement began to formulate its own "public transcript," for there was little common ground of understanding between Christians and non-Christians. The inevitable clash between Romans and Christians occurred as a result of Christianity's expansion and its ideological collision with the Roman religiopolitical transcript. From the earliest expressions of self-identity, Christians rejected the dominative claims of Rome and instead confessed Jesus as *Dominus et Deus*—a public declaration with grave temporal as well as eternal implications.[35]

Since "the question of 'sacrifice' is as much about power as it is about religion," as George Heyman has shown, "it was natural that the clash between Rome and Christianity be steeped in competing sacrificial discourses." [36] The locus of this clash was none other than the very bodies of women and men who were called in front of Roman magistrates like Pliny to "give an account for the hope that was in them" (1 Pet 3:15). The accounts of these collisions are often told in the form of stories under the designation of *martyrium*[37] (report of the martyr's death), or *passio* (passion narrative), or *acta* (acts of the martyrs). *Martyrologies*, as these

---

33. Wilken, *Christians as the Romans Saw Them,* xi.

34. Ibid., xviii–xix. Wilken offers an excellent treatments of the intellectual relationship between Romans and Christians and how the critics helped Christianity articulate the nuances of what they believed, as well as the social ramifications of the exchange. See also Fox, *Pagans and Christians.*

35. Cf. John 20:28; Rom 10:9; 2 Pet 3:18, etc.

36. Heyman, *Power of Sacrifice,* xiii.

37. This is the Latinized form of the Greek noun *martyria* (witness), and the related verb *martyrein* (to bear witness), from which we derive the English "martyr" and "martyrdom" (to die a martyr's death).

texts are known collectively, were very popular among the faithful and a number of them survive.

The self-sacrificial motif on behalf of one's convictions or for the benefit of others was well known among the Greeks and the Romans. Valorizing the deaths of those who went to their deaths voluntarily infused the community with a potent rhetoric of divine call to sacrifice, something Plato recognized in the death of Socrates and which the heroic traditions of the Greeks and the Romans exalted.[38] Christian thought, on the other hand, "arose in response to the facts of revelation, its idiom was set by the language and imagery of the Bible, and the life and worship of the Christian community gave Christian thinking a social dimension that was absent from ancient philosophy."[39] Unlike its classical antecedents where the protagonist almost never had to face the willing sacrifice of one's life for religious reasons, Christians had inherited their notions of martyrdom from their Jewish heritage and especially the martyrdom accounts of the Maccabees who defied Antiochus IV and Seleucid domination and were killed for their unyielding faithfulness to God.[40] Origen looked to the martyrdom of the Maccabees and acknowledged it as "a magnificent example."[41]

The Christians' primary inspiration, however, was in the power and hope of the resurrection of Jesus (1 Cor 15:13–14) whose life and example they were called to emulate. The descriptions of the suffering servant in Isaiah 53 and the obvious connections with Jesus were from very early on the interpretive matrix through which Christians understood their own experiences and times. Jesus had warned them that in response to his call

38. See, for example, Plato's *Phaedo* 57 or Pericles's *Funeral Orations* on behalf of the Athenians who died fighting against the Persians (430 BCE). Pericles speaks of those men as having achieved "the courage of real men" (ἀνδρὸς ἀρετῇ) regardless of their personal flaws and impediments. "They had endured and stood their ground with their bodies and so had arrived at the height of glory (δόξη)" (Thucydides, 2.42.2). See Shaw, "Body/Power/Identity," 269–312. In the Christian tradition, martyrdom was not to be sought voluntarily or be taken lightly; it was a divine call in response to a demand by the secular authorities. If entered not under the proper call and disposition, martyrdom could end differently than in a fitting witness to Christ. One such account is preserved in the *Martyrdom of Polycarp* 3–4, where Germanicus, who stood firm in the faith and his confession is juxtaposed to Quintus who "when he saw the wild animals, turned cowardly."

39. Wilken, *Spirit of Early Christian Thought*, 3.

40. See Frend, *Martyrdom*, 54; also, Shelton, *Martyrdom from Exegesis in Hippolytus*, 35–77.

41. Origen, *Mart.* 23.

to discipleship they would be persecuted at the hands of the *status quo* (e.g. Matt 10:16–42, John 15:18–35). Jesus had called his disciples to see themselves as "blessed" when reviled and persecuted on his account and had assured them of the kingdom of heaven (Matt 5:10–12; Rev 21:7). To quote Wilken again,

> The Church gave men and women a new love, Jesus Christ, a person who inspired their actions and held their affections. This was a love unlike others . . . The Resurrection of Jesus is the central fact of Christian devotion and the ground of all Christians thinking. The Resurrection was not a solitary occurrence, a prodigious miracle, but an event within the framework of Jewish history, and it brought into being a new community, the church. Christianity enters history not only as a message but also as a communal life, a society or city, whose inner discipline and practices, rituals and creeds, and institutions and traditions were the setting for Christian thinking.[42]

It would be misleading, then, to read the accounts of the martyrs primarily as refusals by Christians to offer sacrifice, as their pagan counterparts did.[43] On the contrary, almost sacramental in character, each of these accounts is a rich sacrificial narrative that rejects the dominant religiopolitical paradigm and reinterprets assumed perceptions of power dynamics. Martyrdom was a baptism in blood which brought forgiveness of sins to the martyr,[44] and a eucharist, in which one drank the cup of sufferings of Christ (Matt 20:22). Paul had also spoken of the redemptive role of suffering for the faith in his letter to the church in Philippi

---

42. Wilken, *Spirit of Early Christian Thought*, xv.

43. E.g. *M. Polycarp* 12; *Pass. Scil.* 3–4. Also, Tertullian, *Apol.* 10 notes that the chief charge against Christians was that they refused to sacrifice.

44. Shelton, *Martyrdom*, 56, argues that this redemptive effect of martyrdom is "a positive effect that results in union with God, not a negative purgative notion." See Ign. Rom. 5–6; also, Tertullian, *Bapt.* 16: "We *have* indeed, likewise, a *second* font (itself withal *one with the former*), of *blood*, to wit; concerning which the Lord said, '*I have to be baptized with a baptism*,' when He had been baptized already. For He had come '*by means of water and blood*,' just as John has written [1 John 5:6]; that He might be baptized by the water, glorified by the blood; to make *us*, in like manner, *called* by *water*, *chosen* by *blood*. These two baptisms He sent out from the wound in His pierced side, in order that they who believed in His blood might be bathed with the water; they who had been bathed in the water might likewise drink the blood. This is the baptism which both stands in lieu of the fontal bathing when that has not been received, and restores it when lost."

(Phil 3:10).[45] The martyrs were filled by the Holy Spirit, who gave them words to say to the authorities and to each other, visions of heaven, and supernatural strength to endure sufferings.[46] This was a realized eschatology in which the martyr participated already in the events of the eschaton. To the sacrifice of incense and grain demanded by the state as signs of the loyalty expected from those living under the protection of the gods who promised *Roma aeterna*, the Christian martyrs offered an alternative sacrifice that rejected these illusory claims and guaranteed true eternal life: they offered themselves. In imitation of Christ.[47]

PASSIVE COOPTATION OF POWER

Persecutions directed specifically against the Christians as an identifiable group were too sporadic and local to be counted as normative before the sustained empire-wide persecutions of the mid-third century under Decius (249–251 CE). Yet, even from the earliest years Christians had felt the power and whims of the mob in multiple and various local instantiations (e.g., Acts 14, 16, 19), and had indeed suffered persecutions at the hands of Nero, Domitian, and Trajan. "Christianity was a novel, alien way of life, seemingly disdainful of custom and tradition and making extravagant claims about a man who had lived only recently. Christians, it was thought, jettisoned the wisdom of the past."[48] Towards the end of the

45. Tertullian, *Marc.* 4.39.5, followed the same principle when he presented martyrdom as atonement for sin.

46. Matt 10:19; Mark 13:11; Luke 12:11–12. See, for example, Perpetua's account of her visions in *Passio Sanctarum Perpetua et Felicitatis* 3–9, in Clark (ed.), *Women in the Early Church.*

47. Jacob, "Le Martyre"; Everett Ferguson, "Spiritual Sacrifice." Also, *M. Das.* 5.2; *M. Polycarp* 14; *M. Conon* 6.7; *M. Fel.* 30. See also, Ign. *Pol.*: "We must endure everything especially for God's sake, that he may endure us . . . Await the one who is beyond the season, the one who is timeless, the one who is invisible, who became visible for us, the one who cannot be handled, the one who is beyond suffering, who suffered for us, enduring in every way on our account" (3.1–2).

48. Wilken, *Spirit of Early Christian Thought*, 2. Suetonius, *Nero* 16.2, expresses the common Roman sentiment that the Christians "a race of men given to novel and harmful superstition" deserved to be punished, and Tacitus, *Ann.* 15.44, describes without apology how Nero "inflicted the most exquisite tortures on a class hated for their abominations, called Christians by the populace. . . . Accordingly, an arrest was first made of all who pleaded guilty; then, upon their information, an immense multitude was convicted, not so much of the crime of firing the city, as of hatred against mankind. Mockery of every sort was added to their deaths. Covered with the skins of beasts, they were torn by dogs and perished, or were nailed to crosses, or were doomed to the flames

second century, Christians felt quite keenly Marcus Aurelius's (160–180 CE) stoic disdain for religion and, after a short-lived interim of calm and peace during the reign of Commodus (180–192 CE), Septimius Severus (193–211 CE) carried out the harshest persecutions experienced by the Church to that time. Tertullian wrote his treatise *To the Martyrs* during this brutal period of the so-called Septimian percussions.[49] Since 177 CE, the Senatorial decree *Pretiis Gladiatorum Minuendis* consigned Christians to the arena to face gladiators in an attempt to reduce and regulate the costs of the games throughout the Empire.[50] Burnings, beatings, beheadings, and the "consignment of high-born women converts to the *lupanaria*" were not as uncommon at the turn of the third century.[51]

Intolerant as they were of religious practices that undermined the relationship with the gods or defied the state, for the most part, Romans were not in the business of making martyrs. They preferred the accused recant and profess loyalty to the emperor and the gods. Trajan was quite explicit in his instructions to Pliny: "In the case of anyone who denies that he is a Christian, and makes it clear by offering prayers to our gods, he is to be pardoned as a result of his repentance however suspect his past conduct may be" (Pliny, *Ep.* 10.97).

If suffering in imitation of Christ and for his sake was redemptive, it follows that to deny the faith would have equally grave consequences. To deny Christ was to be cowardly, ranked among the faithless, the polluted, the murderers, the fornicators, the sorcerers, the idolaters, and all liars whose place "will be in the lake that burns with fire and sulphur, which is the second death" (Rev 21:8).[52] The encounter between the magistrate and the martyr was thus revealed to be a battle waged against the forces of Satan.[53] The martyr identified with Christ and appropriated Christ's victory on the cross, defeating Satan and the demons.[54] Christian mar-

---

and burnt, to serve as a nightly illumination, when daylight had expired." (Tacitus's *Annales* can be accessed through the Perseus Digital Library of Tufts University at http://www.perseus.tufts.edu.)

49. Frend, *Martyrdom and Persecution*, 242.

50. *CIL* II 6278 [*ILS* 5163], in Carter, "*Archiereis* and Asiarchs," 41–68.

51. Frend, *Martyrdom and Persecution*, 240, 480n71.

52. Also, Matt 10:38; Luke 14:33.

53. Cf. *M. Carpus.* 6; *M. Crispina.* 1.7; Justin, *1 Apol.* 5; Tertullian, *Spect.* 13; Origen, *Cels.* 7.69.

54. Cf. Eusebius, *Hist. eccl.* 5.1.23 and 27; *M. Apollonius.* 47; *M. Fructuosus.* 7.2; *M. Agape* 1. 2. 4; Hermas, *Similitudes.* 8.3.6; Origen, *Mart.* 42; *Cels.* 8.44.

tyrologies were captivating accounts that borrowed heavily from the rich traditions of sacrificial discourse and transported the reader into a world in which heroic victims from all strata of life were faced with unimaginable forms of cruelty and adversity and were always victorious.

At the opening of Book V of the *Ecclesiastical History* (a section written before the brutal persecutions of his own time could be imagined) the late-third, early-fourth century bishop of Caesarea, Eusebius (ca. 260–342 CE), speaks plainly of the transformative character of these discourses of power as he writes:

> Other writers of historical works have confined themselves to the written tradition of victories in wars, of triumphs over enemies, of the exploits of generals and the valor of soldiers, men stained with blood and with countless murders for the sake of children and country and other possessions. But the narrative of the government of God[55] will record in ineffable letters the most peaceful wars waged for the very peace of the soul, and will tell of those who have been valiant for truth rather than for country, and for piety rather than for their dear ones. It will proclaim for everlasting remembrance the struggles of the athletes of piety and their valor which braved so much, trophies won from demons, and victories against unseen adversaries, and the crowns at the end of all. [56]

Eusebius's goal was not simply to present "facts" in an unbiased manner, for there is no such accounting possible. His goal was to provide "a full account, containing the most reliable information on the subject . . . which constitutes a narrative *instructive* as well as *historical*."[57] The fictional modern notion of impartial documentarianism colors our readings and reception of everything that crosses our horizon, from ancient to contemporary, and we tend to forget that every telling of history is indeed a telling of a *story*. Which stories we choose to tell, how we choose to tell them, to whom we address them, and to what end we tell

---

55. Eusebius's phrase τοῦ κατὰ θεὸν πολιτεύματος (*tou kata theon politeumatos*) appears to draw a contrast between the earthly kingdoms and governments and the kingdom of God.

56. Eusebius, *Hist. eccl.* V.intr..3–4. Adapted from *The Church History of Eusebius*, translated by Arthur Cushman McGiffert, 211. Henceforth *NPNF*. An electronic version of the entire *NPNF* is available at http://www.ccel.org.

57. Eusebius, *Hist. eccl.* V.intr.2.

the stories we choose, all these are inextricably woven together elements of the narrative tapestry we know as *history*.

Martyrdom accounts were meant to reinterpret the way both Christians and non-Christians understood themselves and their situation and to reshape the conventional categories of power. These "athletes of piety" were not the expected heroes of Greco-Roman literature, nor were they limited to the classes of the *nobiles*. The Christian martyrs were a mixed-bag of characters, young and old, educated and uneducated, women and men, slaves, free persons, Romans and foreigners, almost none of whom shared in the classical ideal of heroes. They were women and men who challenged directly the authority of Rome to dictate their conscience and responded "with a classic instance of a public 'no'—the open rejection of a ritualistic litmus test of types of sacrifice and publicly performed ceremonials that constituted an essential surrender of community and the self."[58]

In his novel *Survival in Auschwitz*, a powerful modern autobiographical account of such martyrdom at the hands of an equally omnipotent state, Primo Levi puts in the lips of the elderly Steinlauf what seems to me to be the finest definition of the transformational character of that public "no":

> We are slaves, deprived of every right, exposed to every insult, condemned to certain death, but we still possess one power, and we must defend it with all our strength, for it is the last—*the power to refuse our consent.*[59]

"Judicial punishment and war are domains where ritualized violence upholds the social order through representing the legitimate power of the sovereign," notes Douglas Hedley.[60] As alternative public transcripts of sacrifice, appositional to the ones demanded by Rome, martyrdom accounts are theatrical confrontations "replete with discourses of power that flow through [the martyr's] body, and which are clearly understood to have political significance"[61]—and they are usually presented as such.

---

58. Shaw, "Body/Power/Identity," 275. This is how Shaw describes the Maccabean opposition to Roman domination, which is also a very apt description of the Christian response, for it stems from the same understanding of the unique and exclusive relationship of the Christian with God.

59. Levi, *Survival in Auschwitz*, 41, emphasis added.

60. Hedley, *Sacrifice Imagined*, 140.

61. Shaw, "Body/Power/Identity," 274. From the wealth of excellent scholarship on

They are *theatrical* confrontations because they follow the conventions of the theatrical performances of antiquity. The theater was the primary locus of civic and religious education for the vast majority of people and the various tropes within these theatrical productions were anticipated by the audience. The audience was trained as to the meaning of actions and movements. Entering from the right meant one was coming from the city or the port, while one was understood to be coming from the fields or from abroad if one entered from the left. The audience knew what was happening, who had authority to speak, who transgressed civic or religious norms, and what the expected outcomes ought to be. Everyone had to play one's part for meaning to be conveyed.

From the first formal questions of "Who are you?" and "What is your status?" Roman trials were a matter of such theatrical *confrontations* intent on fixing identities and power relationships. Protagonists and on-lookers alike, everyone participated in a public performance with antici-pated—even if not always uniform or wholly predictable—movements, a call-and-response relationship that created meaning for the audience and assured all of the justice of the outcome. Most often, the accounts of mar-tyrdom that have come to us also show a common pattern of narrative sequence beginning with the authorities issuing an order that creates a moral dilemma. Staying faithful to their religious confession and to God, Christians refuse to obey the order and are thus thrust into immediate confrontation with the law of the government. Since public expressions of religion in Rome were not a matter of belief but of proper action, a trial usually ensues where the reasonable request for participation in the ritual is made by the state without regard for the true belief of the participant.

It is during these movements of trial and the subsequent execution where the most powerful accounts of reversal of power occur. The young are shown to be mature, both in faith and oratorical skill, women exert their autonomy and self control, slaves are proclaimed to be the brothers and sisters of their masters, not only the equals of citizens who share their fate but often their teachers as well. The infirm, the old, those who in the eyes of the world ought not to have power to resist the force of Rome emerge victorious. These were theatrical performances and the audience expected the customary responses from the accused: "convicted of their

martyrdom, language, and identity formation, see also Bell and Hansen (eds.), *Role Models*; Boyarin *Dying For God*; Elizabeth Castelli, *Martyrdom and Memory*; DeSoucey, et al. "Memory and Sacrifice"; Fields, *Martyrdom*; Frend, *Martyrdom and Persecution*; Leemans (ed.), *More than a Memory*; and Scarry, *Body in Pain*.

own guilt by the overpowering rituals of court and 'awe of the law' with which they were faced"[62] they were expected to blush, to sweat, to show signs of fear and shame, bowing, scraping, and weeping to proclaim their repentance and remorse and to ask for forgiveness and life. Seneca had spoken of the expected "recoil effect" as one faced the real danger, the absolute limit of death:

> The other evil [viz., of torture, rather than natural illness] is a great public display. Surrounding it are swords and torches, chains and a fury of wild animals, which it sets loose on the disemboweled innards of humans. Imagine seeing in this place the prison, the crosses, the horses or torture (*eculei*), the metal claw, the stake driven right through the middle of a man until it protrudes through his mouth, limbs torn in opposite directions by chariot wheels, that infamous shirt laced and dipped with flammable substances–and other barbaric things that I have not mentioned. It is not surprising that our greatest fear is of this spectacle, the variety of whose instruments is so great and ma-chinery of which is so terrible. Just as the torturer accomplishes more, the more he displays his instruments of pain and suffer-ing (indeed by show alone those who would have resisted him with endurance are beaten), in the same way, out of the range of things that subdue and domesticate our minds, those are most effective that have aspects which they can display.[63]

It was not so with the Christians. To the magnificent and terrifying display of state power the Christian in these accounts responded with calm defiance, even joy. They did not recoil. In each of the martyrdom accounts, through their movements and gestures, accepting their im-pending torture and execution not as fate but as welcomed destiny, the martyrs signified the drastic shift of hierarchies of power that was occur-ring before the prurient eyes of the crowds.

Condemned under the *Senatus Consultum* to face the beasts and the gladiators in Carthage in the Spring of 203, Vibia Perpetua, a woman of noble birth and a young mother, Felicity, her slave (who herself had given birth just before their ordeal), and their fellow Christians did not recoil, instead, they entered the arena as "noble athletes":

62. Shaw, "Body/Power/Identity," 302–3.

63. Seneca, *Ep.* 14.4–6. This translation is from Shaw, "Body/Power/Identity," 292–93.

The day of their triumph dawned, and they cheerfully came forth from the prison to the amphitheatre, as if to Heaven, with their faces composed; if perchance they trembled, it was not from fear but with joy. Perpetua was following with a bright face and with calm gait, as [a matron] of Christ, as [a] woman pleasing to God, by the power of her gaze casting down everyone's stares. Also Felicitas came forth, rejoicing that she had safely borne her child, so that she could fight the beasts, going from blood to blood, from the midwife to the gladiator, about to wash after childbirth in a second baptism. And when they were led to the gate, they were forced to put on garments: the men, those of the priests of Saturn, the women, however, in those of the priestesses of Ceres. That noble woman fought this right up to the end. For she said, "It was for this reason that we arrived at this situation of our own accord, lest our freedom be smothered. We sacrificed our lives just so that we might not take part in such activities. We made an agreement about this!" Injustice recognized justice: the tribune yielded. They were to be brought in directly, just as they were. . . .

Now after [Saturus] was thrown to the ground, unconscious, and was with the others in the usual place to have his throat cut. And since the crowd demanded that they be put in the center so that their eyes might be added as attendants of murder to the sword that sunk in their flesh, they [*viz.* the martyrs] voluntarily got up and went over to where the crowd wished. Then finally they kissed each other so that they perfected their martyrdom with the sacred kiss of peace. The others, indeed, received the sword without moving and in silence . . . [Perpetua], however, was to taste further pain. She howled as she was punctured between the bones and herself steered the erring hand of the novice gladiator to the own throat. Perhaps so great a woman, who was feared by the impure spirit, could not be killed in any other way than unless she herself wished it.[64]

This was not in keeping with the customs of the Romans. By refusing to conform to the expected prescriptions, Christians defeated all three propositions of the anticipated social transaction: first, they refused to obey an order; second, they denied the amassed crowd the chance to witness *the* final display of power over the subjects; and third, they denied the crown and the governing authorities what Brent Shaw

64. *M. Perp.* 18–21, in Clark (ed.), *Women in the Early Church*, 103–5; see also Salisbury, *Perpetua's Passion.*

calls "the production of truth," the uttering of the prescribed words of confession and "the performance of the required public ritualistic acts of assent."[65] The stoic Seneca expressed a deeply rooted Roman sentiment when he wrote to his friend Lucilius that one ceases to fear only when one ceases to hope (*Ep.* 5.7). The martyrdom accounts taught Christians that one ceases to fear when one recognizes that "Jesus Christ is our hope" (1 Tim 1:1). Bishop Irenaeus of Sirmium († 304 CE) summed up this new paradigm at his trial when he professed that, "Christians are wont to despise death because of the faith they have in God."[66]

In his *Ecclesiastical History* V.1, Eusebius preserves another trial and execution under Marcus Aurelius in 177 CE, this one in Roman Gaul (modern France), just a few years prior to the events in Carthage. This too is a riveting account of martyrdom and shows clearly the reversal of power dynamics that happened during these events. Swept in one of the local pogroms that dotted their times, a group of Christians in the city of Lyon were arrested and brought to trial in front of the magistrate. Featured prominently in the account are the deacon Maturus, "a late convert," Attalus, who had "always been a pillar and a foundation," Sanctus, who "endured marvelously and superhumanly all the outrages which he suffered," and Blandina, a slave woman "through whom Christ showed that things which appear mean and obscure and despicable to men are with God of great glory [cf. 1 Cor 1:27–28] through love toward him manifested in power, and not boasting in appearance." Following their trial, the condemned were brought to the amphitheater where they were expected to yield under unimaginable torture and confess in public the prescribed words that attested to the supremacy of Rome. That was not to be:

> Blandina was suspended on a stake, and exposed to be devoured by the wild beasts who should attack her. And because she appeared as if hanging on a cross, and because of her earnest prayers, she inspired the combatants with great zeal. For they looked on her in her conflict, and beheld with their outward eyes, in the form of their sister, him who was crucified for them, that he might persuade those who believe in him, that every one who suffers for the glory of Christ has fellowship always with

65. Shaw, "Body/Power/Identity," 278. See also *M. Fruc.* 6.3 for death confirming the life of the martyr and proving the truthfulness of Christian teaching.

66. *M. Irenaeus* 4.12, in Musurillo, *Acts of the Christian Martyrs*, 299.

the living God. . . . The blessed Blandina, last of all, having, as a noble mother, encouraged her children and sent them before her victorious to the King, endured herself all their conflicts and hastened after them, glad and rejoicing in her departure as if called to a marriage supper, rather than cast to wild beasts. And, after the scourging, after the wild beasts, after the roasting seat, she was finally enclosed in a net, and thrown before a bull. And having been tossed about by the animal, but feeling none of the things which were happening to her, on account of her hope and firm hold upon what had been entrusted to her, and her communion with Christ, she also was sacrificed. And the heathen themselves confessed that never among them had a woman endured so many and such terrible tortures.[67]

The reversal of power was complete. It was the pagans who were led to confess, not the Christians. The example of Christ, his response during trial and torture, even his physical posture of calm silence and assurance had given Christians a new vocabulary. It transformed profoundly deeply rooted ideologies about human beings, power, the world, and history. The classical Greek concept of *arete*, and its Roman equivalent of *virtus*, both linguistic derivatives of "male/man," signified the ideal of individual greatness. Based on the heroic ideal, Aristotle identified a virtuous person as someone who is prepared to sacrifice himself (women who entered this category were lauded as "manly women") for one's friends or family or homeland and, if necessary, to die for it.[68] Many of the philosophers from the classical to the imperial era expressed similar views. To be humble was to be weak, poor, submissive, slavish, and womanish; it was the physical position of shame, humiliation, degradation and, therefore, to be understood as morally bad. The New Testament revolutionized these values wholly by their total inversion. It presented Jesus who "endured the cross, disregarding the shame" (Heb 12:2) as the one Christians ought to emulate (1 Pet 2:19–20) and Paul's boasting in his lowly status, *tapeinos*, and sufferings in imitation of Christ gave new meaning to humility, transforming it into a virtue. In this new paradigm ὑπομονή (*hypomonē*), endurance, *patientia* replaced the ancient ideal of "glory," and humility (ταπεινοφροσύνη [*tapeinophrosynē*]), the

---

67. Eusebius, *Hist. eccl.* V.1.41–55. The account can be found in http://www.ccel.org/ccel/schaff/npnf201.iii.x.ii.html. For more reactions by pagan onlookers see also *M. Polycarp.* 2; 16; *M. Carpus* 45; and *M. Perp.* 17.3.

68. Aristotle, *Eth. Nic.* 1169a.

voluntary abasement of the self and one's body, "to be low, base, prone, and exposed, was now at the heart of the definition of being good."[69] "In the theater of the national pornography of the Roman state—its public executions,"[70] the new "economy of the body" displayed by the martyrs transformed humility into power and *virtus* was manifested in the form of a slave woman, Blandina. This was a long and slow shift.

"FEAR GOD. HONOR THE EMPEROR"—SEDITION OR CIVIL DISOBEDIENCE?

"'So our gods are not acceptable to you!' said Annulinus. *'But you shall be forced to show them respect if you want to remain alive for any worship at all!' 'That piety is worthless which forces persons to be crushed against their will,'"*[71] replied the martyr Crispina, a prominent Christian woman in Thacora, in the province of North Africa, as she was interrogated by the proconsul Annius Anullinus late in the Fall of 304.[72]

Religion cannot be a matter of compulsion, or so the martyrs claimed. Christians argued that forced assent reduces religion to a moral oxymoron—regardless of what the magistrate says.

The first account of a Christian martyr is the stoning of Stephen (Acts 6:1—8:2) and the earliest recorded prayer of the church for the state is found in the *First Letter of Clement* (60.4—61.3) sent by the church of Rome to the church in Corinth at the end of the first century (ca. 90–95 CE). Scarcely a generation earlier, Paul had written to the churches in Rome to "be subject to the governing authorities, for there is no authority except from God, and those authorities that exists have been instituted by God" (Rom 13:1). Paul had also instructed the Romans to "pay to all what is due to them—taxes to whom taxes are due, revenue to whom revenue is due, respect to whom respect is due, honor to whom honor is due" (Rom 13:7; also, 1 Tim 2:1–2). Jesus had talked about rendering to Caesar what is Caesar's (Matt 22:21). To these, Peter added: "For the Lord's sake accept the authority of every human institution, whether of the emperor as supreme, or of the governors, as sent by him to punish those who do wrong and to praise those who do right . . . Honor everyone. Love the family of believers. Fear God. Honor the emperor" (1 Pet 2:13–15).

69. Shaw, "Body/Power/Identity," 303–4.

70. Ibid., 304–5.

71. *M. Crispina*, 2.1, in Musurillo, *Acts of the Christian Martyrs*, 305.

72. Musurillo, *Acts of the Christian Martyrs*, xliv.

It was the same Peter, however, who, along with John, defined for the Christian community what "honoring the governing authorities" meant and how submitting oneself to the authorities was not to acquiesce to the demands of the state. Following the example of Jesus before the Sanhedrin and Pilate, Peter and John affirmed that obedience to the command of God superseded the orders of the state: "We must obey God rather than any human authority" (Acts 5:29; 4:19). With this seemingly simple declaration, the apostles exposed the true nature of the conflict and identified every other authority, secular or religious, as subordinate to God. The Good News of God's imminent kingdom (Mark 1:15) were interpreted as "the rejection of one emperor, Caesar, by the proclamation of another, namely, Jesus" (cf. Acts 17:6).[73]

Unlike the Maccabees who rebelled against Hellenistic domination because of the Seleucid imposition of religious practices antithetical to Judaism (1 Macc. 11:21) and as a sign of Jewish apocalyptic revivalism (1 Macc. 6:16), the apostles neither rebelled against Rome nor sought a particular national identity separate from the eschatological kingdom of Christ (e.g., 2 Thess 2:1–2).[74] Christians *honored the emperor* and the governors as his appointed authorities by following the example of Christ in refusing their consent *and* by submitting themselves to the consequence of their rejection, including scourging and death. That is what "rendering to Caesar what is Caesar's" would look like in the new economy; a simultaneous "yes" and "no" that points back to God as supreme. In doing so, they overturned yet again the normative paradigms of the classical traditions and showed how, for the Christians, power is gained through submission. A truly countercultural movement the Romans did not comprehend.

Martyrdom, then, was not the fate of the powerless, those finally forced to admit the grandeur of the state. Martyrdom was a witness *to* the state of its subordination to the God of heaven. Paul had already given expression to that: "For your sake we are being killed all day long; we are accounted as sheep to be slaughtered. No, in all these things we are more than conquerors through him who loved us" (Rom 8:36–37). This explicit cooptation of passive resistance or, rather, passivity in resistance,

---

73. Cunningham, *Early Church and the State*, 2.

74. There are numerous resources on Paul's eschatology and on the eschatology of the NT. Some of the best essays are found in Schmidt and Silva (eds.), *To Tell the Mystery*; see especially the essay by Gordon D. Fee, "Pneuma and Eschatology in 2 Thessalonians 2.1–2: A Proposal about 'Testing the Prophets' and the Purpose of 2 Thessalonians," 196–215.

found much fuller expression in the works of the apologists of the second and third centuries who wrote especially during the times of persecution. During this period of three or so centuries, Christian writers
understood that ethical teaching was not simply epistemic, but rather
life-formative. As such, even though the contest was expressed primarily
as between God and idolatry and only secondarily as between church
and state, there were profound political implications which persecution
brought to the fore.[75]

Until almost the middle of the third century and with a few notable
exceptions, Romans saw Christians primarily as a schismatic Jewish sect
whose status as a corrupt off-shoot from the mother religion did not af-
ford them the historical protections extended to the Jews.[76] As we have
already seen, Christianity's claims to exclusivity, its rituals of initiation
and worship, the borderless character of its community, its professed (if
not always practiced) disregard for distinctions based on class or gender,
ethnicity and language, status or age, and all other carefully observed
markers that guided Roman social relationships were antithetical to the
traditional standards and served only to raise the suspicion of the Romans
and, often, their ire. Participation in the public rituals of civic religion
preserved order and gave meaning. So, when public sacrifices were ordered for the welfare of the emperors or collectively offered to the gods on
behalf of the state, the Christian refusal to obey the law, honor the gods,
and submit to the orders of the emperors was an act of civic and religious
blasphemy. It was an act of sedition; or, that is how the Romans saw it.[77]

Based on the example of Christ and the apostles many of the early
Christian writers argued that what is *lawful* is not by definition also *just*.
On the contrary, that which is lawful may even stand in outright oppo-
sition to *divine* justice. That was not a foreign concept to the Romans:

75. Tertullian, *Apol.* 28 considers the political charge secondary to the religious
charge. Grant, "Sacrifices and Oaths," 12–17, also points out that the requirement of
sacrifices and oaths was secondary to the charge of being a Christian.

76. Celsus insisted that Christians were Egyptians twice removed. To be called an
"Egyptian" by the Romans was not an honorific: "The Jews were Egyptians by race, and
left Egypt after revolting against the Egyptian community and despising the religious
customs of Egypt. What they did to the Egyptians they suffered in turn through those
who followed Jesus and believed him to be the Christ. In both instances a revolt against
the community led to innovations." Celsus in Origen, *Cels.* 3.5. Unless otherwise noted,
all English quotations from *Contra Celsum* are from Origen, *Contra Celsum*, translated
by Henry Chadwick.

77. Ferguson, "Early Christian Martyrdom," 79. See, *M. Perp.* 6.3; *M. Crispus* 1; *M.
Apollonius.* 7; *M. Fruc.* 2.6; *M. Carpus* 4, and 21; *M. Agape* 3.4; *M. Justin* (B) 2.1.

Terence had already made the point: *O vere, ius summum, summa malitiae* ("How true is it that complete legality is complete injustice").[78] Throughout the writings of this period the point is made frequently that it is God who appoints the king and who dispenses kingdoms,[79] and it is to this God that Christians owed their loyalty and in whose kingdom they held citizenship (John 18:36; Phil 3:20). As for now, Christians "live in their own countries, but only as nonresidents; they participate in everything as citizens, and endure everything as foreigners . . . They live on earth, but their citizenship is in heaven" (*Letter to Diognetus* 5.5–8).

Christians insisted they were taught to respect the authorities.[80] By their moral influence Christians preserved the order of society.[81] Christians had never rebelled, Tertullian insisted, they were not seditious, nor did they take revenge, or even resist, for they were taught differently.[82] Origen added: "If Christians had started with a revolt, they would never have submitted to the kind of peaceful laws which permitted them to be slaughtered 'like sheep' [(Ps 44:11)] and which made them always incapable of taking vengeance on their persecutors because they followed the law of gentleness and love" (*C. Cels.* 3.8).[83] Christians, they claimed, injured no one, countered enmity with acts of kindness and charity and practicing and alternative civic, based on God's kingdom.[84] Christians offered the state a much greater benefit by praying to the true God for the emperor and the welfare of the empire.[85] Hippolytus put it this way: "This is always the devil's way in persecuting, in afflicting, in oppressing Christians: to stop them from lifting blameless hands in prayer (1 Tim 2:8) to God, knowing that the prayer of the saints obtains peace for the world, punishment for wrongdoers."[86]

---

78. Terence, *The Self-Torturer* (*Heauton Timoroumenos*) 796. A point Jerome repeats in his letter to Innocent, *Ep.* 1.14.

79. Tertullian, *Apol.* 26; Hippolytus, *Comm. Dan.* 3.4; Origen, *Cels.* 8.68; *M. Polycarp* 9; 17; Eusebius, *Hist. eccl.* 5.1.55; *Pass. Scil.* 6; *M. Conon* 3–4.

80. *Diogn.* 5.9; *M. Polycarp* 10; Tertullian, *Idol.* 15.8–11; Origen, *Cels.* 8.65.

81. Origen, *Cels.* 8.75; 70; 73.

82. Tertullian, *Apol.* 37.

83. This translation is from Helgeland, Daly, and Burns, *Christians and the Military*, 39.

84. *Diogn.* 5.7ff.

85. Melito of Sardis, in Eusebius, *Hist. eccl.* 4.26.7–8; Irenaeus, *Haer.* 2.40.3; Tertullian, *Apol.* 30–33; Origen, *Cels.* 7.73; Cyprian, *Demetr.* 20; Hippolytus, *Comm. Dan.* 3.24.

86. Hippolytus, *Comm. Dan.* 31, in Rahner, *Church and State*, 31.

The witness of the New Testament and of the early Christians was not one of an autonomous Christian political order, and yet, it was a wholly new political order. They honored the emperor by putting him in his proper place, under God, and commending him to divine favor.[87] "I will honor the emperor," wrote Theophilus of Antioch (ca. 170 CE), "not by worshipping him, but by offering prayers for him . . . He is not God. He is a man whom God has appointed to give *just* judgment, not to be worshipped."[88] The distinction is crucial: the emperor has been given authority by God to govern according to God's justice, not Rome's.

Christians insisted that their refusal to acquiesce to the simulacra of justice and worship ought not be interpreted as subversion or disloyalty but as a call to the state to repent and acknowledge its proper place under the authority of God (cf. John 19:11). It was civil disobedience.

A first principle of civil disobedience is the proposition that one cannot act contrary to conscience, even under compulsion. One acts or refuses to act, based on a higher conviction which, in the case of the Christian martyrs, was divine law. An equally important feature of civil disobedience is its non-violence.[89] This, too, was an incontestable principle early Christians inherited from the teachings of Christ and the New Testament. The appeal to conscience was often made explicit in the *Acts of the Martyrs* and related literature,[90] which, as Everett Ferguson asserts, belong to this history of non-violent civil disobedience. Ferguson concludes: "Perhaps few exercises of non-violent resistance for the sake of higher law have accomplished as much . . . The fruition of the implications of [the martyrs'] testimony was long time in coming, but the early Christian witness was an important step in desacralizing the State."[91]

---

87. Tertullian, *Apol.* 30; 33–34; Origen, *Cels.* 8.74.

88. Theophilus, *Ad Autolycum* 1.11, emphasis added.

89. Ferguson, "Early Christian Martyrdom," 81. Here Ferguson follows Daube, *Civil Disobedience*, 1–4, 43.

90. The martyr *Agape*, for example declared, "I refuse to destroy my conscience" (*M. Agape* 3.3), and the martyr Phileas added that, "Our conscience with respect to God is prior to all" (*M. Phileas*, col. 9).

91. Ferguson, "Early Christian Martyrdom," 81–83. Leithart, *Defending Constantine*, 326–42, draws out some of the intriguing repercussions of that desacralizing of the Roman state.

THREE

There Will (Not) Be Blood!

It is forbidden to kill; therefore all murderers are punished unless they kill in large numbers and to the sound of trumpets.

—Voltaire, *Religion*

They plunder, they slaughter, and they steal: this they falsely name Empire, and where they make a wasteland, they call it peace.

—Tacitus, *Agricola*

The gods of Rome demanded sacrifice to guarantee their *pax*, and Christians refused to underestimate the potential for violence within such a sacrificial system. Christ, argued Origen in his seminal work *Against Celsus*, had taught his followers otherwise: "No longer do we take the sword against any nation, nor do we learn [the art of] war any more, since we have become sons of peace through Jesus who is our author instead of following the traditional customs, by which we were 'strangers to the covenants' [(Eph 2:12)]."[1] Just a short forty years earlier, Tertullian had made a similar claim: "But how will a Christian go to war? Indeed how will he serve even in peacetime without a sword which the Lord has taken away? For even if soldiers came to John and received advice on how to act, and even if a centurion became a believer, the Lord, by taking away Peter's sword, disarmed every soldier thereafter. We are not allowed to wear any uniform that symbolizes a sinful act."[2]

---

1. Origen, *Cels.* 5.33.
2. Tetrullian, *Idol.* 19.3.

Was the early church, however, uniformly pacifist? And what would it mean for a minority group living under the security provided by the Empire to be *pacifist*? Were Tertullian and Origen representative of a common Christian sentiment or were they just peripheral voices who happen to have come to us? Even more importantly, was rejection of war and military service based on an aversion to killing or was there another reason for that? What about Cornelius?

"RELIGION" WITHOUT "ETHICS," AND A "SMALL, ARTICULATE MINORITY"?

During the past two generations of scholarship many have addressed the relationship of Christians with the Roman army, the reasons for prohibiting, abstaining from, or even joining the legions, but no one has shed as much light on the role of idolatry and the religious syncretism of the armies as central to Christian objections to enlistment as John Helgeland.[3] Helgeland has shown how Roman army religion "created a sacred cosmos in which the soldier lived from the day he enlisted until he died,"[4] and has argued that resistance to that sacred cosmos, that ritualistic mélange of soldiering, was the primary concern for writers like Origen and Tertullian who wrote against Christian involvement in the military.

Throughout his writings on this topic, Helgeland has insisted that Christian objections to war and military service in the pre-Constantinian period were the result not of "ethical" but of "religious" concerns, a rejection of the pervasive Roman army religion. In his attempt to argue against the so-called "pacifist consensus," however, Helgeland seems to have succumbed to the danger of overreaching. Charging with concatenation those who see a basic posture of pacifism in earliest Christianity, Helgeland's argument has led him to reject almost completely that violence and aversion to bloodshed were essential objections for early Christians. Thus, he concludes:

3. Beginning with his 1973 dissertation at the University of Chicago, Helgeland has produced a series of very valuable essays on the topic. These include "Christians and the Roman Army A.D. 173–337"; "Roman Army Religion"; "Christians and the Roman Army from Marcus Aurelius to Constantine"; and "The Early Church and War." See also Helgeland, Daly, and Burns, *Christians and the Military*.

4. Helgeland, Daly, and Burns, *Christians and the Military*, 48.

There is practically no evidence from the Fathers which would support the argument that the early church denied enlistment on the ground that killing and war were opposed to the Christian ethic. The pacifist argument is an artificial construct bringing together passages, torn from their context, and arranged in a way no Father ever could have done; no unequivocal statement to support that argument can be found, and certainly not one of any length such as a paragraph three or four sentences long.[5]

Helgeland is certainly correct that the *immediate* context that occasioned Christian objections were specific acts of public ritual. This much is unquestionable. But is that the whole story? David Hunter has noted that the "unfortunate dichotomy between 'religion' and 'ethics,'"[6] has led Helgeland to identify Roman army religion so narrowly as the locus of patristic objections to war and military service that, methodologically, he is forced to dismiss the other equally essential dimensions of the Christian arguments *contra gentiles*, namely, the non-violent character of the Christian community and the explicit Christian aversion to bloodshed. In his *Apologeticum*, for example, Tertullian repeats the argument of Christian apologists before him that the Christian community does not resort to violence even in self-defense, even when attacked by the lawless mob.[7] Hunter also points out that "even if Roman army religion was Tertullian's main target in *De idololatria* [*On Idolatry*] and *De corona militum* [*On the Crown*], it seems that aversion to bloodshed also was a concern. In the former work Tertullian explicitly addresses the question of military service *apart from* the requirement to make sacrifice or to execute capital punishment," and the same holds true in Tertullian's later discussion in *On the Crown*.[8]

As we saw in the previous chapter, worship of the omnicausal gods was world-formative, not simply epistemic; and the gods demanded sacrifice. Helgeland has correctly identified the "sacred cosmos" created by the Roman army religion as of central importance in the Christian

5. Helgeland, "Christians and the Roman Army," 764–65.

6. Hunter, "A Decade of Research," 93n2. Hunter has provided a thorough critical review of Helgeland, Daly, and Burns, *Christians and the Military* and has shown how the authors' lack of clarity on their own bias and presuppositions resulted in a "study with certain strengths but one that ultimately fails to achieve the balanced perspective the authors claim" (88).

7. Tertullian, *Apol.* 37.1–3.

8. Hunter, "Decade of Research," 88; emphasis original.

rejection of war and military service. Yet, this was not a mere substitution of religious allegiances, nor were the prescriptions against idolatrous practices limited to the *cultus*. It was a tout court rejection of this sacred world as the Romans knew it, of the religion that created it and of the practices that gave it expression. To separate religion and its rituals from the ethical implications for the lives of its adherents is a modern move. Origen's clear statement "no longer do we . . . since . . ." juxtaposes the two competing religious systems as creating two competing ethical systems. Christians did not worship the gods of the Roman, therefore they did not act in accordance with the demands of those gods: "No longer do we take the sword against any nation . . . since we have become sons of peace through Jesus who is our author." One cannot distinguish violence and bloodshed from army religion, any more than one can distinguish the thrust of the *gladius* from the fallen enemy: the latter demands the former. To argue that Christian objections to war and military service was not based "on the ground of possible bloodshed, but on the nature of military life, in particular, the idolatrous army religion," as Helgeland does, is an assumption that contradicts the facts.[9]

Writing together with Helgeland, Robert J. Daly suggests, rather surprisingly, that, perhaps ironically, the medieval two-sword theory had its roots in Origen's perceived ambivalence about the civil magistracy and possible allowance for judicial bloodshed. Daly suggests further that Origen's language acknowledges the possibility of a "righteous war" waged by Caesar and as such was "foundational for later Christian just-war theory."[10] Though it may be true that later Christian thinkers found in Origen's language justification for just war, Daly's suggestion "misses the primary intention of Origen's view in its own historical context. Origen explicitly maintains that violence is not the *Christian* response to injustice."[11] Daly bases his conclusion on the statement made by Origen towards the end of his apology *Against Celsus* (8.68). In this section of the treatise, Origen responded to Celsus's protestation that if everyone followed the example of the Christians and abstained from military service, the emperor would be "abandoned, alone and deserted," and would

---

9. Helgeland, "Christians and the Roman Army from Marcus Aurelius to Constantine," 733.

10. Daly, "Origen," in Helgeland, Daly, and Burns, *Christians and the Military*, 40. This view is also found in Daly, "Military Force and the Christian Conscience," 178–81.

11. Hunter, "Decade of Research," 88.

not be able to stand against the whims of the "most lawless and savage barbarians." Celsus appealed to the Christians' sense of justice and to the civic obligation of all Romans, insisting that it is the Christians' patriotic duty to join the emperor in "what is right, and fight for him, and be fellow-soldiers if he presses for this, and fellow-generals with him" (8.73) because "it is unjust for people who partake of [all the good things which the Emperor offers, including security and wealth,] to offer nothing in return" (8.55). At the end of his long reply, Origen insisted that though Christians "do not become fellow-soldiers with him [i.e., the emperor], even if he presses for this, yet we are fighting for him and composing a special army of piety through our intersessions to God" (*Against Celsus* 8.73). Daly admits that this section of Origen's writings is "the best single passage through which to approach his attitudes towards war, peace, and military service,"[12] yet he moves on to argue that Origen's rejection has to be read through the lens of a spiritual hermeneutic. Thus, Daly uncouples Origen's statement from its historical referent against Celsus and places it within the "specifically Christian vocation and activity as something internal, spiritual, distinct, and separate from worldly pursuits, as opposed to public, practical, and secular pursuits."[13] By doing so, Daly concludes that Origen's response of Celsus's patriotic appeal is in principle "an admission that the wars of the emperor, particularly in the case of a good emperor, are just and necessary."[14] The context and thrust of Origen's argument, however, do not support such a conclusion. It is significant to note that none of this language of interiority appears in Origen's text.[15] Nor is Origen showing any hint that he is allegorizing the situation when he concludes that instead of joining the armies, Christians are of much more use to the emperor if they provide an example to be followed by Romans and barbarian alike: "For if as Celsus has it, every one were to do the same as I, obviously the barbarians would also be converted to the word of God and would be most law-abiding and mild. And all other worship would be done away with and only that of the Christians would prevail" (8.68).[16] Instead of being

---

12. Helgeland, Daly, and Burns, *Christians and the Military*, 41.

13. Ibid., 43.

14. Ibid., 42.

15. Hunter "Decade of Research," 89.

16. Trigg, "Review of J. Helgeland," 206, also argues that Origen objected to military service on moral grounds, not simply to idolatry and imperial worship.

"unrealistic, [a vision that] never could have come about," as Daly calls it,[17] Origen seems to have believed that the results of the Christian example of piety and prayerful intercession would be "every bit as effective in the political and social world as the emperor's soldiers; he claims that peace *and* security would be obtained by prayer. Origen's point is that the Christian *politeia* operates on different principles than that of the pagan. But there is no evidence to suggest that Origen believed it would be any less political."[18]

More recently, Peter J. Leithart has suggested inter alia that even though "Christians are called to manifest and pursue the peace of Christ," since it cannot be proven that the rejection of warfare and military service by Justin, Athenagoras, Origen, Tertullian, Cyprian, Clement, or even Arnobius and Lactantius, in the fourth century, was supported uniformly, or almost uniformly, by all Christians before Constantine, one has to conclude that "the church was never united in an absolute opposition to Christian participation in war"[19] or even killing under certain circumstances. "However vigorously intellectuals like Origen and Tertullian opposed service in the army, and whatever their reasons," argues Leithart, since "we do not know the *practice* of the church, we cannot really know about its convictions."[20] Therefore, "it is entirely possible that [these writers] represented a small, articulate minority that has come to be considered spokesmen only because they had the wherewithal to speak. What did the countless, nameless and forgotten local pastors think?"[21] How did these local pastors "treat the converted soldiers who dropped in wanting to share the Eucharist with them,"[22] especially as the numbers of Christians in the Roman army begun to increase by the end of the second century? The evidence from the early church, Leithart concludes, is "small, divided and ambiguous."[23]

Even though one would not dispute that Christians could be found serving in the Roman legions towards the end of the second century, the dilemma posed by Leithart is simply misleading. However egalitarian it

17. Helgeland, Daly, and Burns, *Christians and the Military*, 43.

18. Hunter, "Decade of Research," 88–89.

19. Leithart, *Defending Constantine*, 273, emphasis original.

20. Ibid., 260–61, emphasis added.

21. Ibid., 259.

22. Ibid.

23. Ibid., 278.

might sound, such an argument ignores the fact that we do indeed know the prescriptions and conditions for baptism in the first three centuries for they have survived in liturgical documents such as the *Apostolic Tradition* and the *Canons of Hippolytus*; we will turn to them in short order. Moreover, even though he acknowledges that "between the New Testament, where we have explicit evidence of Christians in the Roman military [a claim we will address later in this chapter], and the latter part of the second century, we hear nothing about Christian soldiers,"[24] Leithart concludes that the silence does not allow us to speak at all. Whether *from* silence or *to* silence, such arguments ignore the unfortunate fact of history that, if we discount the diverse literary record because it might be representing the views of only a "small, articulate minority," we would have very little left of the Christian story, faith, and practice—let alone of Greek or Roman history. A large portion of the New Testament itself, for example, is written by two writers from the same circle (Paul and Luke), a "small, articulate minority" indeed. The life, teaching, death and resurrection of a Galilean carpenter is given to us by just four.[25]

It would be more appropriate to invert the question and ask whether we have any evidence that Christians were actively encouraged to participate in warfare or pursue military service as a pious, Christian, vocation or civic duty. We ought to ask whether there is a single writer from this period who promotes, or even condones, such a practice. The answer to both is that we do not have a single example of a Christian writer from the first three centuries who would make such a claim. On the contrary, early Christian writers uniformly assumed a basic posture of pacifism. To argue, as Leithart does, that because there were some Christians who either chose to join the legions or (most likely) were converted while in service, but there was only a "small, articulate minority that has come to be considered spokesmen only because they had the wherewithal to speak," soldiering was therefore an *acceptable* Christian practice, is akin to arguing that because certain Christians also frequented temples and engaged in the customary sacred services available to them, yet only one solitary voice from a "a small, articulate minority" was recorded as rejecting such practices in the first century (namely, Paul in 1 Corinthians 6:19–20), that temple prostitution, or *hierodouleia*, or the frequenting of pagan temples, were *acceptable* Christian practices simply because we

24. Ibid., 261.

25. This, of course, is limited to the canonical writings.

do not have the witness of the rest of the multitude of the silent pastors of the Church.

If *ubique, semper, ab omnibus* ("everywhere, always, and by all"), to borrow Irenaeus's phrase, becomes the interpretive litmus test for the relationship between the theology and moral discourse of the church and the multifarious practices of Christians throughout the ages, then we end up with another set of mythological constructs, replacing the ones we try to escape, and come to realize that we cannot make any claim about what Christians believed under any circumstance, on any subject, ever. We cannot know whether early Christians baptized those who came to faith, or whether they gathered together to celebrate the Eucharist, or whether they condoned exposing their children (as their Roman neighbors did), or if they were encouraged to participate in the events of the arena, or if they even confessed Jesus to be God. For, for all these, we have but the evidence from the literati, "a small, articulate minority that has come to be considered spokesmen only because they had the wherewithal to speak."

THE SACRED COSMOS OF ARMY RELIGION AND THE *MYSTERIUM BELLI*

Helgeland is certainly correct when he claims that Roman army religion "created a sacred cosmos in which the soldier lived from the day he enlisted until he died."[26] He is also correct to emphasize that, in order to understand Christian objections to war and military service more fully, we need to recognize how army religion provided a cultic frame of reference for the lives of the soldiers, how rituals served to strengthen and to display power, and why Christians objected to them. Having a better sense of that sacred cosmos of the Roman army also allows us to recognize the polyvocal witness of the early Church.

By the end of the first century CE, the Roman empire reached from the British isles to Persia and from the Black Sea to Thebes in Upper Egypt. The republican ideal of citizen/soldier/farmer retained still its rhetorical appeal, but the cherished model was challenged by the vastness of the territory. Among the many reforms Augustus enacted during his long reign in response to some of these challenges was the transformation of the citizen armies of the republic to a professional standing

---

26. Helgeland, Daly, and Burns, *Christians and the Military*, 48.

army of occupation throughout the provinces, a true *excursus populi Romani*.[27] As the permanent units of the imperial army settled into their respective provinces, from the heavily fortified *Vallum Aelium* on the river Tyne to the outposts of Dura-Europos on the Parthian border, they brought with them not only civic and legal Italic or Roman (i.e., from the city of Rome) traditions, but also the worship of the gods who had looked after Rome as it rose from a collection of villages in the heart of Latium to world domination.

Ever since the time of the Republic, life in the Roman armies was framed by cultic rituals belonging to the sphere of state religion. Oliver Stoll notes that for soldiers, military rituals had the function of "creating, consolidating, and demonstrating loyalty to the supreme, imperial commander—the emperor cult being the hub of political integration covering the entire empire—while simultaneously promoting discipline and the emergence of a corporate identity within each regiment and the professional army as a whole."[28] Rituals of the camp—especially religious ones—provided models for what it meant to be a good soldier and how to show respect to the gods and the emperor as their representative. For Romans, as for soldiers of all times alike, such rituals are also a great distraction and help control the natural fear of death as well as dissipate guilt.[29] In an autobiographical account *What it is Like to Go to War*, Karl Marlantes writes of his time in training and battle during the war in Vietnam, and speaks of the necessity of such rituals to mitigate the psychological and behavioral consequences on the soldiers. He writes:

> To avoid, or at least mitigate, these consequences, warriors have to be able to bring meaning to this chaotic experience, i.e., an understanding of their situation at a deeper level than proficiency in killing. It can help get them through combat doing more harm than they need to. It is also a critical component in their ability to adjust when they return home . . . You can't force consciousness or spiritual maturity. Teenage warriors like to fight, drink, screw, and rock and roll. You can, however, put people in situations where consciousness and spiritual maturity grow rapidly, if those people know what to look for. It's called initiation.[30]

27. For an excellent summary of the transformation and professionalization of the Roman army see Gilliver, "Augustan Reform," 183–200.

28. Stoll, "The Religion of the Armies," 451.

29. Helgeland, Daly, and Burns, *Christians and the Military*, 48.

30. Marlantes, *What It Is Like to Go To War*, 8–9.

The ritual life of the soldier began with the oath of allegiance to the emperor. Taken in front of the regimental colors, the military oath, the *sacramentum,* was binding by religious law.[31] The *sacramentum* was a liturgical practice that was repeated at least three times each year on the occasion of the public *vota,* the sacred oaths that defined the relationship between gods and people. Even upon discharge, after an honorable service of 20–25 years, the military oath had to be dissolved in another religious ceremony, the *sacramentum solver.* The bonds formed and the sacred cosmos created by such rituals could not be displaced. The epitaph of Vitalinus Felix, a veteran of the *legio I Minervia* who served in the lower Rhine and then settled in Lyon to raise a family, is a good example of the close association of soldiers with the deities that protected them. It read:

> To the protective spirits and eternal memory of Vitalinus Felix, veteran of the Legion I Minervia, a very wise and loyal man, seller of earthenware at Lugdunum, who lived 59 years, 5 months and 10 days. He was born on a *Martis dies* [Tuesday, the day dedicated to Mars, the god of war], enrolled for military service on a *Martis dies*, received his discharge on a *Martis dies*, and died on a *Martis dies*.[32]

Whether in civil or military life, the observation of feast-days, the *ferias observare,* was binding for all Romans and, though there were ample allowances, "the principle was fixed and the obligation clear," as Arthur Nock observes.[33] Our best evidence for the religious rituals, observances, and festivals of the Roman legions comes from the region of Dura-Europos, a fortress town on the Euphrates, where a calendar that records the official religious practices of the auxiliary *cohors XX Palmyrenorum* has survived in excellent condition. The *Feriale Duranum*, as the calendar is known, is dated to the mid-third century CE (*c.* 224/5–235) and reveals that the world of the camp needed to be given shape as it could hardly be left to individual initiative.[34] The calendar details the array of guidelines given to soldiers on which sacrifice to perform, on what day, and to whom. Even though the troops of this unit were not Italian in origin but

---

31. Stoll, "Religion of the Armies," 455. See also, Vegetius, *Epitoma Rei Militaris* 2.5; Herodian, *Roman History* 8.74.

32. *CIL* 13.1906 (*ILS* 7231) in Shelton, *As the Romans Did*, 266.

33. Nock, "The Roman Army," 189.

34. Ibid., 194.

came from the city of Palmyra, in Syria, they were to sacrifice on "days of important festivals of the city of Rome, on birthdays of members of the imperial family, and on other days commemorating imperial successes, to the gods who formed part of the Roman state cult, such as Mars the Avenger and Mother Vesta, or to the deified emperors themselves."[35] By participating in the sacred rituals of the camp, by declaring their loyalty to the person of the emperor and worshiping the gods that guarded the Roman state, they were initiated into *Romanitas*—they were formed into Romans and claimed their identity as such.

Replete with religious symbolism and rituals, what Stoll calls, the "corporate rites" of official army religion constituted "corporate identities" as well.[36] Among its festivals, the Roman army had sacred annual ceremonies devoted to the ritual purification of soldiers and weapons before and after the military campaign season. In his *Festivals and Ceremonies of the Roman Republic*, H. H. Scullard preserves an account of the sacred annual rituals of the Roman armies:

> The beginning of the campaigning season in March had been marked by the dancing of the *Salii* [priests of Mars] through the streets [March 1st], the *Equirria* [sacral chariot races held on March 14th], the *Quinquatrus* [March 19th] and the *Tubilustrium* [March 23rd], so its end in October saw the ceremonies of the October horse [the sacrifice of the winning horse of the October 15 race] and today the *Armilustrium* [October 19] when the army had to be purified from the dangerous infection that it may have incurred from contact with bloodshed and strangers. This was a festival in honour of Mars; his Salian priests probably once again danced and sang through the streets, during the sacrifices *tubae* were sounded, and the *arma* and *ancillia* were purified and then put away until the next year. It appears from Plutarch and Varro that the *lustratio* [a purifying sacrifice of animals] was performed on the Aventine "*ad Circum Maximum*" in an open space called *Armilustrium* (it lay south of what is nowadays the church of S. Sabina), the Aventine possibly being the last point in the procession of the *Salii*.[37]

---

35. Kaizer, "Religion in the Roman East," 446–56.

36. Stoll, "Religion of the Armies," 461.

37. Scullard, *Festivals and Ceremonies*, 194–95.

A military campaign began with one of the most ancient and sacred public rites of the Romans, the *suovetaurilia*, the sacrifice of a *sus* (pig), an *ovis* (sheep) and a *taurus* (bull) offered in order to purify the army. At the end of the campaign season in late fall, all instruments of war, from soldiers to arms to the trumpets and the *signa*, everything had to be purified ritually again before settling in for the long winter. Before battle, commanders and emperors alike would consult with the *haruspices*, the diviners who looked for favorable omens from the gods in the entrails of animals; and after battle, the gods needed to be acknowledged again.

Besides honoring the many and varied gods of the Roman pantheon who offered protection to the emperors and the empire and guaranteed victory in battle, Romans were quite tolerant of local and other deities which were invoked as tutelary. The cohorts of the legions would offer weekly gifts of incense and grain to their guardian deities and votives would adorn the camps and the tents of the troops. When off duty, soldiers were free to observe any cult and worship any god they chose as long as the worship of those gods did not conflict with "public law and order" or keep them from fulfilling their obligations.[38] The ubiquitous rituals of the army also conferred immense symbolic importance on the *signa*, the standards and flags of the legions that translated abstract ideas such as *honos* (honor), *virtus* (virtue or valor), *pietas* (piety), and *disciplina* (discipline) into the everyday lives of the troops. It is also important to note that since battle morale, discipline, and cultic structuring of military life belong together, they were collectively the reserved roles of officers. As a result, "military office was not distinguished from the duty of acting as a 'priest,' [and] the person of the officer was representing his unit as a 'bearer' of the emperor cult and state religion. He was responsible for executing the required actions while it sufficed simply for the troops to be present."[39]

To be a soldier in the Roman army was to be in religious observance, in ritual *and* practice. Helgeland is correct in suggesting that "the totality of Roman army religion was an impressive system, one so thoroughly

38. Stoll, "Religion of the Armies," 466. Once a religious practice or group was deemed to be unsuitable or subversive or demoralizing (like the *Isiaci* who were banished from Rome en masse, or when the Druidical *cultus* was put down) its practice, when once forbidden, was a defiance of authority. This was the reason why Pliny the Younger found Christians liable to punishment, regardless of individual offenses or lack thereof. See also Nock, "The Roman Army," 217.

39. Stoll, "Religion of the Armies," 461.

comprehensive that it would be impossible for any Christian in the army to avoid dealing with it in one way or another."[40] Idolatrous practices often occasioned the response, but it was by no means the only concern: ethics, the actions that result from religious observances, was another; for it is impossible to separate religion from ethics. The comprehensive character of any such system creates, by necessity, an environment of rituals and behavior, of presuppositions and expected actions that was impossible for any Christian in the army to escape. Origen saw the relationship quite clearly. He understood that the army was an environment within which warriors are not merely the victims of violence but also perpetrate it. Origen understood that "the sword of war," killing, becomes a *mysterium belli*, "a sacrament of war and strife"; a sacrament that was incompatible with the one inaugurated by Jesus and "a sword of homicide" that stood in opposition to "the sword of the Holy Spirit."[41]

"LOVE YOUR ENEMIES AND PRAY FOR THOSE WHO PERSECUTE YOU"

We saw earlier that religious rituals, including sacrifices, are also social markers of inclusion and exclusion. We identified the piety of the Romans as communal and public and Roman religion not as preoccupied with distinguishing true from false beliefs but rather emphasizing proper behavior and participation in ritual practices. The religion of the Roman army was indeed the focus of key objections by Christian writers against enlistment, but we ought not allow our own concepts of "religion" to underestimate how foundational Jesus's twin commandments to not kill (Exod 20:13; Mark 10:19) and to love one's enemies (Matt 5:43–44) were for the moral topography of the early Christians. Nor should we neglect the positive argument *for* proper worship of God through the sacraments of the Church in favor of the negative one *against* idolatry. For it is in the worship and the sacraments of the Church where the early Christians professed Christ as *Dominus et Deus* and interpreted his story as the "Gospel of Peace" (Eph 6:15).

40. Helgeland, Daly, and Burns, *Christians and the Military*, 54. Also, Helgeland, "Christians and the Roman Army," 732; idem, "Roman Army Religion," 1470–1505.

41. Origen, *Comm. ser. Matt.* 221–22, commenting on Matt 26:25 and the dominical admonition to Peter to "Put your sword back into its place; for all who take the sword will perish by the sword," in Caspary, *Politics and Exegesis*, 88–91.

It is an incontestable fact that Christ did preach nonviolence. It is also an incontestable fact that war, at the end, is "merely another form of sacrificial violence"[42] and warriors are not merely the victims of violence—they also perpetrate it. This was not the message of the New Testament and the patristic writers, even from the earliest years. The *Didache*, a catechetical collection of documents from the turn of the first century, opens by identifying a stark contrast: "There are two paths, one of life and one of death, and the difference between the two paths is great" (1.1). The *Didache* focuses the distinction of these two paths on the dominical commandment to love God and one's neighbor as one's self (1.2) and then proceeds to make explicit how the commandment ought to be interpreted: "Bless those who curse you, pray for your enemies, and fast for those who persecute you" (1.3).[43] Love of enemy as an overwhelming apologetic of love of God and as a pious Christian obligation is a theme that permeates Christian writings of this period. Early in the second century, Justin, the son of pagan parents, was struggling with the philosophical options of his time by the seashore in Ephesus when an old man approached him and told him about Christianity. The lack of fear of death and the kindness he saw in the Christian witness converted him (*Trypho* 3–8). For Justin, Christianity had created a completely new ethic, inconceivable by the competing moral systems of his time: "We, who formerly killed one another not only refuse to make war on our enemies but in order to avoid lying to our interrogators or deceiving them, we freely go to our deaths confessing Christ" (*Apol.* 1.39).[44] The *Second Letter of Clement*, the writings of Irenaeus, bishop of Lyon, Athenagoras' *Plea on Behalf of the Christians*, the *Letter To Diognetus*, the writings of Clement of Alexandria, as well as Tertullian, Origen, Cyprian, Arnobius, and Lactantius, all speak of the irreducible relationship between love of

---

42. Girard, *Violence and the Sacred*, 251. Even if one takes Carl von Clausewitz's proposition that "war is simply the continuation of policy by other means" (*On War*, 69), the rhetoric of war always invokes sacrifice to *patria et familia*, and monuments of remembrance are replete with language of *altar* and offering.

43. Cf. Matt 22:37–39; Mark 12:30–31; Luke 10:27. The theme of love of enemy is almost ubiquitous in early Christian literature. See, for example, 2 *Clem.* 13; Justin, *1 Apol.* 11–16 (esp. 16.1–4); *Dial.* 85, 96; Irenaeus, *Haer.* 2.32; 3.18; 4.13; Athenagoras, *Leg.* 1.4; Clement of Alexandria, *Paed.* 3.12; *Protr.* 10; *Strom.* 4.8; Tertullian, *Apol.* 31, 37; *Adv. Jud.* 3.10; *Cor* 11.2–3; *Spect.* 16; *Pat.* 6; 8.2; *Marc.* 4.16; *Scap.* 1; Origen, *Cels.* 7.25; 7.58–61; 8.35; Cyprian, *Test.* 3.48; *Pat.* 16; Lactantius, *Inst.* 5.10, 6.20.

44. Here Justin is commenting on Mic 4:2, 3 and Isa 2:3–4.

enemy and the Christian call to nonviolence. Love of enemy, insisted Tertullian, is a peculiar idiom found among Christians alone and it separates them from all other people.[45]

We need to note, however, that neither Justin's argument nor that of the other early Christian writers, was one of passive acceptance of the *pepromenon*, a fatalism that acquiesced to fate at the hands of an omnipotent state. If interpreted as such, Christian pacifism loses its scriptural underpinnings and ignores the fact that Jesus called his disciples to engage in active peace-making. The scriptural call to nonviolence locates the positive call to love—especially the enemy—at the nonnegotiable center of the Christian message.[46] This reversal of power that originates voluntarily from the one in the perceived position of weakness and is directed towards the strong is expressed in the form of prayer for one's persecutor and aims to bring the enemy into the Christian communion (*cf.* Rom 12:21). In this active pacifism, this *eirenopoietic* relationship with the world, Justin insisted, Christians were mandated to "cultivate piety, justice, love of humanity (*philanthropia*), faith, and hope, the kind that comes from the Father through the crucified one."[47] Christians do not kill or participate in war because the rule of Christ demands otherwise. In the fourth century, Lactantius put it this way:

> When God forbids killing, he doesn't just ban murder, which is not permitted under the law even; he is also forbidding to us to do certain things which are treated as lawful among men. A just man may not be a soldier, [since justice itself is his form of service], nor may he put anyone on a capital charge: whether you kill a man with a sword or a speech makes no difference, since killing itself is banned. In this commandment of God no exception at all should be made: killing a human being is always wrong because it is God's will for man to be a sacred creature.[48]

45. Tertullina, *Scap.* 1.3: *Amicos enim diligere omnium est, inimicos autem solorum Christianorum.*

46. On the positive call to love versus the "negative counterpart and normal mode of realization," nonviolence, see Helgeland, Daly, and Burns, *Christians and the Military*, 15.

47. Justin, *Dial.* 110.3, my translation. For full text see Justin Martyr, *Dialogue with Trypho*, 165.

48. Lactantius, *Div. Inst.* 6.20.15–17. Unless otherwise noted, all excerpts from Lactantius' *Divine Institutes* are from the Bowan and Garnsey translation. Lactantius is somewhat of a transitional figure in the history of Christian attitudes to war and killing. Throughout most of the *Divine Institutes*, which was composed between 304–311 CE

"This is pacifism pure and simple," says Louis Swift.[49] So understood, the pacifism of the early Christians has to be interpreted as a concrete social event that gives the command to love the enemy a public and implicitly political dimension, "a fully rounded religiophilosophical and political position."[50] Christians are called to be peacemakers and, for their early writers, that *eirenopoietic* articulation of the kingdom on earth had its roots in their understanding of the imminence of the eschaton and the very character of Jesus.

Almost eighty years before Lactantius, Origen had argued against Celsus that Christians could not participate in warfare even for a cause that would be designated as just by the Roman criteria of self-defense or justice. If Christians "were allowed to take up arms in defense of their possessions and to kill their enemies," argued Origen, "the Christian Law-giver would not have made homicide absolutely forbidden. He would not have taught that his disciples were never justified in taking such action against a man even if he were the greatest wrongdoer. [Jesus] considered it contrary to his divinely inspired legislation to approve any kind of homicide whatsoever" (*Cels.* 3.8).

This was not the naïve posture of idealist bishops and philosophers blind to the affairs of the world. As we have already seen, every one of these writers had experienced the cruelty of war and persecution. Justin was martyred. Tertullian had witnessed the cruelty of the Septimian persecutions, the imprisonment, torture, and execution of family members and fellow Christians. And so did Origen. Origen saw his father, Leonides, arrested, imprisoned, and executed in Alexandria. Tertullian and Cyprian witnessed the same cruelty in Carthage. Irenaeus was a presbyter of the church in Lyon when Blandina and her fellow Christians were condemned *ad bestias*. They understood that wars were inevitable[51] and that social order may necessitate violence on the part of the magistracy, but they also understood that what is asked of soldiers is to kill, and even though the camp may not turn (young) men into killers,

---

(during the so-called Great Persecution) and was intended to explain Christianity to the educated public of the day, he is consistently opposed to any for form of bloodshed. However, after the end of the persecution and the ascension of Constantine, his outlook changed and it seems to reflect a change in the Christian community at large.

49. Swift, *Early Fathers*, 63.

50. Helgeland, Daly, and Burns, *Christians and the Military*, 1, 14–15.

51. Cf. Cyprian, *Mort.* 2.

"it removes the societal restrains on the savage part of us."[52] That was not an option for the Christian.

The patristic writers decried the thinly veiled attempts by the state to hide the horrors of war in language of "valor" and "justice" and lamented the pretense of arguments based on peace. Cyprian identified the problem well: "When individuals slay a man, it is a crime. When killing takes place on behalf of the state, it is called virtue."[53] Even in self defense, or in pursuit of a just cause, wrote Arnobius, echoing the long patristic tradition, "it is not right to repay evil for evil; it is better to suffer an injury than to inflict one and to shed one's own blood rather than pollute one's hands and one's conscience with the blood of another."[54] The Fathers rejected a double standard for private and public morality, even in this area, and a number of them made the explicit connection between bloodshed and moral pollution, enunciating an inherent conflict between acts of violence and the celebration of the Christian mysteries. Addressing himself specifically to Christians, Cyprian insisted that "after the reception of the Eucharist the hand is not to be stained with the sword and bloodshed."[55]

"LET EVERYONE STAY AS HE WAS AT THE TIME OF HIS CALL": CONVERTS AND CATECHUMENS

Early Christians knew their scriptures. They new the stories of the Old Testament well and the books that now form the New were becoming quickly available. By the middle of the second century there were already established traditions of liturgy, catechesis, and practice in large cities such as Antioch, Alexandria, Carthage, and Rome, and even though there might have been a variety of local instantiations, the principles were the same. Even with Jesus's high praise for the faith of the centurion (Matt 22:21), John the Baptist's exchange with the soldiers (Luke 3:14), and the centurion Cornelius who came to faith (Acts 10), we have no evidence for Christians serving in the Roman army either as soldiers or in the auxiliary units prior to the reign of Marcus Aurelius (162–180 CE) and the story of

---

52. Marlantes, *What It Is Like*, 12.

53. Cyprian, *Don.* 6. In the early fourth century Lactantius repeated the same sentiment and insisted that violence and war were one issue on which Christians differed decisively from pagans (*Inst.* 1.18.8–10, 5.8.6, 6.6.22.24).

54. Arnobius, *Nat.* 1.6.

55. Cyprian, *Pat.* 14. See also, Swift, *Early Fathers*, 48–50.

the famed *legio XII Fulminata*. The story of the campaign in the summer of 173 CE against the Quadi, just across the Danube in modern-day Serbia, is told by both Christian and pagan sources. Both Christian writers and the Roman historian Dio Cassius agree that during the offensive, the Thundering Legion was itself surrounded by numerically superior forces. Cut off from any source of water, thirsty and exhausted by the heat of the Balkan summer, the Romans came to the point of surrender when the so-called "miracle of the rain" occurred. Lightning struck the Quadi and the sudden shower provided much needed relief for the Romans who won the battle and the war. While both accounts contribute the rain to divine intervention, Tertullian insists that it was the prayers of Christian soldiers of the legion that brought the rain. The Roman historian Dio Cassius, on the other hand, knew nothing of Christians among the ranks and attributed the miracle to the intercession of the Egyptian magician Harnouphis who prayed to Mercury to save the legion.[56] While the Christian claim seems to be "an apologetic invention,"[57] it marks the first time Christian writers speak of Christians among the Roman legions.

Around the time he penned *The Crown* and *Idolatry*, Tertullian also wrote his famed *Apology*, a work set up as a defense in a Roman trial, to present and defend the Christian faith to the pagan world. In the rhetorical fervor of the "trial" Tertullian attempts to persuade his Roman audience that Christianity is not simply a fringe group that ought to be ignored, or worse, extinguished, and declares:

> We are but of yesterday, yet we have filled every place among you—cities, apartment houses [or: islands], fortresses, towns, market places, the very camps, tribes, town councils, the palace, the senate, the forum. We have left nothing to you but the temples of your gods. We can count your armies; there is a greater number of Christians in one province. For what kind of war would we not be fit and ready, despite our inferior numbers, we who willingly submit to the sword, if it were not for the fact that according to our doctrine we are given the freedom to be killed rather than to kill?[58]

---

56. Tertullian, *Apol.* 5.6. Tertullian has received this story form Apollinaris of Hierapolis (†c. 175). cf. Eusebius, *Hist. eccl.* 5.4.3–5.7. Also Dio Cassius, *Hist. Rom.* 82.8.1–10.5.

57. Hunter, "Christian Church," 171n25.

58. Tertullian, *Apol.* 37.4–5.

Tertullian's claim is, of course, much more rooted in rhetorical enthusiasm rather than the sociological realities even of his own city of Carthage. Since there is no reason to reject Rodney Stark's "crude estimate," the total number of Christians in Carthage at the turn of the second century totaled no more than about 1,000–2,500, approximately 0.35–0.50 percent of the population of roughly 250,000–500,000 people.[59] Additionally, an evaluation of the 176 surviving epitaphs from the first four centuries that can be identified as those of Christian soldiers, reveals that only eight can be dated with certainty from the pre-Constantinian era, and the majority come form the city of Rome itself.[60] The number is not very great but it does witness to Christian soldiers in the army.

Christians had heard Paul's admonition to the Corinthians for Christians to remain in the condition in which they were called (1 Cor 7:20) and it seems that by Tertullian's time some were appealing to examples from the Old and New Testaments for pursuing a rather profitable career in the army (or remaining in the army after conversion) or aspiring to positions of authority within the magistracy. Tertullian's response was a thorough rejection of the argument. He wrote:

> Now the question is whether a believer can become a soldier and whether a soldier can be admitted into the faith, even if he is a member only of the rank and file who are not required to take part in sacrifices or capital punishments. There can be no compatibility between the divine and the human sacrament,[61] the standard of Christ and the standard of the devil, the camp of light and the camp of darkness. One soul cannot serve two masters: God and Caesar. Moses, to be sure, carried a rod; Aaron wore a military belt, and John (the Baptist) is girt with leather [i.e., like a soldier]; and if you really want to play around with the subject, Joshua the son of Nun led an army and the people waged war—and Peter waged war, if I may sport with the matter (if I permit myself a joke). But how will a Christian go to war?

59. Cf. Dunn, *Tertullian*, 5. Stark, *Rise of Christianity*, 7. Some studies raise the total population of Carthage to approximately 700,000 persons, but that might be too generous an estimation. See also, Decret, *Le Christianisme*.

60. Henri Leclerq in the article, "Militarisme," in *Dictionnaire d'archéologie chrétienne et de liturgie*, has collected and analyzed all 176 epitaphs of Christian soldiers. Reported in Ruyter, "Pacifism and Military Service," 67n12.

61. Like the Christian mysteries, the military oath was called a *sacramentum*, and was a liturgical act invoking the gods as witnesses.

Indeed how will he serve even in peacetime without a sword which the Lord has taken away? For even if soldiers came to John and received advice on how to act, and even if a centurion became a believer, the Lord, by taking away Peter's sword, disarmed every soldier thereafter.[62] We are not allowed to wear any uniform that symbolizes a sinful act.[63]

Tertullian raised both the arguments against idolatry and against violence at the same time. He made no distinction between the two. Waging Caesar's wars is based on the *sacramentum*, the sacred relationship affirmed by the oath of allegiance to the emperor and the state that puts the soldier at the service of a lord other than Christ. Christ's sacrament stands in opposition and demands Peter to sheath his sword. Tertullian did not simply reject the idolatry that infuses military life: he explicitly rejected violence as forbidden by Christ.

It was an unarguable assumption that the Roman emperor would always be pagan and early Christians never even considered the question of what should be done if a Christian became commander-in-chief of the army. No one expected that armies would ever march under Christian standards. Yet, the military imagery and metaphors of the New Testament (e.g., 1 Thess 5:8, Eph 6:10–18, 2 Cor 6:7, 2 Tim 2:3–4) are quite potent and convey well the gravity of the arguments of the biblical authors; and even though the language might have raised Roman curiosity, later Christian writers continued to use the imagery in great profusion. In the early second century, on his way to be martyred in Rome, Ignatius of Antioch wrote to Polycarp, the bishop of Smyrna, and gave him a last admonition: "Be pleasing to the one in whose army all of you serve [cf. 2 Tim 2:4], from whom also you receive your wages. Let none of you be found a deserter. Let your baptism remain as your weaponry, your faith as a helmet, your love as a spear, your endurance as your armor (cf. Eph 6:11–17). Let your works be your deposits, that you may receive the back pay you deserve."[64] In *First Clement* (c. 90–95 CE) the writer pleaded with the Corinthians to obey ecclesiastical discipline, which placed bishops over the laity and borrowed from the military imagery found in the Old

---

62. *Lit.* "the Lord, in disarming Peter, unbelted every soldier thereafter."

63. Tertullian, *De Idol.* 19.1–20.

64. Ign. *Pol.* 6.2. It was customary for Roman soldiers to be paid only half of their salary, with the other half deposited to their account with the financial officer of the legion to be received when honorably discharged at the end of their 20–25 years of service.

Testament: "Therefore, brothers, let us serve with all eagerness as soldiers under his [Christ's] blameless commands."[65] Even Tertullian himself used strong military language in *Apology* 50. The use of strong military imagery and language, however, was no endorsement of Christian participation in the military or war, for even the most cursory reading of these texts would reveal that their authors were speaking about war and armies in a spiritual sense. Paul himself had made that clear: "For though we live in the world, we do not wage war as the world does. The weapons we fight with are not the weapons of the world. On the contrary, they have divine power to demolish strongholds" (2 Cor 10:3–4; also, Eph 6:12).

THE INCARNATION: A RADICAL SHIFT IN HISTORY

Early Christian writers were bound by the biblical texts and found it hard to dismiss the Old Testament conquest and war narratives. Various allegorical interpretations provided a *via media* between of the Old Testament narratives, on the one hand, and love's superseding mandate in the "Gospel of Peace" (Eph 6:15), on the other. Most often, however, the Incarnation provided a new interpretive lens, a radical shift in history, and the dominical juxtaposition in Matthew, "You have heard it said . . . but I tell you . . ." was understood as the fulfillment of the Law (Matt 5:17–20). Tertullian used the formula "For though . . . but now the Lord . . ." and the language of the old law as being fulfilled by the new law: "The old law vindicated itself by the vengeance of the sword, to take an eye for an eye and to repay injury for injury. But the new law was to focus on clemency and to turn bloodthirsty swords and lances to peaceful uses and to change the warlike acts against rivals and enemies into the peaceful pursuits of plowing and farming the land" (*Adv. Jud.* 3.10). Origen understood that Jesus is the kingdom of God in his own person, the *autobasileia*: "For he is the king of heaven, and as such he is *autosophia* [wisdom in person], and *autodikaiosune* [justice in person], and *autoaletheia* [truth in person], is he not therefore, also *autobasileia* [the kingdom in person]?"[66] I believe that most early Christian writers saw that there is something fundamental in the move from a bordered national identity with a religion to defend and a people and lineage

---

65. *1 Clem.* 37.1. *First Clement* does not use language borrowed from the Roman military; rather, it borrows the terminology of the Septuagint, especially 2 Kings 1.

66. Origen, *Comm. Matt.* 14.7, my translation.

to protect, to a universal call to discipleship and a new family of God through Jesus; a family that transgresses national identities and gender and societal constructs through the realigning effects of baptism (Gal 3:28; Eph 2:14), a family that brings all into a new kingdom (Rom 6:1–3; Gal 3:27) whose only defense is the empty tomb (1 Cor 15)—the proof that all violence has been subsumed and conquered on the Cross. The result is a resounding alienation from the structures of loyalty and ownership that orient this world because of the new Lord, Jesus.

The anonymous second-century *Epistle to Diognetus* had already presented to the Roman authorities the case that Christians were not seeking power and prestige, and that even though they "obey the established laws" and were orderly in their civic affairs, in truth they were "foreigners" and "nonresidents," for "their citizenship is in heaven": "They are cursed, yet they bless; they are insulted yet they bless; they are insulted, yet they offer respect. When they do good, they are punished as evildoers; when they are punished, they rejoice as though brought to life. By the Jews they are assaulted as foreigners and by the Greeks they are persecuted, yet those who hate them are unable to give a reason for their hostility."[67]

BAPTISM AS CIVIL DISOBEDIENCE?

At the conclusion of a long but successful four-year war with the Persians co-emperors Diocletian and Galerius returned to Syria, late in the year 299 CE.[68] While in Antioch, as was his custom, Diocletian offered a sacrifice to the gods so that the haruspices might divine the future by reading the entrails of the animals. It was then, Lactantius tells us, that some Christians in the household of the emperor "signed their foreheads with the immortal sign," the sign of the cross, to ward off demons. The ritual failed and the diviners were unable to find the expected marks in the entrails. Diocletian ordered the sacrifice repeated. The Christians crossed themselves again. The ritual failed again and again. The master of the rituals diagnosed the problem as ritual pollution caused by the presence of profane men interrupting the sacrifices. "At this point the emperor became enraged and ordered not only those present at the rites

67. *Diogn.* 5.1—6.4, translation from Holmes, *The Apostolic Fathers*, 701–5.

68. For an account of the Persian campaigns and the origins of the Diocletian persecution, see Barnes, *Constantine and Eusebius*, 15–27.

but everybody in the palace to offer sacrifice. Anyone who refused was to be scourged, and the emperor had letters sent out to his commanders ordering troops even in the lower ranks to be compelled under pain of dismissal for refusing."[69] A great number of soldiers left the army.[70] Three years later, the oracle of Apollo at Didyma was silenced by "the just on earth" who obstructed the rituals once again. The immortal gods had been tested and the future of the empire was at stake. Diocletian chose the festival of the *Terminalia*, on 23 February 303, "as the day which would terminate the Christian religion."[71] This time the camp and the palace had to be purged for good. Soldiers did not have the option of resigning: they had to sacrifice or be executed for treason.

When treating a contentious topic, the danger is often to surrender to overly broad and uncritical assumptions on either side of the issue and not to take into account the pluralism of practice endemic in multivalent communities, such as those of early Christianity. So it is with the participation of Christians in military service, and even war. And even though early Christians writers were unanimously opposed to the idolatry and violence of the camp, abhorred war, and rejected military service as an option for Christians, there is the paradox that, by the end of the second century, there were Christians to be found among the troops. And by the turn of the third century there were enough Christians in the palace and scattered throughout the legions of the provinces that the emperor Diocletian felt he needed to purge the army. How could that be?

By the middle of the third century, the eschatological enthusiasm of the second seems to have dissipated and the numerical growth of Christianity meant that a number of practical issues that were not imaginable before had to be addressed, and Tertullian and Origen were not alone in raising objections. The church order document known as *The Apostolic Tradition* is an almost contemporary witness to the complexities facing the growing Christian movement. A piece of "living literature"[72] that went through various editions, the *Apostolic Tradition*

---

69. Lactantius, *Mort.* 10.1–5; *Inst.* 4.27.4–5.

70. Eusebius, *Hist. eccl.* 8.1.7; 8.4.2–3.

71. Barnes, *Constantine and Eusebius*, 21.

72. Bradshaw, Johnson, and Phillips, *The Apostolic Tradition*, 13. The *Apostolic Tradition* has survived in Latin, Sahidic, Arabic, and Ethiopic. In other versions it is known as *Apostolic Constitution, Canons of Hippolytus,* and *Testamentum Domini.* For an exceptional treatment of the evolving regional views of the church order documents see, Alan Kreider, "Military Service," 415–42.

is sometimes attributed to Hippolytus of Rome and its origins date to the mid-to-late third century. The document contains instructions for ordination, ministry, catechesis, baptism, etc., and versions of it were widely used for many centuries. Like Tertullian, the *Apostolic Tradition* recognizes the realities of life and the practical issues facing women and men who wanted to join the Church. It recognizes that people come to Christ from all walks of life, women and men with established professions and lucrative careers as well as those who were poor in need of jobs, rich who became such by keeping brothels and selling slaves, slaves who have no control over their bodies and free citizens who do, those who were raised as pagans and those who grew up in Christian families. The Church had to account for all these and many more. The church order document addresses the trades and professions that are permissible for Christians and the ones that are forbidden. In section 16, it speaks to the catechumens and lists the alternatives: pimps and brothel keepers, prostitutes, magicians, makers of spells and pagan priests, astrologers and soothsayers, they should desist immediately or be rejected from baptism and the Church. So should gladiators, who were most often slaves, or public officials of gladiatorial games, who were free citizens. The Church recognized that among those who wanted to join the Church and participate in the mysteries were also soldiers who had been converted while in service. Section 16.8–9 gives explicit instructions: "A soldier in command must be told not to kill people; if he is ordered so to do, he shall not carry it out. Nor should he take the oath [the *sacramentum*]. If he will not agree, he should be rejected. Anyone who has the power of the sword, or who is a civil magistrate wearing the purple, should desist, or he should be rejected."[73] As for those who professed to be Christians, whether catechumens or already baptized, and sought to join the military, the instructions were also very clear: "If a catechumen or a believer wishes to become a soldier they should be rejected, for they have despised God."[74] Parallel to the *Apostolic Tradition* is the variant

---

73. *Apostolic Tradition* 16.8–9. This translation is from the Sahidic and is found in Hippolytus, *On the Apostolic Tradition*, 100.

74. *Apostolic Tradition* 16.10, in Hippolytus, *On the Apostolic Tradition*, 100. Another variant is known as *Canons of Hippolytus*. In Canons 13 and 14 of *Hippolytus* the instructions read: "[13] Whoever has received the authority to kill, or else a soldier, they are not to kill in any case, even if they receive the order to kill. They are not to pronounce a bad word. Those who have received an honor are not to wear wreaths on their hands (i.e. reject the honor). Whosoever is raised to the authority of prefect or the

known as *Testamentum Domini* which preserves this wording of Canon 14: "Let a catechumen or a believer of the people, if he desires to be a soldier, either cease from his intention, or if not let him be rejected. For he has despised God by this his thought, and leaving the things of the Spirit, he has perfected himself in the flesh, and has treated the faith with contempt."[75]

Contrary to what some have argued,[76] then, both the theologians and the pastors of the early church were of one mind: Christians could neither kill nor participate in structures that do so, even when ordered. Baptism, it seems, was another call to civil disobedience.

Those who came to faith while in military service were to refuse the order to kill and leave the army, if they could, just like brothel keepers and pagan priests were to abandon their (often lucrative) professions and careers, or else suffer the consequences of their disobedience to carry out the orders they were given, just like gladiators who refused to kill or other slaves who refused the will of their masters. As for those who were already Christians but wanted to join the military out of a sense of civic obligation or as a profitable career, the ecclesiastical pronouncement was as clear as it was severe: such persons have "despised God by this thought, and have treated the faith with contempt."

Then, there were those who argued that they could serve without truly "meaning the words of the oath" or being soiled by the office and its responsibilities. In his *Apology*, Justin had already argued that, contrary to the Roman dichotomy between interiority of belief and the external proper ritual practice, not to affirm what the oath says would be simply a moral oxymoron, a lie, to which Christians could not assent (1.9). Tertullian applied the same argument to Christians seeking positions of power and influence within the magistracy under the pretext that they would not be tainted or corrupted by its structures and demands.

---

magistracy and does not put on the righteousness of the gospel is to be excluded from the flock and the bishop is not to pray with him. [14] A Christian must not become a soldier, unless he is compelled by a chief bearing the sword (i.e., conscription). He is not to burden himself with the sin of blood. But if he has shed blood, he is not to partake of the mysteries, unless he is purified by a punishment, tears, and wailing. He is not to come forward deceitfully but in the fear of God," in Bradshaw, Johnson, and Phillips, *The Apostolic Tradition*, 91.

75. *Testamentum Domini* 2.2, in Bradshaw, Johnson, and Phillips, *The Apostolic Tradition*, 91.

76. Cf. Leithart, *Defending Constantine*, 255–78.

> A dispute has lately arisen as to whether a servant of God can hold a position of honor or authority if he can keep himself free of any appearance of idolatry by means of some special grace or through his own wisdom, just as Joseph and Daniel, who, served with honor and power, wearing the insignia and the purple of the governor of Egypt and Babylonia, yet without being tainted by idolatry. We may grant that someone could hold a position in a purely honorary way if you can believe that it is possible for him to avoid sacrificing or authorizing sacrifices, without paying for victims [viz. sacrificial animals], without managing the upkeep of temples, without taking care of temple taxes, without putting on shows [spectacula] at his own or at public expense or presiding over the staging of them, without issuing solemn pronouncements or edicts or even taking an oath. Provided he can do this and also avoid the functions of his office, that is without passing judgment on a man's life [i.e., capital punishment] or honour—for you can put up with a decision on financial matters—without condemning or forejudging, without putting anybody in chains or prison or torturing, if it is believable that all this is possible, [then he may serve].[77]

And he concluded:

> So what will you accomplish, if you use this attire (viz. of purple of the magistracy) but do not perform the function connected with it? Nobody can give an impression of cleanness in unclean clothes (i.e. the office is already polluted by long standing practice and tradition). If you put on a tunic soiled of itself, it may perhaps not be soiled through you, but certainly you will not be able to be clean because of it.[78]

We have seen that a first principle of civil disobedience is the proposition that one cannot act contrary to conscience, even under compulsion. One acts, or refuses to act, based on a higher conviction which, just like in the case of the Christian martyrs, was divine law.

This civil disobedience and refusal of governmental demands takes the specific form of a choice between the military and Christ in the *Acts of the Military Martyrs* (events that took place from the end of the second century to the beginning of the fourth, right before the rise of

---

77. Tertullian, *Idol.* 17.2–3.

78. Ibid., 18.4.

Constantine as the sole ruler of the Empire). Among them, the centurion Marinus († c. 260–262 CE) was confronted in Caesarea Maritima by his commander when it was revealed he was a Christian. Given three hours to reconsider his fate, Marinus went for a walk. The bishop of Caesarea, Theotecnus, met him and brought him to the church where he revealed for him the true nature of his dilemma: "Once inside, [the bishop] placed Marinus right in front of the altar, and drawing aside Marinus' cloak pointed to the sword attached to his side. At the same time he brought a copy of the divine Gospels and he set it before Marinus, asking him to choose which he preferred." Marinus chose the Gospels and was executed.[79] The recruit Maximilian († 295 CE), from the city of Tebessa in Numidia, became the first recorded conscientious objector by refusing military service: "I cannot serve," Maximilian declared, "because I am a Christian."[80] In 298 CE, Marcellus, a centurion with the *legio II Traiana* stationed in Tingis, renounced military service both because of the pagan religious practices and because his Christian conviction would not allow him to fight any more.[81] The soldier Dasius († 303 CE) was serving with the *legio XI Claudia* in Durostorum when he, too, rejected his very identity as a soldier along with the religious practices of the Roman army.[82] The veteran Julius was probably serving with Dasius in Durostorum and was martyred in the same year. Though a Christian for the twenty-seven years of his military service, Julius renounced his identity as a soldier and refused to sacrifice decrying: "All the twenty-seven years in which I made the mistake, so it appears, to serve foolishly in the army."[83]

What then of those who those soldiers we know to have been Christians during at least part of their service? What were their reasons for joining or not leaving upon converting? Did they join as a means of social advancement or job security? Was it love of country or a means to gain Roman citizenship? Was it the expected *cursus honorum* in which sons of privilege were expected to participate before assuming civic careers? Was it the militarism of the late third century that brought the Empire to an almost constant state of fear of invasion? Did they find an

79. *M. Marinus* 4.

80. *M. Max.* 2.1.

81. *M. Marc.* (Recension M) 1.1; 4.3.

82. *M. Das.* 6.1.

83. *M. Jul.* 1.3–4; 2.1. A purge of the army similar to the one initiated by Diocletian also occurred under the emperor Decius (249–251 CE).

excuse in conscription? How they did it we can only conjecture. There are probably as many reasons as there were soldiers. What we do know is that both the theological and the ecclesiastical witness of the Church unanimously objected to the practice. We also know that when the antithesis between what Christians said they believed and what they practiced was pointed out—usually by the state—when a choice between loyalty to emperor and Christ was demanded, when the state did not turn a coopting blind eye to Christians among its ranks, the consequences for the Christians were grave.

Or, it could simply be that, as Helgeland suggests, some "probably modeled their Christianity along the lines of Roman polytheism—Mars is for victory, spring nymphs are for fresh water, Jupiter Dolichenus is for weapons that do not break in combat, and Christ, is for when your weapon does break and you die."[84]

WHAT ABOUT CORNELIUS?

In Acts 10, Luke presents to us the story of Cornelius, "a centurion of the Italian Cohort" and a "devout man who feared God" (10:1–2). Peter was prompted by God to visit Cornelius and bring him the good news of the love of God as manifested through the life, death, and resurrection of Jesus of Nazareth (10:37–43). Peter begun by assuring him that what Cornelius had heard was true: "You know the message [God] sent to the people of Israel, preaching peace by Jesus Christ—he is Lord of all" (10:36). As Peter was speaking, the Holy Spirit fell upon all who were gathered and Cornelius and his Gentile household was baptized in the name of Jesus Christ (10:44–48). Peter did not ask Cornelius to leave his army career. Nor did he ask him to cease from exercising the official duties of his post. All Peter did was welcome him in the Name. Is the story of Cornelius, then, "explicit evidence of Christians in the Roman military," as some have argued,[85] or of an ambiguity towards military service found in the New Testament?[86]

Leaving aside the obvious connection with Luke 4:14–20 and the fact that Luke's point in this story is *not* Cornelius's station but the in-breaking of the kingdom of God through national and ethnic barriers,

---

84. Helgeland, Daly, and Burns, *Christians and the Military*, 55.

85. Leithart, *Defending Constantine*, 261.

86. Cf. Swift, *Early Fathers*, 19–23, and others.

or as Luke puts it: "God has given even to the Gentiles the repentance that leads to life" (11:18), we need to ask what is *not* being said in this story, as much as what *is* being said.

What is being said is clear enough: Cornelius is a Roman, a centurion, and of the Italian Cohort. What is not being said in the account in Acts 10 is what Cornelius did, or what he was forced to do, after Peter left him. We know that, as a centurion, Cornelius had very specific, prescribed, and long-standing duties even in peacetime—especially in peacetime. Whether a *Primus Pilus*, a centurion of the First Cohort (as, probably, in Luke 7:5; 23:47) or one of the other fifty-eight centurions of his legion, Cornelius's "military office was not distinguished from the duty of acting as a 'priest,' [since] the person of the officer was representing his unit a 'bearer' of the emperor cult and state religion."[87] As such, Cornelius was responsible for executing the required religious actions. We have already seen that all divisions of the imperial army participated in the worship of those gods and were given very specific guidelines on which sacrifice to perform, on what day, and to whom. We have seen that soldiers would sacrifice "on days of important festivals of the city of Rome, on birthdays of members of the imperial family, and on other days commemorating imperial successes, to the gods who formed part of the Roman state cult, such as Mars the Avenger and Mother Vesta, or to the deified emperors themselves"[88] and it was the centurions, like Cornelius, who would perform those sacrifices in front of the assembled cohorts, and on their behalf.

As a centurion, Cornelius would have to lead his cohort in the offering of the *sacramentum*, three times each year. And here we have to ask: Could Cornelius, who had just moved from the ranks of the "God-fearers" to a newly baptized Christian, confessing Jesus as *omnium Dominum*, "Lord of all," as Luke attests (10:36), now stand in front of his cohort and offer sacrifices to the gods and proclaim Caesar *Dominus et Deus*? If he could, then Luke was wrong, Cornelius did not accept that "Jesus Christ is Lord of all" and Peter was mistaken in baptizing him in the Name. If Cornelius could not stand in front of his cohort and proclaim Caesar Dominus et Deus, then Rome had an answer for him—and, often, it was not simple dismissal from the army (as the *Acts of the Military Martyrs* evidence).

87. Stoll, "The Religion of the Armies," 461.

88. Kaizer, "Religion in the Roman East," 446–56.

The burden of proof on the question of why did not Peter ask Cornelius to leave military service, then, is not on those who see a coherent pacifist stance in the early Church, but on those who insist that Luke's silence is, somehow, condoning the continuation of such a service. Why didn't Peter ask Cornelius to leave military service? The answer seems simple enough: because he didn't have to—Rome would take care of that.

It is not true that, as Leithart claims, the period of silence is evidence that the early Church actively condoned military service, or perhaps indicative that Christians served in the Roman army openly, as Christians. Such claims seem to be misreading the importance of religion and the ritual system of the Roman army and the attention Rome paid to it. If Christians could not serve openly in the Roman army—affirming Caesar as *Dominus et Deus*, thrice each year—how can we argue that the church condoned such a duplicitous stance?

Christians countered the Roman *libido dominandi* with a new language about power based on the hope of resurrection and the sovereignty of God, and the Church's ethical teachings were an expression of that hope. The prohibitions against killing, war, and resisting evil did not simply derive from an assumption about violence as inherently evil, but rather from the early Christian understanding of the sovereignty of God. To the coercive power of the state articulated in the demand for devotion to the gods of the empire and the emperor as their vicar on earth, the example of Christ provided Christians with a new interpretive matrix that allowed them to follow a completely new paradigm of power and sacrifice—and their undergirding instrumentalities of violence in all its pluriformity, including killing—based on civil disobedience, and a passive cooptation of power that found its strength in non-violent resistance, in imitation of Christ. At the end, Louis J. Swift puts it best: "If violence had any place in the Christian's life, it would appear that it must be a violence which is endured rather than inflicted, a violence which is suffered in imitation of the Founder as a way of transcending human passions and breaking the endless cycle of injury and retaliation."[89]

---

89. Swift, *Early Fathers*, 17.

FOUR

General Introduction to the Texts

From the earliest, post-apostolic, writings to the writings of Lactantius and the church order documents of the later fourth century, the primary documents included in this collection continue to form a well-established canon of patristic writings on the topic at hand. Throughout this essay, however, I have argued that, in order to gain a more fully-orbed understanding of the responses of the earliest Christian writers to war and military service, we cannot limit ourselves exclusively to those excerpts that contain references to these two foci; rather, we have to place both sentiments and statements within their socioreligious and historical context. When we open our horizons to see the discussions more fully, we realize that idolatry was not the single locus of Christian objections to war and military service—quite often, it was not even the most important issue—and we come to recognize the importance of the dominical command to love one's enemies and pray for one's persecutors, as the constructive center in much of the Christian argument.

We begin with the famous correspondence between the Governor of Bithynia, Pliny the Younger, and the emperor Trajan (111 CE), known as *Letters* 96 and 97. They provide the first extra-biblical account of the practices of Christian communities. In spite of its brevity, *Letter* 96 provides an incredibly rich description of the sociological constitution of the Christian communities in Bithynia by a Roman magistrate who had no sympathy for the community or their way of life. It includes a detailed description of Christian gatherings and worship, preserves the public oath to harm no one, and recounts the relationships of Christians with their neighbors. The *Didache*, or the *Teaching of the Twelve Apostles*, preserves the earliest catechetical instructions outside the New Testament and as such gives us a look into the character, expectations, and practices of earliest Christianity. This self-expression is continued in the *Epistle to Diognetus* which, even though it does not speak specifically to the issue of war and military service, presents a most eloquent description of the theology of Christians as sojourners and aliens that permeated the conscience of the first few generations of Christians. Together, these documents place the work of the apologists, both Greek and Latin, within its proper sociological, religious, and even ecclesial context, and allow us to engage their arguments more fully.

With *First Clement* and Ignatius of Antioch we enter the world of the apologists of the second and third centuries. This is a period of deep theological, philosophical, and sociological reflection for the Christian communities. As Christians of the second and early third centuries tried to understand their relationship with the culture, philosophy, religion(s), and practices of the Roman world that enveloped them, and as the communities in their various locales moved beyond the second and third generations of converts into well-established patterns of worship and initiation, it was only natural that questions of participation in the empire's wars and constructs of power would have to be addressed. Tertullian and Origen provide the most expansive treatments on the topic and thus form the core of the earliest Christian witness, along with those like Cyprian and, later, Lactantius, who wrote in times of persecution. By the end of the third century, the militarism and expansionism of Rome had made a career in the army quite lucrative and, some times, even mandatory. The rapid growth of the Church to all parts of the empire and throughout the social strata of Roman society also meant that a number of Christians did not find military or civic service (as) objectionable. How many Christians were among the legions we do not know, but what *The Acts of the Military Martyrs* do tell us is that a number of soldiers came to a crisis of conscience and abandoned their military service, while others were brought to that moment of crisis by their fellow soldiers. In each case recorded in the *Acta* the choice was quite clear, as were the consequences.

Lastly, the documents that belong to the church order genre deal with ethics within the notion of worship, catechesis, and pastoral life and care. They preserve for us some of the clearest examples of instructions for those who wished to join the Church and expectations for those already baptized. These documents also illuminate both the continuity as well as the variance between the theological treatises and admonitions of famous early Christian writers and the struggles of local congregations to deal with the everyday lives and realities of the faithful.

In the first chapter we saw David Hunter's suggestion for a "new consensus" that takes into account both the pacifist and non-pacifist positions. Hunter suggested that, first, because early Christians were as repelled by the idolatry of the Romans as much as they were by killing, the most vocal of early Christian opponents of military service, such as Tertullian and Origen, based their rejection as much upon their "abhorrence of Roman army religion" as they did on their objections to the shedding of blood. Second, by the end of the second century there is evidence that the practices of some Christians diverged from the theological principles of the writers of the Church (a trend that grew throughout the third century). The third point Hunter identified was that, "the efforts of Christians to justify participation in warfare for a 'just' cause (most notably that of Augustine) stand in fundamental continuity with at least one strand of pre-Constantinian tradition."[1] In this book, I have challenged Hunter's third notion of the "new consensus" (which is based on Swift's claim that in the pre-Constantinian period both pacifist and non-pacifist positions existed side by side and neither was able to supplant the other). In its place I have proposed what I believe to be supported by the literary evidence, namely that, even though the *practices* of some Christians might have been contrary to the clear voice of the Church, the pre-Constantinian Church spoke with remarkable *unanimity* against participation in war and military service.

For the documents that are included in this collection, I have consulted the most recent critical editions of the Greek and Latin texts and have provided new English translations where ones were needed. Many of these documents exist online in translations from the late-nineteenth and early-twentieth centuries and sometimes, due to the linguistic sensitivities of the time they were produced, those translations do not carry the full force of the language of the original authors. Where modern translations that carry the spirit of the author are available, I have included those, or I have adapted the text so that readers who are interested may read the whole work of the ancient authors and engage their arguments more fully.

1. Hunter, "Decade of Research," 93.

FIVE

The Earliest Sources

PLINY THE YOUNGER (61/62-113 CE)

Gaius Plinius Caecilius Secundus, known as Pliny the Younger (61/62–ca. 113 CE), was born at Como, in the northern Italian region of Lombardy, in 62 CE He was only eight years old when his father, Caecilius, died, and he was adopted by his maternal uncle, the elder Pliny, author of the "Natural History." As a young man, Pliny studied rhetoric under Quintilian and Nicetes Sacerdos, and he gained a reputation as a jurist, specialized in the prosecution of financial cases. Following the ordinary *cursus honorum*, he served as military tribune in Syria and upon his return to Rome he received various political and administrative appointments. During this time Pliny gained a reputation for honesty and competence and an expertise in public administration. Having survived the "thunderbolts," as he called them, that fell around him during Domitian's reign of terror (described in detail by Tacitus in *Agricola*) Pliny was appointed by emperor Trajan to the office of tribune in 98 CE at the unusually early age of thirty-nine. In 111 CE, Pliny was sent to his final post as governor of the combined provinces of Bithynia and Pontus, on the south coast of the Black Sea. Bithynia was a province in turmoil and Trajan needed a trusted and capable administrator to put its affairs back in order. During the decade before Pliny arrived as governor, the province of Bithynia had brought charges against two successive governors, Julius Bassus (102–103 CE) and Varenus Rufus (106–107 CE) for financial mismanagement and Pliny had successfully defended both governors against the charges. When he arrived in September 111, Pliny's mandate was to figure out what was wrong with the affairs of the province and address the issues.

From his correspondence with Trajan, it becomes evident that Pliny identified three categories of problems: first, there was political disorder in the province; second, municipal bankruptcy due to unregulated public spending; and third, irregularities in administration. It was in his tour of Bithynia and Pontus that Pliny first encountered a group of people called "Christians," and it was within the context of the threat of political disorder that he responded to them. Because of the risk of spreading disorder, Trajan had banned the formation of all societies, especially ones that were not open to public scrutiny. Christian gatherings and mysteries fell under this category. Pliny sent a letter, *Letter 96*, to Trajan describing the group and their practices as well as the measures he had already taken in response. From Pliny's letter we learn for the first time that Christians had been in the provinces for at least two or three generations, and that some who had been Christians or had grown up in Christian families had returned to traditional Roman religion, some "even twenty years ago." We learn that many were Roman citizens while others were not; they were of all ages and socioeconomic strata, from the cities and rural areas alike. Pliny also informs Trajan that there were anonymous lists circulated accusing women and men of being Christian, and therefore worthy of summary punishment. While some chose to offer the requisite obeisance—curse the name of Christ, and offer a sacrifice of loyalty to the emperor—others did not and were executed. *Letter 96* is also the first description of a Christian worship service by a non-Christian source. Pliny characterizes the Christian gatherings as innocent in nature (that is, not seditious) and provides a stunningly beautiful description of the Christian commitment to the commandments of Jesus for purity of life and honest witness to the world. Pliny says he extracted the details of the regular services during the torture of two slave women, "whom they call deaconesses."

Having concluded that Christianity was nothing more than a "depraved sort of cult [*superstitio*] carried to extravagant lengths," Pliny suggested to Trajan that whatever the nature of their belief, since it was forbidden, the practice was a defiance of authority and the Christians' "obstinacy and unyielding inflexibility should be sufficient reason for punishment." Trajan's reply is recorded in Letter 97 and affirms Pliny's estimation and practice.

Letter 96, Gaius Plinius to the Emperor Trajan[1]

It is my custom to refer to you, Sir, everything about which I have questions, since you are the one best able to resolve my hesitation and correct my ignorance.

I have never been present at the interrogation (*congitio*) of Christians. Therefore I do not know what punishment is required or how far it is to be carried out, nor the legal grounds for an investigation, or how severely it should be prosecuted. Nor am I clear whether any distinction should be made in respect to the age of the persons, or if the young and the old should be treated alike; whether a pardon should be granted in the case of those who recant, or if there is no advantage for a person completely ceasing to be a Christian; whether it is the name ["Christian"] which is punishable, even if not involved in crime, or if it a crime to be associated with the name.

In the meantime, this is how I handle the cases of those who have been handed over to me as Christians. I ask them in person if they are Christian, and if they admit it, I ask them a second and a third time, and warn them of the danger of their situation. If they persist, I order them executed; and I have no hesitation in this for, whatever it was they professed, I am convinced that their stubbornness and inflexible obstinacy is sufficient reason for punishment. There have been others who were similarly insane with this cult, but since they were Roman citizens, I sent them to Rome for trial.

Now that I have begun to handle this situation, as is often the case, the numbers and kinds of charges are becoming more widespread. An anonymous list has been circulated which contains the names of a great number of persons. I have decided to dismiss charges against anyone on this list who stated they were not, nor had they ever been Christians, if they repeated after me a prayer of invocation to the gods and made an offering of wine and incense to your statue, which I had brought in the court along with the statues of the gods for this purpose, and in addition they were to curse Christ: none of these, I understand, genuine Christians will ever do.

---

1. The Latin text of the *Letters* can be found online at The Latin Library: http://www.thelatinlibrary.com/pliny.ep10.html.

Others, whose names were given to me by an informant, first said they were Christians and then denied it. They said that they had been [Christians] and then stopped, some three years ago, others even twenty years ago. They all venerated your statue and those of the gods, and cursed Christ. They also stated that the sum total of their guilt or error was that they meet regularly on a given day before dawn, singing responsively a hymn to Christ as to a god, and also swearing a sacred oath (*sacramentum*) not to commit any crime, never to commit theft or robbery or adultery, or break an agreement, or fail to return a deposit entrusted to them when asked to do so. When this ceremony was finished, it was their custom to go their separate ways and come together again later to take food of an ordinary and simple kind; but after my edict which banned all political societies, they had given up this practice. At this time, I thought it necessary to extract the truth by torture from two slave women, whom they call Deaconesses (*ministrae*). I found nothing more than a depraved and unrestrained cult (*superstitio*).

I have therefore postponed further interrogations and hastened to consult you. This situation seems to me to be worthy of your consideration, especially in view of the large number of people falling into this danger; for a large number of people of every age and class, both men and women alike, are being brought to trial, and this seems likely to continue. It is not only in cities, but also in villages and rural areas which are being infected with this contagious cult (*superstitio*).

It seems to me that it is still possible to check and reverse this direction, for it is quite clear that the temples of the gods which had been empty for so long, have begun to be filled again, and the sacred rites which had been allowed to lapse are being performed again, and flesh for sacrificial rites is now sold at the shops everywhere, though until recently no one would buy it. It seems reasonable to conclude that a great many people could be persuaded to reform if there were a legal procedure for repentance.

Letter 97, Emperor Trajan to Pliny:

You have done what is right, my dear Pliny, in handling the cases of those who were brought to you under the charge of being Christians, for it is not possible to establish a universal rule out of a specific formula. These people must not be searched out; if they are brought before you and the charge against them is proven, they must be punished, but in the case of anyone who denies he is a Christian and makes it clear that he is not by offering prayers to our gods, such one is to be pardoned as a result of his repentance, however suspect he may have been in the past. But anonymous lists must have no place in the court proceedings. They create the worst example and are not at all in keeping with our times.

THE *DIDACHE* (CA. 80–120 CE)

The *Didache*, or *The Teaching of the Twelve Apostles*, belongs to the "church order" category of documents and is a collection of catechetical instructions for use in the church, dating from around the end of the first century to the beginning of the second. The first section, is a set of ethical instructions knows as the "two ways" section in which those who were initiated into the Christian community were given moral guidance as to "the path of life" and the "path of death." The first four chapters reflect Jesus's teaching, especially in the so-called Sermon on the Mount (Matthew 5–7, Luke 6), and explain in depth and in practical terms the meaning of the commandment to love God and one's neighbor, emphasizing love for one's enemies as a unique Christian characteristic. In so doing, the *Didache* opens for us a very important window to the ethical expectations of the early Church and allows us to see what was expected of Christians before they came to baptism (ch. 7), and how the community understood itself and its sacraments (chs. 8–10). In the section presented here, the catechumens are given the hermeneutical lens that is to form the rest of their understanding of the Christian life.

Didache 1.1–6[2]

1. [1] There are two ways, one of life and one of death, and there is a great difference between the two ways.

   [2] This then is the way of life: First, you shall love God, who made you; Second, you shall love your neighbor as yourself.[3] And

---

2. The Greek text of the *Didache* can be found in *The Apostolic Fathers*, edited by Bart D. Ehrman.

3. Matt 22:37–39; Mark 12:30–31; Luke 10:27; Deut 6:5; Lev 19:18.

whatever you do not want to happen to you, do not do to another.[4] [3] This is the teaching of these words: Bless those who curse you and pray for your enemies, and fast for those who persecute you. For what credit is it to you if you love those you love you? Do not even the Gentiles do this as well?[5] But you should love those who hate you,[6] and you will have no enemy. [4] Abstain from fleshly and bodily passions.[7] If someone strikes you on your right cheek, turn the other to him as well[8] and you will be perfect. If someone compels you to go one mile, go with him two.[9] If anyone takes your cloak, give him your shirt as well.[10] If anyone seizes what belongs to you do not demand it back,[11] for you are not able to do so. [5] Give to everyone who asks you, and do not demand it back,[12] for the Father wants something of his own gifts to be given to everyone. Blessed is the one who gives according to the commandment, for that one is innocent. Woe to the one who receives. If anyone receives because one is in need, this one is innocent. But the one who receives without a need will have to explain why and for what purpose he received, and he will be thrown into prison and will be interrogated about what he did, and he will not be released from there until he pays back every last cent.[13] [6] For it has also been said concerning this: "Let your gift sweat in your hands until you know to whom to give it."

FIRST CLEMENT (CA. 80–100 CE)

The letter known as *First Clement* is one of the earliest extant Christian documents outside the New Testament. Sent from the churches in Rome to the churches in Corinth before the turn of the century, *1 Clement* was

---

4. Cf. Matt 5:44–47; Luke 6:31.

5. Cf. Luke 6:28.

6. Cf. Matt 7:12; Luke 6:27–28, 32–33, 35

7. 1 Pet 2:11

8. Matt 5:48.

9. Matt 5:41.

10. Luke 6:29; cf. Matt 5:40.

11. Luke 6:30.

12. Ibid.

13. Cf. Matt 5:26; Luke 12:59.

written to address the factiousness that had resulted from competing claims to leadership. It seems that a group of younger Christians had rebelled against the established leadership of the churches and deposed even presbyters (3.3; 44.6; 47.6). The appeal came from the churches in Rome for "peace and harmony" (63.2), and the whole affair is interpreted in spiritual terms, as a conflict between "spirit and order" and between orthodoxy and heresy. The strong military imagery used in chapter 37 echoes the language in 2 Tim 2:3 and frames the appeal to the restoration of the deposed presbyters to their positions, submitting to their authority, and living in peace with each other, against the clear warnings on the dangers of disunity. Within the context of the Corinthian situation, then, 1 *Clement* 37.1–5 cannot be interpreted as endorsing either war of military service, but, on the contrary, it needs to be placed alongside the language of Eph 6:10–17. Likewise, 1 *Clement* 61.1–3, which echoes Romans 13 and 1 Timothy 2, is a prayer on behalf of governing authorities whom the writer sees appropriately as appointed by and accountable to God.

1 Clement 37.1–5[14]

37. [1] Therefore, brothers, let us serve with all eagerness as soldiers under his blameless commands. [2] Let us consider the soldiers who serve under our commanders, in what good order, with what readiness, with what obedience they execute orders. [3] Not all are prefects[15] or chiliarchs[16] or centurions or captains of fifty[17] and so forth, but each in his own rank executes what is ordered by the king and the leaders. [4] Those who are great cannot exist without the small, nor the small without the great. There is a certain blending in all

14. The Greek text of the 1 *Clement* can be found can be found in *The Apostolic Fathers*, edited by Bart D. Ehrman.

15. In command of the legions of the province.

16. Commanders of a thousand troops.

17. Helgeland, "Christians and the Roman Army," 734: "When Clement pleaded with the Corinthians to obey the ecclesiastical discipline which placed bishops over the laity, . . . most likely appropriated this description of an army (he never said it was the Roman army) from the 'Septuagint' where the exact words for those same detachments are used (except for the word for prefect, of course). The words for the leader of fifty is found referring to the army of the Seleucids, and was, therefore, probably taken over in the translation of the 'Septuagint' [2 Kings 1]."

things, and therein lies the advantage. [5] Take our own body. The head is nothing without the legs, just as the feet are nothing without the head. Even the most insignificant parts of our body are necessary and useful for the whole body. Yet all parts come together and are subjected to a single order so as to keep the whole body safe.

1 Clement 61.1–3

61. [1] You, O Master, have given them the authority to rule through your magnificent and indescribable power, so that we may both recognize the glory and honor you have given them and subject ourselves to them, resisting nothing that conforms to your will. Grant to them, O Lord, health, peace, harmony, and stability, in order that they may administer the rule that you have given to them without stumbling. [2] It is you, Heavenly Master, King of the Ages, who gives human beings glory, honor, and authority over the creatures of the earth. Guide their plans, O Lord, according to what is good and acceptable before you, so that by administering with piety in peace and meekness the authority you have given them they may attain your mercy. [3] You, who alone can do these and even greater good things for us, we praise through the high priest and benefactor of our souls, Jesus Christ, through whom the glory and majesty be yours both now and for all generations and forever. Amen.

IGNATIUS OF ANTIOCH (†CA. 116 CE)

It is undeniable that whatever the disposition of a writer (Christian and non-Christian alike) towards war and military service, strong military language and imagery conveys the urgency and gravity of a situation. Early tradition holds that Ignatius was the second or third bishop of Syrian Antioch (Ign. *Rom.* 2.2) after Peter and Euodius (Eusebius, *Hist. eccl.* 3.22.36). Ignatius was arrested during the reign of Trajan (98–117 CE) and was forced to journey to Rome where he was condemned to die *ad bestias* in the amphitheater. On the long way to the capital, Ignatius wrote six letters to churches of Asia minor and Rome and a personal letter to Bishop Polycarp of Smyrna. Throughout his letters Ignatius emphasized the need for unity in the church and dedication to the faith under episcopal authority. In his letter to Polycarp, Ignatius uses military imagery and makes it clear that love and endurance in faith is what is demanded of Christians.

To Polycarp 6[18]

6. [1] All of you should pay attention to the bishop so that God may pay attention to you. I am giving my life on behalf of those who are subject to the bishop, the presbyters, and the deacons. May it be granted me to have a place with them in [the presence of] God. Labor together with one another, compete together like athletes, run together, suffer together, lie down together, rise together as God's household stewards, attendants, and servants [2] Be pleasing to the one in whose army all of you serve (cf. 2 Tim 2:4), from whom also you receive your wages. Let none of you be found a deserter. Let your baptism remain as your weaponry, your faith as a helmet, your love as a spear, your endurance as your armor (cf. Eph 6:11–17). Let your works be your deposits, that you may receive the back pay you deserve.[19] Be patient, therefore, with each other in gentleness, as God is with you. May I have joy in you always.

JUSTIN MARTYR (CA. 100–165 CE)[20]

Justin was born in Flavia Neapolis (modern Nablus) in Samaria, in Palestine, to a Greek-speaking pagan family that held Roman citizenship. Only few details survive of his early years. He received a Greek philosophical education in Flavia Neapolis and it was in his quest for true knowledge among the various philosophical schools that he came to Christianity through the witness of an old man who walked along with him at the sea shore in Ephesus and explained the Old Testament and the Gospel to him: "My spirit was immediately set on fire, and a love for the prophets and of those who are friends of Christ, took hold of me."[21] Justin

---

18. The Greek text of the Ignatius's letter *To Polycarp* can be found in *The Apostolic Fathers*, edited by Bart D. Ehrman.

19. Ign. *Pol.* 6.2. It was customary for Roman soldiers to be paid only half of their salary, with the other half deposited to their account with the financial officer of the legion to be received when honorably discharged at the end of their 20–25 years of service.

20. The Greek texts are from Goodspeed (ed.), *Die ältesten Apologeten*.

21. Justin, *Dial.* 8.1.

left Asia Minor for Rome (ca. 140), where he taught Christianity in the manner of a philosopher, during the reign of Antoninus Pius. He moved back to Palestine in 151–155, and then returned to Rome a second time (155/56–65/66), where he continued to teach, presenting Christianity as "the only sure and beneficial philosophy."[22] This approach to philosophy brought Justin in direct conflict with a number of the other philosophical schools active in Rome, including the cynic philosopher Crescens. Eventually, he was arrested and martyred (ca. 165/66, early in the reign of Marcus Aurelius). The *Acts of the Martyrs* preserve Justin's death scene. Having been charged for holding meetings, Justin and six of his companions were brought before the prefect of Rome, Junius Rusticus, to be interrogated and were ordered to sacrifice to the gods. Confessing to be Christians, Justin and his companions refused to offer the requisite sacrifices and were condemned to be beaten with rods and beheaded. Eventually, their bodies were carried off in secret by other Christians who buried them with honor.

Justin wrote his *First Apology* in the 150s—most likely when he returned to Palestine—and addressed it to the emperor Antoninus Pius (138–161 CE). Composed during Justin's second stay at Rome, the *Dialogue with Trypho* reports a discussion Justin had with the Jew Trypho at Ephesus, shortly after the Jewish rebellion against Rome (132–135 CE), known as the Bar Kochba revolt. The first of the Greek Apologists, Justin presents a defense against the common charges of novelty, atheism, immorality, and sedition, by tracing the fulfillment of the Old Testament prophesies of the Messianic age to Christ and by arguing that Christianity if the only true philosophy. Justin argues for the diachronic character of Christianity against the charges of novelty and atheism, and offers the moral life of the Christians and their active transformation away from killing and war into acts of kindness and love of enemy as proof against the charges of immorality and atheism. Jesus inaugurated the "age of peace" promised in Mic 4:1–4 and Isa 2:2–4 welcoming every "race of people" into his community. By being joined into a new people through baptism, Christians conquer the enmity that existed among people and between nations, and the grounds for warfare cease to exist. Christians do not raise arms even in self-defense and would rather be martyred than kill anyone. On the contrary, the patience, kindness,

---

22. Ibid.

honesty, and disregard for ethnic and racial differences by the Christians are attracting their pagan neighbors to God (1 *Apol.* 1.16.1–4).

One also needs to note here that Justin's famous pupil, Tatian, refused military command (*Or.* 11.1) and attributed wars to the inspiration of demons (*Or.* 19.2–4).[23]

1 Apology 1.14.3

14. [3] We who hated and slaughtered one another, we who would not welcome to our homes people of a different race because of their customs, now, since the coming Christ we live and eat with them, and we pray for our enemies, and we try to persuade those who hate us, unjustly, to live according to the good counsel of Christ, so that they may share with us in the good hope of the things that come from God, the ruler of all.

1 Apology 1.15.9

15. [9] And concerning our affection for all people, [Christ] taught us these things: "If you love those who love you, what new thing do you do? For even fornicators do the same. But I tell you: Pray on behalf of your enemies, love those who hate you, bless those who curse you, and pray on behalf of those who act despitefully towards you" [cf. Matt 5:44; Rom 12:14].

1 Apology 1.16.1–4

16. [1] And concerning our being long-suffering and ready to serve all, and free from anger, this is what he [Christ] said: "To the one who strikes you on one cheek, offer the other also; and to the one who takes your shirt do not forbid your coat also; [2] whoever shall be angry is in danger of the fire. And everyone who compels you to go with him one mile, follow him two. Let your good works shine before all people so that, by seeing them, they may glorify your Father who is in heaven" [Matt 5:16, 22, 39–41]. [3] For we ought not to rebel; nor does [Christ] want us to imitate the wicked, but he has exhorted us, by our patience and kindness, to guide all people out of

---

23. Tatian, *Oratio ad Graecos.*

shame and desire for evil. [4] And we have the proof of this in the many examples of those who used to be on your side but who have turned from the way of violence and tyranny, who were overcome by observing their neighbors' steadfast way of life, or by observing the strange patience of their fellow travelers when they were taken advantage of, or by experiencing the [honest] way they did business with them.

1 Apology 1.17.2–3

17. [2] We try to pay taxes and assessments, everywhere and more ready than everyone, to those who have been appointed by you, just as we were taught by him [Jesus]. For at that time some came and asked him if it was necessary to pay taxes to Caesar. And he replied, "Tell me, whose image is on the coin?" and they said, "Caesar's." And he replied to them again, "Give to Caesar what is Caesar's, and to God what is God's."[24] [3] That is why we worship God alone, but in regards to other things, we serve you gladly, acknowledging you as kings and rulers of people, and we pray that along with your royal power you may be found to have sound judgment.

1 Apology 1.39

39. [1] When the Spirit of prophecy speaks of things to come, he says: "For the law will go forth from Zion and the Word of the Lord from Jerusalem, and he shall judge between the nations and arbitrate among many peoples; and they shall beat their swords into plowshares and their spears into pruning hooks, and nation will not lift up sword against nation, neither shall they learn to war any more"[25] [Mic 4:2, 3; Isa 2:3, 4]. [2] We can show you that this has really happened. [3] For twelve men went forth from Jerusalem, and they were common men, not trained in speaking, but by the power of God they testified to every race of people, just as they were sent by Christ to teach all the word of God; and now, we who used to kill each other not only do we not fight our enemies but, in order that we might not

---

24. Matt 22:15–22; Mark 12:13–17; Luke 20:20–26.
25. The quotation is from the LXX.

even lie nor deceive our inquisitors, we gladly die bearing witness to Christ. [4] In fact, it would be possible for us to follow the saying: "The tongue has sworn, but the mind remains unsworn";[26] [5] but it would be ridiculous for the soldiers whom you have recruited and enrolled to embrace their confession to you before their own life and their parents and their homeland and all that is familial, even though you can offer them nothing incorruptible, and for us, who love incorruptibility, not to endure all things in order to receive what we long for from him who is able to give it.

Dialogue with Trypho 85.7[27]

85. [7] "Friends," I replied, "listen to the Scripture I obey when I act this way. Jesus commanded us to love even our enemies, as Isaiah had also announced in many passages, in whose words is [included] also the mystery of our new birth, and of all those who, in simplicity, expect Christ to be revealed [(or, to come again)] in Jerusalem and strive to please him in their every action.

(In 85.8–9, Justin quotes at length Isa 66:5–11 from the Septuagint.)

Dialogue with Trypho 96.2-3a

96. [2] Now, you can see clearly that this has actually happened. For in your synagogues you curse all those who have become Christians through [the crucified one], and the gentiles put into effect your curse by killing those who merely confess to be Christians. To all we say, "You are our brothers [cf. Isa 66:5], recognize the truth of God." And since neither you nor they are persuaded by us, you struggle to force us to deny the name of Christ, but, we overcome and endure preferring to die, confident that God will give us all the blessings which he promised us through Christ. [3] And in addition to all these, we pray that you may experience the mercy of Christ. For he

26. Justin rejects that Christians could swear an oath of loyalty to Caesar without really meaning it, even though it was allowed by Roman custom. See also, Tertullian, *Apol.* 27.2.

27. My translation. For full text see Justin Martyr, *Dialogue with Trypho*, translated by Thomas B. Falls.

taught us to pray even for our enemies, saying: "Be kind and merciful, just as your heavenly Father is" [Luke 6:36].

Dialogue with Trypho 110.3-4a

110. [3] And we who were full of war and the slaughter of one another and every kind of iniquity, have in every part of the world converted our weapons of war [into implements of peace], "our swords into ploughshares, our spears into farmer's tools" [Mic 4:3] and we cultivate piety, justice, love of humanity (*philanthropia*), faith, and hope, the kind that comes from the Father through the crucified one; . . . [4] Now it is obvious that no one can frighten us or subdue us who believe in Jesus throughout the world. For it is evident that, though we are beheaded and crucified, thrown to the wild beasts, the chains, the fire, and all the other forms of torture, we will not renounce our confession; the more such things happen, the more do others, in great numbers, come to faith and become worshipers of God through the name of Jesus. Just as when one cuts off the fruit-bearing branches of a vine, other branches shoot afresh and blossom again and bear fruit, so it is with us. For the vine that was planted by God and Christ the savior is his people.

EPISTLE TO DIOGNETUS (CA. SECOND HALF OF SECOND CENTURY CE)

The Epistle to Diognetus is generally recognized as one of the most eloquent examples of early Christian literature. It belongs to the apologetic corpus along with the writings of Aristides (ca. 145 CE), Justin Martyr († 165 CE), Athenagoras (170–180 CE), and Theophilus of Antioch († ca. 180 CE). Its author is unknown, as is the recipient, but the overall arc of the argument is fairly clear. Addressed to an educated Greco-Roman audience, *The Epistle to Diognetus* seeks to respond to three specific charges levied against early Christians, namely, that Christians practiced incest (they married their "brothers and sisters"), performed cannibalistic rites (they ate flesh and drank blood), and they sacrificed infants. Greeks and Romans regarded Christians as "atheist" because they refused to honor the traditional gods and customs of the ancestors, and because they did not participate in the public religious rituals that unified civic society.

As a result, sedition also became a popular charge against Christians. In sections 5.1—6.4, the writer of *The Epistle to Diognetus* responds to the perceived threat to the well-being of the state and insists that the Christian way of life is morally superior and that Christians respond to persecution with kindness and love for those who persecute them.

Epistle to Diognetus 5–6 [28]

5. For Christians are not distinguished from other people by country, or language or custom. [2] Nowhere do they live in cities of their own, or speak a strange dialect, or live life in a peculiar way. [3] This teaching of theirs has not been discovered by the intellect and thought of busy people, nor do they promote any human doctrine, as some do. [4] Yet while they live in both Greek and barbarian cities, according to the lot each received, and follow the local customs in clothing and food and in the rest of life, they demonstrate the remarkable and admittedly paradoxical character of their own citizenship. [5] They live in their respective countries, but only as resident aliens;[29] they participate in all things as citizens and they endure all things as foreigners. Every foreign country is their homeland, and every homeland is foreign. [6] They marry like everyone else and have children, but they do not expose them when they are born. [7] They share their table but not their bed.[30] [8] They are in the flesh, but they do not live according to the flesh. [9] They live on earth, but their citizenship is in heaven. [10] They obey the established laws, and in their own lives they surpass the laws. [11] They love everyone and by everyone the are persecuted. [12] They are unknown, yet they are condemned. They are put to death, and they are brought to life. [13] They are poor and make many rich. They lack all things, and they abound in everything. [14] They are dishonored, and they are glorified in their dishonor. They are slandered, yet they are vindicated. [15] They are reviled, yet they bless. They are insulted, yet they bestow honor. [16] When they do good, they are punished as evildoers. When they are punished, they rejoice as though brought

28. The Greek text of *Diognetus* can be found in *The Apostolic Fathers*, edited by Bart D. Ehrman.

29. Or, sojourners.

30. That is, they share their food, but not their spouses.

to life. [17] By the Jews they are assaulted as foreigners, and by the Greeks they are persecuted; and those who hate them are unable to give a reason for their hostility.

6. [1] To put the matter simply, what the soul is to the body, Christians are to the world. [2] The soul is spread through all the members of the body, and Christians throughout the cities of the world. [3] The soul dwells in the body, but is not of the body; likewise Christians dwell in the world, but are not of the world. [4] The soul, which is invisible, is guarded in the visible body; in the same way, Christians are recognized as being in the world, and yet their religion remains invisible. [5] The flesh hates the soul and wages war against it, even though it has suffered no wrong, because it is hindered from indulging in its pleasures. And the world hates the Christians, even though it has suffered no wrong, because they are opposed to its pleasures. [6] The soul loves the flesh that hates it, along with its members; Christians love those who hate them. [7] The soul is imprisoned in the body, but it holds the body together; Christians are detained in the world as in a prison, yet they hold the world together. [8] The soul, which is immortal, lives in a mortal dwelling; likewise, Christians live as sojourn among perishable things, waiting for the imperishable which is in heaven. [9] The soul, when poorly treated in regards to food and drink, becomes better; and Christians when punished daily increase all the more. [10] God has appointed them to such a position, and it would not be right for them to decline it.

ATHENAGORAS (†CA. 180 CE)[31]

Athenagoras was a learned and eloquent Athenian philosopher who converted to Christianity around the middle of the second century. Written in 177 CE, Athenagoras's *Plea for Christians* (or, *Plea on Behalf of the Christians*) was addressed to emperors Marcus Aurelius and his son Lucius Aurelius Commodus, and stands unique among the extant Greek and Latin Christian apologies from the second century. The "Philosopher and Christian," as W. R. Schoedel calls Athenagoras, employs the full range

31. For the Greek text and an introduction to Athenagoras see Athenagoras, *Legatio Pro Christianis*, edited by Miroslav Marcovich. Sections of the Greek text from Athenagoras, *Legatio and De resurrectione*, edited by W. R. Schoedel.

of his philosophical erudition and Christian education and the full force of his rhetorical skill to convince Marcus Aurelius against the customary accusations of cannibalism, incest, and atheism (see Justin Martyr).

Like Justin and *Diognetus*, Athenagoras turns to Jesus's ethical commands to love one's enemies to prove that the charges against Christians are illogical and unjust (chaps. 1–3). Athenagoras is the first of the Christian apologists to establish the principle of monotheism on primarily philosophical grounds (chaps. 4–6) and, after a short excursus on the superiority of the Christian faith in God (chaps. 7–8), he presents a strong expositions of the unity of God and the doctrine of the Trinity (chaps. 9–10). Having shown that the God of the Christians is the only true God, Athenagoras shows that the demands placed upon Christians to worship the Roman gods are both illogical and unnecessary (chaps. 12–14). In the middle of that discourse on the unity and superiority of God, or perhaps because of it, Athenagoras provides an articulate defense against the charge of immorality (chs. 4, 11, 31–37) by emphasizing Jesus's commands for purity in all things and underscoring the love of enemy, even when persecuted. He concludes that it this spirit of piety that gives rise to the Christians aversion to bloodshed and killing in any form, including abortion, infanticide, and the (very popular) gladiatorial games: "Even watching a man being slain is next to killing him" (35.5). It was during this period (in early 177 CE) that Marcus Aurelius had enacted the legislation *Senatus Consultum de Pretiis Gladiatorum Minuendis*. With this legislation, the emperor had given local magistrates the authority to condemn criminals to death, providing cheap alternatives for the carnage of the gladiatorial games. Blandina and her fellow martyrs in Lyon were executed under this legislation.

Plea on behalf of the Christians P–1.4.

P. To the Emperors Marcus Aurelius Anoninus and Lucius Aurelius Commodus, conquerors of Armenia and Sarmatia, and more than all, philosophers.

1. [1] In your empire, greatest of sovereigns, different peoples have different customs and laws, and no one of them is hindered by law or fear of punishment from following one's ancestral ways, however ridiculous these may be. Someone from Ilium calls Hector a god, and reveres Helen, taking her for Adrasteia, while the Lacedemonian

venerates Agamemnon as Zeus, and Phylonoe, the daughter of Tyn-dareus, [and those from Tenedos worship Tennes]; the Athenian of-fers sacrifices to Erechtheus as Poseidon. The Athenians also per-form religious rites and celebrate mysteries in honor of Agraulus and Pandrosus, even though these women were considered guilty of impiety for opening the box. In short, among every nation and people, people offer whatever sacrifices and mysteries they wish. The Egyptians count among their deities even cats, and crocodiles, and serpents, and asps, and dogs.

[2] And to all these both you and the laws give permission, con-sidering it, on the one hand, impious and wicked to not believe in god at all, and on the other, that it is necessary for each person to worship the gods one prefers, in order that through fear of the divine, people may be kept from wrongdoing. With us, on the contrary—for do not, like the crowd, be let astray by hearsay—the mere name is de-spised. It is not names that deserve to be hated, but the unjust act that calls for penalty and punishment. Accordingly, while admiring your mildness and gentleness and your peaceful and benevolent attitude towards all, everyone enjoys equal rights; and the cities, according to their rank, share in equal honor; and, through your wisdom, the whole empire enjoys profound peace.

[3] But you have not cared for us who are called Christians in this way; and although we commit no wrong but, as it will be shown in this discourse, we are of all people most piously and righteously disposed toward God and your reign, you allow us to be harassed, plundered, and persecuted, the mob making war upon us only be-cause of our name. We venture, therefore, to state our case before you (and you will ascertain from what we say that we suffer unjustly, and contrary to all law and reason) and we beseech you to show some consideration to us also, so that we may cease to be slaughtered on account of false accusers.

[4] The injury we suffer from our persecutors is not aimed [mere-ly] at our property [lit., money] or our civil rights or our honor or anything of less importance—after all, we hold these things in con-tempt (although they appear of great importance to the masses), for we have learned not only not to return blow for blow, or to bring to court those who plunder and rob us, but to those who strike us on the

one cheek to offer the other, and to those who take away our shirt to give also our coat—for when we have given up our property, they plot against our very bodies and souls, pouring upon us a host of criminal charges about things we cannot even imagine, but which belong to these very prates and to the whole tribe of those who are like them.

Plea on behalf of the Christians 11.1–2, 4

11. [1] Do not wonder if I relate our doctrine in detail to you. I will speak with precision so that you might not be misled by the commonly held and irrational opinion, but that you may have the truth clearly before you. For by presenting to you what we believe as being not of human origin but as uttered and taught by God, we will persuade you not to consider us as atheists. [2] What, then, are these teachings by which we are brought up? "I say to you, Love your enemies, bless those who curse you, pray on behalf of those who persecute you, so that you may be sons of your Father who is in heaven, who causes his sun to rise on the evil and the good, and sends rain on the just and the unjust" [Matt 5:44–55].

[4] [No one among the philosophers has been able to purge one's soul to such an extend as to love one's enemy] Yet among us, you will find uneducated persons, and artisans, and old women who, even if they cannot prove the benefit of [our faith] through words, through their deeds they prove the benefit that results from our devotion [*or*, faith]; for they do not memorize speeches, but rather they exhibit good works; when struck, they do not strike back, and when they are robbed, they do not bring charges; to everyone who asks of them, they give, and they love their neighbors as themselves.

Plea on behalf of the Christians 35

35. [1] What person of sound mind, then, will say that we are murderers? For it is not possible to eat human flesh if we have not first killed someone. [2] Since the first charge is false, if someone was to ask them [our accusers] about the second one, if they have seen what they claim, no one would be so shameless as to say that he has. [3] And since we have slaves, some more, others fewer, we could not help

but be seen by them; yet even among them, no one has been found to bear such false witness against us. [4] For when they know that we cannot endure to see someone be put to death, even justly, how can one of them accuse us of murder or cannibalism? Who does not make haste[32] to be at the contests with the gladiatorial and the wild beasts that you have sponsored? [5] But because for us even watching a man being slain is next to killing him, we have forbidden watching such spectacles. How, then, can we, who do not even look on, lest guilt and pollution rubs off on us, put people to death?

Plea on behalf of the Christians 37

37. [1] And now that I have disposed of the several accusations and proved that we are pious, and gentle, and temperate in spirit [lit., soul] nod your royal head in approval. [2] For who are more justified in receiving the things they ask, than those who, like us, pray for your reign that it may pass from father to son, as is most right, and that our empire may increase and advance, all becoming subject to you? [3] And this is also for our advantage, that we may lead a peaceful and quiet life, and that we may serve readily in whichever way we are called to do so [cf. 1 Tim 2:2].

CLEMENT OF ALEXANDRIA (CA. 150–CA. 215 CE)

Clement is the last of the Greek apologists. Early tradition spoke of him as being born in Athens in the middle of the second century. Clement was born into a pagan family and, like Justin and Athenagoras before him, he wandered into a variety of philosophical schools of his time before he ended up in Alexandria, in Egypt, and met with Pantaenus, the head of the Catechetical School of the church at Alexandria. Clement speaks of his Christian teachers as "blessed and memorable men" who spoke "plain and living words." Ordained a presbyter, Clement succeeded Pantaenus as the head of the Catechetical School in 190 CE. Clement taught in Alexandria for more than twenty years before the Septimian persecutions (202–203 CE) forced him to leave the city, first for Jerusalem, then Antioch and, eventually, to Cappadocia (in modern

---

32. Or, "consider it important."

Turkey), where he died ca. 215 CE. Among Clement's pupils were the famed Origen and Alexander, who later became bishop of Jerusalem. An eloquent and prolific writer, Clement sought to demonstrate the intellectual character of Christianity and to show how true philosophy found its fulfillment in the Christian faith. In his writings Clement returns constantly to the Old and New Testaments and puts the scriptures in sophisticated conversation with the philosophers and poets of antiquity to show how the truth of God had permeated all facets of human inquiry, preparing the way for Christ.

Clement did not develop a thorough argument on war and Christian participation in military service, like his contemporaries Tertullian and Origen, but he wrote at length on the moral life of the Christian community and the transformative character of Christ. Bound by the language and imagery of scripture, Clement used ample military analogies in the line of Paul's language, comparing Christians to soldiers and warriors (*Strom.* 6.14.112) and referred to Christ as a military commander (*Paed.* 1.7.54). Clement praises Moses as a prophet, a legislator, a politician, a philosopher, and skilled as a military commander equal to the rulers of Egypt (*Strom.* 1.24.162) and acknowledges the appropriateness of certain military practices in the Old Testament (*Strom.* 2.18.82), yet, like Tatian, he considers wars as inspired by demons (*Protr.* 3.42.1) and concludes that in the New Economy, Christians are "a peaceful race," trained in peace, not in war (*Paed.* 1.12.99) honoring God with "the word of peace alone" (*Paed.* 2.4.42).

On the topic of military service, the most disputed passage from Clement's writings comes from his *Protrepticus*, or *Exhortation to the Greeks*. Clement acknowledges that there are soldiers who have been converted while in service, and seems to repeat Paul's admonition to the Corinthians for Christians to remain in the condition in which they were called (1 Cor 7:20). Clement uses the examples of farmers, sailors, and soldiers and says to the latter: "If you are in the army when you were seized by the knowledge of God, obey the Commander who gives just commands" (10.100.3). Some have taken this as affirming military service to be an acceptable option for Christians, albeit limited to soldiers who convert to the faith while already in service. Louis J. Swift has argued that "it would appear that Clement no more expected the Christian soldier to abandon his profession than he expected the farmer or the sailor to do so."[33] But neither Clement's previous use of such language nor the arc of his argument seem to support such a conclusion. Clement used the analogies of military command and sailing in *Christ the Educator* to describe Jesus, our educator, as the good shepherd who protects his flock, the military commander who brings his troops to safety, and the captain who steers the ship away from danger into the heavenly harbor (1.7.53–54). Later, Clement also describes Christ as "our great General, the Word, the Commander of all" who leads everyone "peacefully to the sacred concord of [his] citizenship" (1.8.65). It seems more likely, then, that Clement is in accord with Tertullian and Origen, instructing soldiers who converted to Christianity to obey their new "Commander who gives just commands" rather than the military hierarchy of the legions.

When considering the issue of obeying orders and judging them as just or unjust, however, there is one further issue we need to keep in mind, namely, the reality of military life and command. The Roman army was composed of professional, volunteer soldiers who were highly trained and disciplined. Soldiers who valued their own life and the lives of their comrades; soldiers who understood that breakdown in formation during battle or discipline, even in peacetime, would lead inevitably to death. Roman soldiers followed the orders of generals and officers they respected and trusted explicitly. Mutiny and insubordination were not options for the Roman armies,[34] and generals had the power to execute summarily any soldier under their command. The argument that Christian writers like Clement would instruct converted soldiers to pass judgment on the commands they received and weigh whether they could be followed based on their new Christian ethic or that soldiers who became Christians would have thought it possible to do so, ignores the realities of military life, discipline, and command. Conscientious objection was not an option for the Roman army.[35]

---

33. Swift, *Early Fathers*, 52. For a similar argument see also Helgeland, "Christians and the Roman Army," 154.

34. Mutinies among the legions were usually the result of dangerous commanders or breaking of promises made to the troops. Suetonius tells of how Julius Caesar quelled a mutiny brewing in the Tenth legion, when the soldiers were not discharged as promised, by a single word, addressing them as "Citizens" instead of "soldiers" (*Jul.* 70).

35. As we are going to see later with the *Acts of the Military Martyrs*.

Exhortation to the Greeks, 10.100.2–5, 108.4–5[36]

10.100. [2] It is man's very nature to be on intimate terms with God. [3] In the same way we do not compel the horse to plow or the bull to engage in the hunt, but direct each animal to the kind of work which is natural to it, we call upon man, who is truly a heavenly creature and who has been made for the vision of heaven, to come to a knowledge of God. Laying hold of what is intimately and peculiarly his own as distinct from other living things, we advise him to outfit himself with godliness as an adequate preparation for his eternal journey. If you are a farmer, we say, till the earth, but acknowledge the God of farmers; if you love seafaring, sail on, but remember to call upon the celestial Helmsman. If you are in the army when you were seized by the knowledge of God, obey the Commander who gives just commands.

10.108. [4] If you count yourself among the people of God, heaven is your country and God is your lawgiver. And what are the laws? "You shall not kill; you shall not commit adultery; you shall not commit pederasty; you shall not steal; you shall not bear false witness; you shall love the Lord your God."[37] And the ones that complement these are eloquent laws and words of sanctity, engraved in the hears of people: "You shall love your neighbor as yourself," and "to the one who strikes you on the one cheek, present also the other," and "you shall not lust, for by lust alone you have commited adultery."

Exhortation to the Greeks, 11.116

11.116. It has been God's eternal purpose to save the flock of people, for which [flock] the good God sent the good Shepherd. And the Word, having unfolded the truth, showed people the height of salvation, so that either by repenting they might be saved, or by disobeying they might be judged. This is the proclamation of righteousness: to those you obey, good news, [and] to those who disobey, judgment. It is as when the blaring trumpet sounds and calls the troops together, and proclaims war. Will not Christ, who has blared a song of peace to

---

36. The Greek text is from Clement, *Le Protreptique*. Translation is adapted from Swift, *Early Fathers*, 52.

37. Here Clement follows the order of the *Didache* 2.

the very ends of the earth, gather together his own soldiers of peace? Indeed, O People, he did assemble a bloodless army by his blood and his word, and to them he entrusted the kingdom of heaven. Christ's trumpet is his gospel. He blew it, and we heard. Let us put on the armor of peace "putting on the breastplate of righteousness" and taking up the "shield of faith" and putting on "the helmet of salvation." Let us sharpen "the sword of the spirit which is the word of God" [cf. Eph 6:14–17; 1 Thess 5:8]. This is how the Apostle arranges us in the battleline of peace. These are our invulnerable weapons. Armed with them, let us take our position against the evil one. Let us "quench the flaming arrows of the evil one" with sharp [swords] wet from the waters of baptism by the Word, giving grateful thanks for the benefits we have received, and honoring God through the Divine Word.

Christ the Educator 1.7.54.2–3[38]

1.7.54 [2] As the general directs the phalanx, taking care to preserve the safety of his soldiers, and as the helmsman steers the ship being mindful to keep safe those who sail with him, so also this *Pedagogue* [Jesus, our Educator in piety] guides the children to a mode of life that leads to salvation, because he cares for us. And, generally speaking, of what we ask of God (in accordance with reason) to be done for us, much more will come to pass for those who believe in the Educator. [3] And just as the helmsman does not always yield to the winds, but sometimes, turning the prow towards them, opposes the forces of the hurricanes, so also the Educator never yields to the winds that blow in the world, nor does he turn his child over like a ship to them to be dashed by a savage and licentious way of life, but rather wafted on by the favorable wind of the Spirit of truth he holds firmly onto the child's tiller (I mean his ears) until he brings the child safely to land at the heavenly harbor.

Christ the Educator 2.4.42.1–3

2.4.42 [1] In reality, a human being is an instrument made for peace, while, if you care to investigate, you will find out that these other ones are

38. The Greek text is from Clement, *Le pédagogue*, 3 vols.

instruments of conflict, for they either enkindle desires or inflame the passions. [2] The Etruscans, for example, use the trumpet for war, the Arcadians use the pipe, the Sicilians use stringed instruments, and the Cretans the lyre, the Lacedemonians the flute, the Thracians the horn, the Egyptians the drum, and the Arabs the cymbal. [3] But as for us, we make use of one instrument alone: only the Word of peace, by whom we honor God, no longer with ancient harp or trumpet or flute which those trained in war use.

Salvation of the Rich 34.3.[39]

34. [3] Do not be deceived, you who have tasted of truth and have been deemed worthy of the great redemption. But contrary to the rest of people, gather for yourself an army without weapons, without war, without bloodshed, without anger, without stain, and army of pious old men, of orphans loved by God, of widows armed with gentleness, of men adorned with love. With your own wealth obtain as guards for your body and your soul, people such as there, whose commander is God; for whose sake a sinking ship rises, steered by the prayers of saints alone; and disease at its height is subdued, put to flight by the laying on of hands; and the attack of robbers is disarmed, its weapons stripped by pious prayers; and the violence of demons is crushed, checked by confident commands.

39. The Greek text is in Clement, *Exhortation to the Greeks. The Rich Man's Salvation. To the Newly Baptized.*

SIX

Tertullian
(ca. 160–ca. 220 CE)

No Christian writer of the first four centuries has written as much on war and military service or on the relationship between the Church and the state as has Tertullian.

Tertullian is often called "the father of Latin theology" and he is one of the most important theologians of the first four centuries, second only to St. Augustine (354–430 CE.). His lasting influence on Western Christianity is vast and is due, in no small measure, to the number of his works that survived through the centuries. Latin theologians turned often to Tertullian for theological direction and insight as it is in his writings that we first encounter terms like *sacramentum, trinitas, persona, substantia,* and *satisfactio* in their Christian, theological sense.[1]

Septimius Tertullianus grew up a pagan in Roman Carthage in the second half of the second century CE and received the standard Greek and Latin education of his time. He studied rhetoric, philosophy, and medicine before converting to Christianity in his thirties. He almost never spoke of his early life and the portrait that has reached our time comes from Eusebius and Jerome in the late fourth century. According to Jerome, Tertullian was ordained a presbyter in the church at Carthage (*Vir. ill.* 53), while Eusebius mentions that his father was a proconsular centurion, and identified him with the Roman jurist Tertullianus (*Hist. eccl.* 2.2.4). These assumptions have informed much of the discussion of Tertullian as a person and have colored the understanding of the nature

---

1. Dunn, *Tertullian,* 10.

of his work, especially during the first three quarters of the twentieth century.[2] Based on these assumptions, Tertullian is often presented as a legalist (presumably a remnant of his training in jurisprudence) and an uncompromising puritan whose rigorism forced him to break with the Catholic Church at the end of the second century and to find a more passionate expression in the schismatic movement known as Montanism (or, the New Prophecy). Tertullian's affiliation with Montanism, in turn, leads some to interpret his work and thought after ca. 206 CE as a movement further into rigorism and separatism.

Beginning with Timothy D. Barnes's critical study of Tertullian in 1971, a more complex narrative of Tertullian's life has emerged, and a more accurate chronology of his works has shed much needed light on the development of this thought. The idea, for example, that his father was a centurion, that Tertullian was a priest, and that he should be identified with the Roman jurist Tertullianus, all have been successfully challenged, as has the nature and effect of Montanism in second-century North Africa. All these assumptions are crucial in understanding Tertullian's arguments and the positions for which he advocated so forcefully. At the end, a much different portrait emerges.[3]

Tertullian belonged to the educated elite of second-century Carthage and wrote in both Latin and Greek. Of Tertullian's writings, thirty-one treatises are accepted as genuine, while a number have not survived. As one considers the totality of his writing career, it becomes evident that, throughout the years, Tertullian's thinking about issues deepened and even changed. Yet, when interpreting his works, it is important to note that all of his writings were occasioned by either a controversy, a point of dispute, or an error that needed to be corrected. Tertullian was an apologist, an advocate, and a polemicist. As Geoffrey Dunn notes, Tertullian did not preach, engage, or write simply to contemplate the mysteries of God, or edify a congregation. Whether engaging Christians or non-Christians, Tertullian "preached, interpreted Scripture and wrote in order to argue. He was a pugilist with a pen."[4] Following the conventions of his time, Tertullian wrote from a *rhetorical perspective*

---

2. Johannes Quasten's treatment of Tertullian exemplifies the commonly accepted wisdom of the middle of the twentieth century. See Quasten, *Patrology*, 2:246–47.

3. Barnes, *Tertullian*; Fredoille, *Tertullien*; Tabbernee, *Montanist Inscriptions*; Rankin, *Tertullian and the Church*; Osborn, *Tertullian*. In this account of Tertullian's life and thought I will rely heavily on Geoffrey Dunn's excellent study of the man and his work.

4. Dunn, *Tertullian*, 9.

and, unlike many of his contemporary Christian writers, he did not write treatises as much as he wrote prescriptions and advocacy papers.[5] Conscious of his audience and aiming to win an argument, Tertullian wrote passionately and often used stark language that sometimes seems trenchant, even sarcastic, and with no room for tepidity. Being aware of the rhetorical purpose of Tertullian's writings helps us to interpret what he wrote and understand that "sometimes it is not a question of him changing his mind over time but of writing with particular readership in mind. In apologetic works [for example] written to imperial officials, he was not as critical of the Roman system as he was in works addressed to an exclusively Christian audience."[6]

Nowhere is this more evident than in the discussion of Tertullian's writings on war and military service. Those who see a dramatic change in Tertullian between the writing of the *Apology* (placing this work shortly after his conversion) and the arguments presented in *Idolatry* and *The Crown* (on the assumption they were written some fifteen years later) often do not take into account either his rhetorical perspective or the recent reevaluation of the fourth-century account of his life. As a result, an "early Tertullian" who first condoned Christian service in the army and presented "the Christian as an ideal citizen of the empire, enjoying the benefits and shouldering its responsibilities—including military service"[7] is often juxtaposed to a "Montanist Tertullian," a rigorist and an obstinate separatist who changed his outlook on the relationship with the state and military service because of his association with a rigorist and "schismatic" movement; perhaps even prompted to do so by the unexpected and brutal Septimian persecutions of the late second century.

William Tabbernee has shown that such an understanding of Montanism does not represent the reality of Tertullian's lifetime. Instead of being a schismatic, separatist movement that verged on misanthropia, Tertullian's Montanism was "a prophetic renewal movement informed by the Holy Spirit,"[8] that ought to be understood as charismatic, ascetic, enthusiastic, innovative, spiritualist, ecstatic, and rigorous.[9] And

5. Ibid., 29.

6. Ibid., 8.

7. The views presented in, e.g., Helgeland, *Christians and the Roman Army*, 737; and Gero, "*Miles Gloriosus*," 298, are common among writers of general histories.

8. Tabbernee, *Montanist Inscriptions*, 24. See also chapters 1, 8–13 in idem, *Prophets and Gravestones*.

9. Dunn, *Tertullian*, 6.

Tertullian's work cannot be properly divided into the pre- and post-Montanist periods, as is often done, for there is "no dramatic or sudden catharsis" in Tertullian's literary career; nor should his embracing of the New Prophesy be read as making a significant change of direction in his religious and theological orientation.[10] When one takes into account questions of audience, rhetorical purpose, and the more recent chronology of his works (which places the writing of the *Apology* very close to that of *Idolatry* and *The Crown* and not fifteen years apart) one sees that Tertullian's ideas do indeed become sharper over time but he is much more consistent in his views on issues of state, war, and military than it seems at first read.[11]

Tertullian's rhetorical flourish and witty aphorisms make his writing quite memorable and eminently quotable. Perhaps one of Tertullian's most often (mis)quoted axioms is "What indeed has Athens to do with Jerusalem? What concord is there between the Academy and the Church?" (*Praescr.* 7.9). Tertullian's point in *Prescription against Heretics* is not that Christians ought not study philosophy, or that Christian faith is indifferent—worse yet, contrary—to reason. Rather, Tertullian is pointing out that classical philosophical methods of enquiry have nothing to do with the teaching authority of Scripture. Scripture was authoritative for Tertullian and, like most other early Christian writers, he used it in almost every chapter of every work.[12] As Dunn points out,

> Tertullian's stated hermeneutic was his belief in the simplicity of Scripture. It could interpret itself, he claimed at one point, and had a method of its own, such that all apparent inconsistency could be explained (*Against Praxeas* 18.2). Indeed, the principle he put forward was that one text of Scripture must always be interpreted in the light of a greater number of texts (*Against Praxeas* 20.2), and that later texts much agree with earlier ones (*Against Praxeas* 20.3).[13]

But most of all, and again in accord with almost every early Christian writer, Tertullian read Scripture christologically, including the Old Testament and the exodus and conquest narratives. Thus, at times Tertullian

10. Ibid., 7.

11. Ibid., 8. See also Evans, "On the Problem of Church," 21–36.

12. The only exceptions were his apologetic works that were written for a pagan audience; Dunn, *Tertullian*, 19.

13. Ibid., 22.

would argue for an allegorical or typological or spiritual interpretation of a scriptural passage, whereas at other times he would advance a more literal interpretation.[14] For him, Christ was the culmination of all Scripture and Jesus's teachings were the definitive interpretive lens. Christianity was the new *philosophia*, properly understood, the new way of life, whose morality was based on divine revelation and, therefore, placed much greater demands for holiness and right living.[15]

Yet, Tertullian did not simply abandon Athens for Jerusalem; nor did he equate Athens with reason and Jerusalem with faith. His was not an anti-rationalist argument for faith but, quite the opposite, a radically rationalist point of view which rejects falsehood of any kind.[16] Justo González has shown that for Tertullian, "the question is not one of reason versus faith as sources of authority but is rather a question of two different sorts of reason. One is the reason of 'Athens'; the other the reason of 'Jerusalem.' One could be called 'dialectic reason' the other would then be 'historical reason.'"[17] "Athens" begins with the theoretically possible, the philosophically articulated necessity, and argues that reason ought to conform to that; while "Jerusalem" begins with what has actually occurred, as revealed in Scripture, and argues that reason ought to conform to the historical event. If one takes the resurrection from the dead, for example, the point is made clear: "Athens" begins with the theoretical impossibility of resurrection and conforms its reason to reject that Jesus rose from the dead. "Jerusalem," on the other hand, begins with the divinely revealed historical event that Jesus rose from the dead and reasons for the resurrection of the dead (cf. 1 Cor 15:32). Tertullian makes use of the same language of paradox in *The Flesh of Christ* (5.4) when he presents the story of Jesus: "The Son of God was born: there is no shame, because it is shameful. And the Son of God died: this is believable because it is unfitting. And, having been buried, he rose again: it is certain because it is impossible."[18] The fact is that in spite of how

14. Ibid.

15. *Pall.* 6.2; *Apol.* 45.3.

16. Sider, "Credo Quia Absurdum?," 417–19.

17. González, "Athens and Jerusalem Revisited," 22.

18. Tertullian, *Carn. Chr.* 5.4: *Natus est Dei Filius; non pudet, quia pudendum est: et mortuus est Dei filius; credible est quia ineptum est: et sepultus resurrexit; certum est quia impossibile est.* Tertullian's saying is not, as has often been misquoted, *credo quia absurdum est* ("I believe because it is absurd"), but rather, *credible est, quia ineptum est* ("It is believable, because it is foolish"). Borrowing from Aristotle's *Rhetoric* 2.23.22, Tertullian stands in a long tradition of antiquity that shows an argument from probability can

improbable this may seem to Athenian philosophical presuppositions, reason has to conform to the historical event, not the other way around.

The same holds true with Tertullian's view of the incompatibility of military service and Christian confession. Even though the philosophical presuppositions of political theory and state pragmatics may present the preservation of the state, its defense, and even flourishing, as a necessary condition to which Christian reasoning (theology) ought to conform, Tertullian turned to the fact of the Gospel of Peace articulated by Jesus, and sought to conform Christian reasoning (theology) to the revealed kingdom of God, namely, to the fact that: "In disarming Peter, the Lord disarmed every soldier" (*Idol.* 19.3). In this, Tertullian was consistent throughout his life.[19]

Even from his earliest writings Tertullian sought to address issues of everyday life and instruct Christians who lived in an overwhelmingly pagan society. The city of Carthage had a direct and long-standing connection with Rome, but was also a crossroads where ancient Punic, Egyptian, Berber, Greek, and Eastern religions, learning, and commerce intersected, creating a unique cosmopolitan center. Christianity burst into the scene sometime during the first half of the second century and within a generation the Christian community in North Africa offered its first recorded martyrs. Twelve Christians from the region of Scilli were executed on 17–18 July 180 CE after offering the most defiant testimony to the proconsul Vigellius Saturninus at Carthage. Promised safety if they would return to the traditional Roman rites and denounce the "new religion" Speratus spoke for the five women and seven men and said: "I do not recognize the empire of this world. . . . [and in all I do] I acknowledge my lord who is the emperor of kings and of all nations."[20]

---

be drawn from the sheer improbability of the story. As Sider, "Credo Quia Absurdum?," 417, notes, Aristotle's principle, followed by Tertullian, was that "some stories are so improbable that it is reasonable to believe them." Moffatt, "Aristotle and Tertullian," 170–71, shows how the paradox of the *certum quia impossibile* was accepted as an obvious axiom of historical proof.

19. Dunn, *Tertullian*, 45.

20. *Pass. Scil.* 6. The text of the *Passio* can be found in Musurillo, *Acts of the Christian Martyrs*, 86–89. It is worth noting that the five women and seven men all have local North African names, and came from the non-citizen rolls. As Frend, *Martyrdom and Persecution*, 314 points out, the *Passio* makes clear that "there is no compromise here. Moreover, the reward for rejecting the 'mos Romanorum' was immediate entry into Paradise. 'Hosie martyres in caelis sumus.' This was to be the rallying-cry of African Christians against the Imperial authorities for the next two centuries. The religion of the Book allowed no other conclusion."

In *The Shows* and *Idolatry*, Tertullian addresses Christians and argues for the incompatibility of the socioreligious constructs that framed existence within the Roman megalopolis as contrary to the Christian faith (*Spect.* 5–14). He reminds Christians that the Roman way of life was violent and God had "prohibited the killing of human beings under any pretext by that one summary precept: 'You shall not kill'" (*Spect.* 2.8). Tertullian asserts that almost every human activity within the world that surrounded them was under the aegis of pagan deities. The Roman spectacles of the theater, the amphitheater, and the circus, were all dedicated to the gods and as such, they were not simple entertainment but were infused with religious elements and rites. To participate in them, argued Tertullian, "even as a spectator, was to engage in idolatry or to be tempted to immorality and violence, the practice of which the Christian had vowed to abandon at baptism."[21]

This was serious business, especially for such a small minority at the fringes of the Roman empire's second largest city.[22] By disassociating themselves from the accepted and expected Roman ways of life, Christians were also disallowing themselves from the myriad of professional opportunities that surrounded them: from the industries that manufactured statues used as idols (*Idol.* 8): from astrology and the lucrative craft of divination, from school teaching (as teachers were expected to educate their pupils in the pagan religious myths that gave meaning to life), from trades that produced or advanced lust, from training gladiators, and from serving in the myriad of public offices. In all they did, Christians were called to leave comfort and security behind (*Idol.* 12). More explicitly, because it involved violence and was based on the military oath (which could not be reconciled with loyalty to God), military service was completely forbidden to a Christian (*Idol.* 19). Tertullian saw how difficult a task it was to be a Christian in a non-Christian environment and "he wanted his fellow Christians to be clearly distinguishable from their pagan neighbors in the way they lived their lives."[23]

In the *Apology*, Tertullian engages in a forensic defense of Christians against the popular charges of atheism, and treason, and against the

21. Dunn, *Tertullian*, 41.

22. Carthage was the second largest city of the empire, with an estimated population of 250,000–500,000 people at the end of the second century CE. There is no reason to estimate the Christian population to more than a few thousands, perhaps only 1,000–2,500 at the turn of the century.

23. Dunn, *Tertullian*, 42.

prurient rumors of incest, murder, and cannibalism. He dispatches with the absurdity of the latter accusations first (*Apol.* 7–9) by highlighting that in popular imagination rumor is received as fact (*Apol.* 7.8–14) and cannot be refuted if the audience is ready to accept the unthinkable as true. He then moves on to present the Christian ethic as proof that such accusations are not credible, declaring that Christians "would prefer to die outright rather than live with such crimes upon their consciences" (*Apol.* 8.9). Tertullian admits the charges of atheism by giving a brilliant twist to the very logic of the accusation itself: Christians ceased worshiping the pagan gods "when [they] discovered that they did not exist" (*Apol.* 10.2). He then proceeds to counter the charge of treason by assuring his readers that Christians pray for the welfare of those in authority (*Apol.* 30), asking "for them long life, undisturbed power, security at home, brave armies, a faithful Senate, and upright people, a peaceful world, and everything for which a man or a Caesar prays" (*Apol.* 30.4). Christians recognize the proper ordering of Caesar as subordinate to God and therefore pray for him to the One who appoints all authorities (*Apol.* 33.2–3). Tertullian's primary concern in the *Apology* was for his readers not to get the impression that "Christians were somehow a separatist sect, even though they refrained from involving themselves in pagan religious activities, affairs of state or the spectacles of public entertainment"[24] (*Apol.* 37.5–6; 38; 42.4–7).

If the primary audience for the *Apology* was the pagan court of public opinion, Christians are explicitly addressed in *The Crown*. During the last part of the second and the beginning of the third century, the Severan reforms resulted in the unprecedented militarization of the Empire and many new inducements were offered to citizens, even those of the most remote provinces, to join the armies of Rome. This new reality meant that Tertullian faced in his own lifetime a situation unimaginable just a few decades earlier, namely that not only was Christianity making inroads into the camp, but now a military career was seen as an attractive option for some baptized Christians.

The occasion for the *The Crown* was most probably a donative provided for the army by the emperors Caracalla and Ceta shortly after their accession in 211 CE. During the parade, in a camp close to Tertullian's home (either at Lambaesis or Carthage), one Christian soldier refused to wear on his head the honorific garland, the *corona*, that had been awarded

---

24. Dunn, *Tertullian*, 41.

to the troops. Being derided by this fellow soldiers, the dissident individual was brought to the tribune for disciplinary action (*Cor.* 1.1–2). In the course of his public examination, the soldier replied that the reason he refused to wear the crown "like everyone else" was simply: "Because I am a Christian" (*Cor.* 1.2). On hearing this, his fellow soldiers clamored for his punishment, while the other Christians among the ranks criticized him for drawing attention to their religious identity (*Cor.* 1.4).

Tertullian presents a fourfold argument in support of the soldier's defiance, by expanding on a series of dominical sayings. He begins by denying the possibility of divided loyalties and serving two masters: by wearing the crown, soldiers demonstrated their allegiance to the emperor which, in fact, Christians could not do, since their allegiance was to God alone (*Cor.* 10; 11.1; 12–14; cf. Matt 6:24; Luke 16:13).[25] Then Tertullian appeals to the Christian obligation not to shed blood by asking: "Is it likely we are permitted to carry a sword when our Lord said that he who takes the sword will perish by the sword?" (*Cor.* 1.2; cf. Matt 26:52.). Next he pointed out "the radical implications of the cultural separatism incumbent on the believer"[26]: the Christian, "a son of peace," (Luke 10:6) is forbidden to avenge even one's own private wrongs by resorting to a court of law (*Cor.* 1.2; cf. Matt 5:40), therefore, *a fortiori* one must not be a soldier, "a man of violence." Finally, Tertullian focuses on the acts of idolatry that the soldier is forced to do in the course of his service (*Cor.* 11.3; cf. 1 Cor 8:10). The conclusion was unambiguous: a Christian could not enlist since it would involve deserting the camp of light for the camp of darkness (*Cor.* 11.4).

Facing the practical question of whether a baptized Christian may remain in the army, Tertullian concludes that those who converted during service ought to leave the army as soon as possible (*Cor.* 11.4–7), for in attempting to satisfy both Roman and Christian precepts, "the Christian would be torn apart."[27]

---

25. Just a few years later St. Cyprian expressed the same objection to the crowning based on the same grounds that Christians who had already received the seal of Christ on their foreheads, could not now place it subordinate to the Roman *corona*. Cyprian argued: "From the accursed and wicked veil with which the enslaved heads of those who sacrifice at the Capitol are veiled, your head remained free. Your forehead, pure with the seal of God, could not wear the garland wreath [*corona*] of the Devil and instead kept itself free for the garland wreath of God" (*Laps.* 2.26–28).

26. Gero, "*Miles Gloriosus*," 294.

27. Helgeland, "Christians and the Roman Army," 743.

Both Evans and Dunn have shown that what at first appears to be a difference in Tertullian's attitude towards Christian engagement with the state and the army between the writing of the *Apology* and *Idolatry* and *The Crown*, is not a change in his personal view but rather a question of audience and rhetorical purpose. Tertullian's own view concerning the incompatibility of military service and Christian confession seems to have remained unchanged throughout his writing career.[28]

Apology 16.8[29]

As we saw in chapter 3, the *signa*, the standards and flags of the legion were considered sacred and were housed in a sanctuary, the *aediculum*, in the camp. Tertullian makes the visual association of the Christian use of crosses in worship with the fact that the *signa* were displayed on cruciform wooden pikes to highlight the idolatrous nature of military life.

16. [8] Among the Romans, the whole of the soldier's religion is to venerate the standards, to swear by the standards, to set the standards before all the gods. All those rows of images on the standards are but ornaments hung on crosses. Those hangings of your standards and banners are but robes upon crosses. I laud your thoughtfulness. You did not wish to consecrate crosses naked and unadorned.

Apology 25.14–26.1

Here Tertullian criticizes the Roman *libido dominandi* and establishes that the greatness of Rome was due to the devastating wars and violence of the past and present. In this he echoes Tacitus's lament, *ubi solitudinem faciunt, pacem appellant* "they create a wasteland and call it peace" (*Agr.* 1.30).

25. [14] [It was not Roman devotion to religion that made them great,] on the contrary, how could they be great because of their religion, since their greatness resulted from their indifference to religion? Unless I am mistaken, every kingdom or empire is gained by wars and extended by victories. Yet, wars and victories generally consist in the capture and destruction of cities. This business is not accomplished without its injury to the gods. Walls and temples are indiscriminately

---

28. See Dunn, *Tertullian*, 44–45; also Evans, "On the Problem of Church and Empire," 21–36.

29. Adapted from Tertullian, *Apology*, translated by Glover, 85.

destructed, citizens and priests are slaughtered without distinction, and treasures are plundered whether they belong to temples or citizens alike. [15] The sacrileges of the Romans are as many as their trophies; their triumphs over the gods as many as those over nations . . . [17] Certainly, it cannot be true that those people have attained greatness as a reward for their adherence to religion, who have done such harm to religion in the very act of growing strong.[30]

26. [1] Examine it, then, and see if the One who dispenses the kingdoms, is not proven to be whose is the world that is ruled and those who rule it; if he who has existed before all time and who made the world into a coherent system of times is not the One who has ordained the changes of empires, each at its own time in the course of time; if it is he who raises cities and destroys them, under whom the human race once lived without cities at all.

Apology 27.1–4, 28.1–3, 29.1–5

27. [1] This much is enough to refute the charge of offending divinity, since we cannot be thought to offend that which we have shown does not exist. Therefore, when we are called upon to sacrifice, we take a first stand against it, being faithful to our conscience; . . . [2] Some think it madness that, though we could offer sacrifice right here and now and go away unharmed, even preserving our mental reservation,[31] we prefer to be obstinate rather than safe; [3] that is to say, you give us advise on how to cheat you. But we recognize the origin of these suggestions, who it is that prompts all this, how, sometimes by cunning deception, sometimes by cruel rage, he works to throw us off from our constancy. [4] This spirit endowed with the nature of demons and angels, who wars against us because it is separated from God, our enemy because God gives us grace, using as its battleground your minds, which have

---

30. Helgeland, "Christians and the Roman Army," 735: "Rome owed its greatness to wars it had waged. War, however, always results in destruction: cities, priests, and citizens suffer as well as armies. In addition, Rome suffered because, in destroying the religions of conquered nations, it destroyed its own religion. Rome's greatness was not a gift of the gods but a spoil of war."

31. See Justin, *1 Apol.* 39. The point Tertullian is making here is that even though for the Romans one's belief was not the issue, but rather the proper public exercise of the rite, that is not an option for Christians.

been attuned and suborned to him resulting in perverse judgment and savage rage against us.

28.[32] [1] Moreover, it is clearly unjust to force free persons to sacrifice against their will, for under all other circumstances, a willing mind is required for discharging one's religious obligations. . . . Now, it is by the same spirits, assuredly, that you have been taught to force us to offer sacrifice for the well-being of the emperor; and you are led by necessity [i.e., edict] to force us [to sacrifice], just as much as it is our duty to face the danger. [2] We have come, then, to the second charge alleged against us, that of offending a more august majesty. You pay your obeisance to Caesar with great fear and craftier timidity than to Olympian Jupiter himself. And rightly so, if you but knew it! For who among the living, whoever he might be, is not more powerful than any of your dead ones? [3][33] But it is not reason that makes you do this so much as regard for power that can act on the instant. So that in this too you will be found irreligious to those gods of yours, when you show more fear for the rule of a man. In fact, among you perjury by all the gods together comes quicker than by the genius of a single Caesar.

29. [1] First, then, let it be established whether those to whom sacrifice is offered can grant safety to the emperor or to anyone at all, and then charge us with the crime of treason . . . [2] Certainly, they should first protect their own statues, images, and temples, which, I believe, Caesar's soldiers have to keep safe with guards. Moreover, the very materials of which they are made, I think, come from Caesar's mines, and entire temples depend on Caesar's agreement [lit: nod]. [3][34] Many gods until now have felt Caesar's wrath. . . . If the god's are so completely in Caesar's power, and belong to him so completely, how can they have Caesar's welfare in their power? [4] So, we are committing a crime against the emperors because we do not subordinate emperors to their property, and we do not make a joke of our duty regarding their health, for we do not think it rests within hands that

---

32. 28.1–2 adapted from Tertullian, *Christian and Pagan*, edited and translated by Sider, 51–52.

33. 28.3 adapted from Tertullian, *Apology*, translated by Glover, 149.

34. 29.3–5 adapted from Tertullian, *Christian and Pagan*, edited and translated by Sider, 52–53.

are soldered on which lead! [5] But then you are irreligious ones who seek health where it is not, who ask it from those who have no power to give it, and who neglect the one in whose power it lies. And, in addition to all this, you assail those who know how to ask for it, and who can obtain it, too, since they know how to ask!

Apology 30.1–7; 32.1–2; 33.1–3

30.[35] [1] For, in our case, we pray for the welfare of the emperors to the eternal God, the true God, the living God, whom even the emperors themselves prefer to have propitious to them before all other gods.[36] They know who has given them power; they know who has given them life; they feel that he is the only God in whose power alone they are; . . . against him they cannot avail, through him they know they do avail. From him comes the emperor, from whom came the man also, before he became the emperor; from him comes the emperor's power, from whom as well came the breath of life . . . [4] Looking up to heaven, we Christians—with hands outstretched, free from sin, with head uncovered, for we have nothing to be ashamed of, and, yes, without a monitor,[37] for we pray from the heart—constantly beseech [God] on behalf of all emperors. We ask for them long life, undisturbed power, security at home, brave armies, a faithful Senate, an upright people, a peaceful world, and everything for which a man or a Caesar can pray. [5] These I cannot ask of any other but only of him [God] from whom I know I shall receive them, since it is he alone who gives and I am the one to whom answer to prayer is due, for I am his servant, who worships him alone, who is slain for his teaching, who offers to him that rich and greater sacrifice which he himself required, I mean prayer, rising from a pure body, an innocent soul, a sanctified spirit [cf. Rom 12:1], [6] not the few grains of incense a penny buys—tears of an Arabian tree—or two drops of wine, or the blood of a worthless ox longing to die, and, in addition to all other kinds of pollution, an unclean conscience, so that I

---

35. 30.1–3, Adapted from Tertullian, *Christian and Pagan*, edited and translated by Sider, 54–55.

36. See *1 Clem.* 61.

37. In Roman ritual a monitor made certain that the words of supplication were precise, as the verbal formula was more important than the intention.

wonder why, when your victims are examined by the most vicious of priests, it is not those who offer the sacrifice that are being examined rather than the sacrifices themselves. [7] While thus, then, we spread ourselves before God, let the hooks pierce us, the crosses suspend us, the flames engulf us, the swords slash our throats, the beasts leap upon us. The very posture of the Christian at prayer is preparation for any punishment. Let this be your work, my good magistrates, wrench out the soul that prays to God for the Emperor. Here lies the crime—where the truth of God is, where devotion to him is.

31. [1] But perhaps we have been flattering the emperor and have lied about those prayers we alleged, just to escape persecution! Your mistake gives us the opportunity to prove our claims. If you indeed think that we have no interest in the emperor's welfare, look into the words of God, our books, which we do not hide; in fact, many a chance hands it over to outsiders. [2] Learn from them with what superabundant charity we are commanded to pray to God even for our enemies, and to beg for blessings for our persecutors [Matt 5:43–45; Rom 12:14]

Tertullian's eschatological understanding expected the end to come as a barbarian invasion and the Roman Empire was part of God's plan. In *Res.* 24.18, where he comments on 2 Thess 2:1–7 and the rise of the Antichrist, Tertullian writes, "What obstacle is there but the Roman state, the falling away of which, by being scattered into ten kingdoms, shall introduce Antichrist upon its own ruins?"[38]

32. [1] There is also another, more pressing, obligation for us to pray for the emperors, for the stability of the empire and the interests of Rome. We know that the great catastrophe that hangs over the whole world, that is, the very end of time which threatens with frightful calamities, is held back for a time by the continued existence of the Roman Empire. This event we have no desire to experience, and, in praying that it may be deferred, we favor the continuance of Rome. We do not wish to experience these things, and while we pray for their postponement we are helping the continuance of Rome.

---

38. This is a common understanding among Christian writers. See also Tertullian, *Scap.* 2.6; Lactantius, *Inst.* 7.25.7–8; and Augustine, *Civ.* 20.19.

[2] Moreover, we do make our oaths, not "by the *genii* of the Caesar," but by their welfare, which is more venerable than all the *genii*. . . . In the emperors, we respect the judgment of God, since he has set them over the people [cf. Rom 13:1–7]. [3] We know that in them is that which God has willed, and so we wish that what God has willed be safe and sound, and we consider this a great oath.

33. [1] We are under obligation to respect [the emperor] as the one chosen by our Lord. So, I might well say: "Caesar belongs more to us, since he has been appointed by our God." [2] As he is mine, I do more for his welfare, not only because I pray for it to him who can truly grant it, or because I who ask am one who deserves to receive, but also because I set the majesty of Caesar below that of God, I commend him the more to God to whom alone I subordinate him. And I do subordinate him to God; I do not make him equal to God. [3] . . . If he is a man, it is to his interest as a man to cede to God. Let him be satisfied to be called emperor.

Apology 37.1–10

37. [1] If then, as we have said above, we are expressly commanded to love our enemies, whom have we to hate? And if when someone injures us we are forbidden to retaliate, so that the action may not make us alike [the rest of the world], whom then can we injure? [2] Look at this yourselves and think it over. For[39] how many times, partly in compliance with a brutish passion, partly in obedience to the laws, have your judges showed a most savage cruelty to Christians! How often without your authority has the hostile mob of their own mere motion invaded us with showers of stones and fire! The mob, I say, who acted with the furies of a Bacchanal spare not even a dead Christian, but tear him from the quiet of a tomb, the sacred refuge of death, and mangle the body, hideously deformed already, and rotting to pieces; and in this rueful condition drag it about the streets. But now in all this conspiracy of evils against us, in the midst of these mortal provocations, what one evil have you observed to have been

---

39. For this part of 37.2 I quote W. M. Reeve's translation because of the poetry of his language that conveys the power of Tertullian's rhetoric. The translation can be found at http://www.tertullian.org/articles/reeve_apology.htm.

returned by Christians? [3] Yet I ask, banded together as we are, ever so ready to sacrifice our lives, what single case of revenge for injury are you able to point to, thought, a single night with a few torches could achieve an ample vengeance, if it were considered right among us to repay evil with evil? But away with the thought that those who are taught by God should either revenge themselves with human fire or resent the fire that is sent to refine them.

[4] . . . We are but of yesterday, yet we have filled every place among you—cities, apartment houses [or: islands], fortresses, towns, market places, the very camps, tribes, town councils, the palace, the senate, the forum. We have left nothing to you but the temples of your gods. [5] We can count your armies; there is a greater number of Christians in one province. For what kind of war would we not be fit and ready, despite our inferior numbers, we who willingly submit to the sword, if it were not for the fact that according to our doctrine we are given the freedom to be killed rather than to kill?

[6][40] Even unarmed and without any uprising, merely by standing aside, simply through an invidious withdrawal, we could have fought against you. For if such a multitude of people as we are had broken loose from you and had gone into some remote corner of the earth, the loss of so many citizens, of whatever kind they might be, would certainly have made your power blush for shame; in fact, it would even have punished you by this very desertion. [7] You would have had to look around for people to rule; there would have been more enemies than citizens left to you. [8] For, now, the enemies whom you have are fewer because of the number of Christians. These you have preferred to call the enemies of the human race. [9] But who would rescue you from those secret enemies that are constantly destroying your spiritual and bodily health—I mean, the demons, which we ward off from you without any reward and without pay? [10] Instead of thinking of any compensation for so great a protection, you have preferred to consider as enemies a class of people who are actually indispensable to you. To tell the truth, we are enemies, not of the human race, but of the human error.

---

40. Adapted form Tertullian, *Christian and Pagan*, edited and translated by Sider, 57–58.

Tertullian continues with the same argument in *Apol.* 42.2–3. He is intent on refuting the charge of social uselessness and withdrawal from social life, the life of the city, a grave charge of *misanthropia* (*odium generis humanis* in Tacitus, *Ann.* 15.44.5), which the Romans took very seriously. The assertion "we serve in the army" is part of a series of activities Christians share in common with their Roman neighbors (that is, *with you*). Here Tertullian continues his claim from 37.4 and 37.8, where he also claims, "we have left nothing to you but the temples of your gods." Tertullian's rhetorical hyperbole, then, serves a suasive role within the genre of an *apology* and needs to be weighted accordingly.

Apology 42.1–3[41]

42.[42] [1] But on still another charge of misconduct are we arraigned: they say we are worthless in business. How can they say that? Are we not people who live right with you, people who follow the same way of life, the same manner of dressing, using the same provisions and the same necessities of life? For we are not Brahmans or naked sages of India who dwell in forests, withdrawn from life. [2] We bear in mind that we owe thanks to the Lord our God who created us; we disdain no fruit of his works; obviously, we do restrain ourselves from an immoderate or excessive use of them. So it is not without a forum, not without a meat market, not without baths, shops, factories, inns, market days, and the rest of your business enterprises that we live with you—in the world. [3] We are sailors along with you; we serve in the army with you; we farm and trade along with you; in addition, we share with you our arts; we place the products of our labor at your service. How we can appear worthless for your business, when we live with you and depend on you, I do not know.

Apology 50

50.[43] [1] "Why, then," you say, "do you complain because we persecute you, if you desire to suffer, since you ought to love those through whom

---

41. Swift, *Early Fathers*, 39, quotes only 42.2 in arguing for Tertullian's support for military service in the *Apology*, but the whole context of 42.1–3 does not support such a conclusion.

42. Adapted from Tertullian, *Christian and Pagan*, edited and translated by Sider, 64.

43. Adapted from ibid., 69.

you suffer what you desire?" Certainly, we are willing to suffer, but in the way that a soldier endures war. No one actually has a liking for suffering, since that inevitably involves anxiety and danger. [2] However, a man fights a battle with all his strength and, though he complained about there being a battle, he finds delight in conquering in battle, because he is attaining glory and reward. There is a battle for us, because we are called to trial in court so that we may fight there for the truth while our life hangs in the balance. And the victory is to hold fast to that for which we have fought.[44] This victory has attached to it the glory of pleasing God and the reward of eternal life. [3] We have won the victory when we are killed; we escape at last when we are led forth. . . . [12] Carry on, good magistrates; you will become much better in the eyes of people if you sacrifice the Christians for them. Crucify us, torture us, destroy us! Your injustice is the proof of our innocence. That is why God permits us to suffer all this. . . . [13] Yet, your tortures accomplish nothing, though each is more refined than the last; rather, they are an enticement to our sect [or: school]. We become more numerous every time we are hewn down by you: the blood of Christians is seed. . . . [15] For, who is not stirred by the contemplation of it to inquire what is really beneath the surface? And who, when he has inquired, does not [join] us? Who, when he has [joined], does not desire to suffer so that he may procure the full grace of God, that he may purchase from him full pardon by paying with his own blood? [16] For, by this means, all sins are forgiven. That is why we give thanks immediately for your sentences of condemnation.[45] Such is the difference between things divine and human: when we are condemned by you, we are acquitted by God.

Against the Jews 3.10[46]

The treatise *Adversus Iudaeos* is usually translated *Against the Jews*, but probably ought to be titled, *Against the Judaizers*.[47] Tertullian enters the

44. Cf. Minucius Felix, *Oct.* 37.1–6.

45. "Probably a reference to the Martyr's words, 'Thanks be to God,' on hearing the sentence of condemnation" (Tertullian, *Christian and Pagan*, edited and translated by Sider, 70n167).

46. For an introduction and a full English text see Dunn, *Tertullian*, 63–104.

47. Another viable option is *In Answer to the Jews*. What is important is that this

argument between a convert to Judaism and a Christian and tries to present a systematic response to the relationship between the Old and New Testaments, Judaism and Christianity. Though the work was left unfinished, in the first eight chapters Tertullian argues that since Israel rejected God's grace, the Church, constituted of gentiles, has taken over as the people of God and the Old Testament must now be interpreted spiritually (ch. 1). Circumcision (ch. 3), the observance of Sabbath (ch. 4), and temple sacrifices (ch. 5) have been replaced by the New Covenant and are no longer necessary for salvation. In place of the ancient law of retribution is the law of love. Finally, in Jesus the prophecies of the Old Testament are fulfilled as he is proclaimed an everlasting king of a universal kingdom (chs. 6–7), inaugurating the *Age of Peace* described in Isa 2:3–4 and Mic 4:2–3. The primary portion of the treatise ends with an exposition of Daniel's Messianic prophecy (ch. 8), while chapters 9–14 are more notes than an integral part of the treatise.

3. [10] The old law vindicated itself by the vengeance of the sword, to take an eye for an eye and to repay injury with revenge. But the new law was focusing on clemency and turning bloodthirsty swords and lances to peaceful uses and to change the warlike acts against rivals and enemies into the peaceful pursuits of plowing and farming the land.

Patience 3.7–9; 6.3—7.1; 8.1–3[48]

Written between 200–203 CE, the treatise *De patientia* paints the picture of the ideal Christian in imitation of Christ. Patience finds its source in faith, and faith, in turn cannot exist without it. Afflictions, insults, and even persecution, ought to be welcomed by Christians as means of growth in the virtue and pleasure of patience, love of enemy, and the exercise of charity. In chapter 8, Tertullian discusses how and why a Christian should respond to abuse and violence, while in 13.7, he refers to martyrdom as the "second baptism." Cyprian of Carthage referred to Tertullian's treatise frequently in his own *De bono patientiae*.[49]

---

is not a treatise against Jews, but an exposition for Christians who are attracted to the antiquity and traditions of Judaism and are considering conversion.

48. Here I include the translation of S. Thelwall, found in *ANF* vol. 3, for it retains the uncharacteristically quiet spirit of Tertullian's treatise.

49. Quasten, *Patrology*, 2:298–99.

Patience 3

3. [7] While [Christ] is being betrayed, while he is being led up "as a sheep for a victim," (for "so he no more opens his mouth than a lamb under the power of the shearer," [cf. Isa 53:7]) he to whom, had he willed it, legions of angels would at one word have presented themselves from the heavens, approved not the avenging sword of even one disciple. [8] The patience of the Lord was wounded in [the wound of] Malchus [cf. John 8:10–11; Luke 22:49–51]. And so, too, he cursed for ever the works of the sword; and, by the restoration of health, made satisfaction to him whom himself had not hurt, through Patience, the mother of Mercy.[50]

Patience 6

6. [3] So faith, illumined by patience, when it was becoming propagated among the nations through "Abraham's seed, which is Christ" [cf. Gal 3:16], and was superinducing grace over the law, made patience her pre-eminent coadjutrix for amplifying and fulfilling the law, because that alone had been lacking unto the doctrine of righteousness. [4] For people were of old accustomed to require "eye for eye, and tooth for tooth" and to repay with usury "evil with evil;" for, as yet, patience was not on earth, because faith was not either. Of course, meantime, impatience used to enjoy the opportunities which the law gave. That was easy, while the Lord and Master of patience was absent. [5] But after He has supervened, and has united the grace of faith with patience, *now* it is no longer lawful to assail even with *word*, nor to say "fool" even, without "danger of the judgment." Anger has been prohibited, our spirits retained, the petulance of the hand checked, the poison of the tongue extracted. [6] The law has found more than it has lost, while Christ says, "Love your personal enemies, and bless those who curse you, and pray for your persecutors, that you may be sons of your heavenly Father." Do you see whom patience gains for us as a Father? 7. [1] In this principal precept the universal discipline of patience is succinctly comprised, since evil-doing is not conceded even when it is deserved.[51]

50. *ANF* 3:708.
51. *ANF* 3:711.

Patience 8

8. [1] In this world we have exposed our very life and our very body to all manner of injury and we endure this injury with patience. Shall we, then, be hurt by the loss of lesser things? Far from a servant of Christ be such a defilement as that the patience which has been prepared for greater temptations should forsake him in frivolous ones. [2] If one attempt to provoke you by manual violence, the monition of the Lord is at hand: "To him," he said, "who strikes you on the face, turn the other cheek likewise." Let outrageousness be wearied out by your patience. Whatever that blow may be, conjoined with pain and contumely, it shall receive a heavier one from the Lord. You wound that outrageous one more by enduring: for he will be beaten by him [*viz.* Christ] for whose sake you endure. [3] If the tongue's bitterness break out in malediction or reproach, look back at the saying, "When they curse you, rejoice" [cf. Matt 5:11]. The Lord himself was "cursed" in the eye of the law [cf. Gal 3:13]; and yet is he the only Blessed One. Let us servants, therefore, follow our Lord closely; and be cursed patiently, that we may be able to be blessed.[52]

Idolatry 17.2–3; 18.4–8[53]

In this section of *Idolatry*, Tertullian responds to Christians seeking positions of power and influence within the magistracy under the pretext that they would not be tainted or corrupted by its structures and demands, nor would they be soiled by the oath of office they took (which included words of allegiance to the emperor as the representative of the Roman state) as they could simply repeat the words without affirming their meaning. Contrary to the Roman dichotomy between interiority of belief and the external proper ritual practice, Tertullian argued that to not affirm the words of the oath taken freely would be simply a moral oxymoron, a lie, to which Christians could not assent.

17. [2] A dispute has lately arisen as to whether a servant of God can hold a position of honor or authority if he can keep himself free of any appearance of idolatry by means of some special grace of through

52. *ANF* 3:712.

53. Tertullian, *De Idololatria,* edited and translated by Waszink and van Winden, 59, 61.

his own wisdom, just as Joseph and Daniel, who, served with honor and power, wearing the insignia and the purple of the governor of Egypt and Babylonia, yet without being tainted by idolatry. [3] We may grant that someone could hold a position in a purely honorary way if you can believe that it is possible for him to avoid sacrificing or authorizing sacrifices, without paying for victims [viz. sacrificial animals], without managing the upkeep of temples, without taking care of temple taxes, without putting on shows [spectacula] at his own or at public expense or presiding over the staging of them, without issuing solemn pronouncements or edicts or even taking an oath. Provided he can do this and also avoid the functions of his office, that is, without passing judgment on a man's life [i.e., capital punishment] or honour—for you can put up with a decision on financial matters—without condemning or forejudging, without putting anybody in chains or prison or torturing, if it is believable that all this is possible, [then he may serve].

18. [4] So what will you accomplish, if you use this attire [i.e. the symbol of power] but do not perform the function connected with it? Nobody can give an impression of cleanness in unclean clothes. If you put on a tunic soiled of itself, it may perhaps not be soiled through you, but certainly you will not be able to be clean because of it. Further, you, who take an argument from the cases of Joseph and Daniel you must know that we cannot always compare things old and new, rude and polished, only begun and fully developed, servile and free. [5] For these men, even by their circumstances, were slaves. But you are nobody's slave, in so far as you are solely the slave of Christ, who even freed you from the imprisonment of this world. You will thus have to act according to your Lord as pattern. He walked in humility and obscurity, uncertain about his dwelling place . . . [7] He rejected the worldly splendour which he did not want, and he condemned what he rejected, and what he condemned, he consigned to the pomp of the devil. . . . [8] If you have sworn off the devil's pomp, know then that all that you touch of it is idolatry. Let moreover this fact remind you that all the powers and dignities of this world are not only foreign but even hostile to God: that by their agency punishments have been fixed against God's servants

and also that by their agency the punishments prepared for the impious remain unknown.

Idolatry 19.1–3

In *Idolatry* 19, Tertullian addresses the excuses that some Christians brought forward for pursuing a military career, or staying after conversion. Some, it seems, argued that since the lower ranks, unlike officers, did not have to conduct sacrifices or order capital punishment (*Idol.* 19.1), they could remain untainted if they only served as such. Others made appeals to the rod (*virga*) of Moses, the buckle (*fibulum*) of Aaron, and the belt (*lorum*) of John the Baptist. Since these items were part of the Roman soldier's equipment, Tertullian's interlocutors invoked these biblical examples to legitimate their military profession. Tertullian also dismisses the more relevant examples of Joshua and his host. Within the context of his argument, even the instance of the soldiers who came to John the Baptist and "received a rule to be guided by" [*De Idol.* 19.3] is not normative, for the dominical response supersedes all others: "The Lord, by taking away Peter's sword, disarmed every soldier thereafter" [*De Idol.* 19.3].[54]

19. [1] In that last section, decision may seem to have been given likewise concerning military service, which is between dignity and power. But now the question is whether a believer can become a soldier and whether a soldier can be admitted into the faith, even if he is a member only of the rank and file who are not required to take part in sacrifices or capital punishments. [2] There can be no compatibility between the divine and the human sacrament,[55] the standard of Christ and the standard of the devil, the camp of light and the camp of darkness. One soul cannot serve two masters: God and Caesar. Moses, to be sure, carried a rod;[56] Aaron wore a military belt, and John (the Baptist) is girt with leather [i.e., like a soldier]; and if you really want

54. In the *Acta Marcelli* the martyr signifies his rejection of military service by throwing off his belt (reiecto etiam cingulo militari coram signis legionis). Harnack, *Militia Christi*, 117.

55. The military oath was called a *sacramentum*, and was a liturgical act invoking the gods as witnesses.

56. A *Virgam* was the vine switch, or rod, in the Roman army that was a mark of the centurion's rank.

to play around with the subject, Joshua the son of Nun led an army and the people waged war—and Peter waged war, if I may sport with the matter (if I permit myself a joke). [3] But how will a Christian go to war? Indeed how will he serve even in peacetime without a sword which the Lord has taken away? [Matt 26:52; 2 Cor 10:4; John 18:36]. For even if soldiers came to John and received advice on how to act, and even if a centurion became a believer, the Lord, by taking away Peter's sword, disarmed every soldier thereafter.[57] We are not allowed to wear any uniform that symbolizes a sinful act.

The Crown 1.1–6; 11.1–7; 12.1–5; 15.1–4

De corona militis is Tertullian's most sustained critique of Christian presence in the military. His argument is fourfold, beginning with the incommensurability of competing loyalties to Caesar and Christ (Cor. 10; 11.1; 12–14; cf. Matt 6:24; Luke 16:13), followed by an appeal to the Christian obligation to not shed blood (Cor. 1.2; cf. Matt 26:52.). The third part of the argument is that since the Christian, "a son of peace," (Luke 10:6) is forbidden to avenge even one's own private wrongs by resorting to a court of law (Cor. 1.2; cf. Matt 5:40), therefore, a fortiori one must not be a soldier, "a man of violence," either. Tertullian closes his argument by focusing on the acts of idolatry the soldier is forced to do in the course of his service. (Cor. 11.3; 12, 15; cf. 1 Cor 8:10)

The occasion for the The Crown was most probably a donative provided for the army by the emperors Caracalla and Ceta shortly after their accession in 211 CE. During the parade probably of the renown legio III Augusta, in a camp close to Tertullian's home, either at Lambaesis or Carthage, one Christian who refused to wear on his head the honorific garland, the corona, that had been awarded to the troops. Being derided by this fellow soldiers, the dissident individual was brought to the tribune for disciplinary action (Cor. 1.1–2). In the course of his public examination, the soldier replied that the reason he refused to wear the crown "like everyone else" was simply: "Because I am a Christian" (Cor. 1.2). On hearing this, his fellow soldiers clamored for his punishment, while the other Christians among the ranks criticized him for drawing attention to their religious identity (Cor. 1.4). In this treatise, Tertullian also faces the practical question of whether a baptized Christian may

57. Lit. "the Lord, in disarming Peter, unbelted every soldier thereafter."

remain in the army and concludes that those who converted during service ought to leave the army as soon as possible (*Cor.* 11.4–7).

The Crown 1.1–6[58]

1. [1] I record a recent occurrence. The bounty of our most excellent Emperors was being dispensed in a military camp. The soldiers were approaching with laurel crowns on their heads. One man present was first and foremost a soldier of God; the other Christians had thought they could serve two masters, but he was more faithful than they. He was the only one with head bared; his crown remained in his hand unused. By this act he stood out publicly as a Christian. [2] People begin to point him out; those further away jeer; those closer by snarl at him. A general hubbub soon builds up. He is denounced to the tribune—he had already come out of his place in the ranks. The tribune immediately asks: "Why are you dressed differently?" He says that he is not allowed to dress like the others. He is told to give his reasons. "I am a Christian," he replies. "Proud warrior" [*miles gloriosus*] of God! A vote is taken; the case is recorded; he is sent for sentence to the prefects. [3] There and then he removes his heavy cloak (he is beginning to be lightened of his burden); he takes his cumbersome boots off his feet (he is beginning to stand on holy ground [cf. Exod 3:5]); he hands over his sword (his Lord did not need one to defend himself [see John 18:10–11]); the laurel wreath falls from his hand. Instead he is clad in the crimson of the blood he expects to shed; he is shod with the preparation of the gospel; he is girded with the word of God sharper than any sword—thus he puts on the whole armour of which the apostle speaks [cf. Eph 6:13–16; Heb 4:12]. Then as one who is to receive a far better crown, the dazzling laurel crown of the martyr, he waits in prison for the bounty which Christ will give him. [4] Views are expressed about him (I hesitate to call them the views of Christians, as they were no different from those of non-Christians): he was headstrong, rash, eager to die, he had made things difficult for Christians by getting himself interrogated on a matter of dress—whereas the truth of the matter is that he was the only brave man among all his Christian fellow-soldiers, in fact the only Christian at all. Obviously

---

58. Wiles and Santer (eds.), *Documents in Early Christian Thought*, 133–34; used by permission.

the next step for people who have rejected the prophecies of the Holy Spirit is to plan how to refuse martyrdom too. [5] They complain that peace which has served them so well for so long is being endangered. Some no doubt, following the Scriptures, are clearing out, packing their bags and preparing to flee from city to city [cf. Matt 10:23]. That is the only bit of the gospel they are keen to remember. I know their pastors too—lions in peace and deer in battle. But will deal elsewhere with the public confession of Christ and the issues it involves. [6] For the moment I want to take up a different objection—namely "Where are we forbidden to be crowned?" [i.e., to be honored by the state, as in receiving medals, etc.] Here is the nub of this particular case. Some ask the question out of genuine ignorance; them I seek to instruct. Others do it with the definite intention of exculpating the offense; them I seek to refute—and particularly those crowned Christians themselves who seem to find consolation in the raising of the question on the ground that if the matter is open to question the offense must be regarded either as non-existent or at least open to doubt. That it is neither non-existent nor open to doubt is what I shall now show.

The Crown 11.1–4[59]

11. [1] Now, to come to the very heart of this question about the soldier's crown, should we not really first examine the right of a Christian to be in the military service at all? In other words, why discuss the merely accidental detail, when the foundation on which it rests is deserving of censure? Are we to believe it lawful to take an oath of allegiance to a mere human being [i.e., to Caesar] over and above the oath of fidelity to God? Can we obey another master, having chosen Christ? Can we forsake father, mother, and all our relatives? By divine law we must honor them and our love for them is second only to that which we have toward God [Exod 20:12]. The Gospel also bids us honor our parents [Matt 15:4; Mark 7:10; Luke 18:20], placing none but Christ Himself above them. [2] Is it right to make a profession of the sword, when the Lord proclaims that he who takes the sword shall perish by the sword [Matt 26:52]? Will the son of peace [cf. Eph 6:15] take part in battle when he should not even go to court?

59. Adapted from Tertullian, *Disciplinary, Moral and Ascetical Work*, translated by Arbesmann, Daly, and Quain, 255–57.

[cf. 1 Cor 6:7]? Will a Christian, taught to turn the other cheek when struck unjustly [Matt 5:39; Luke 6:29], guard prisoners in chains, and administer torture and capital punishment? [3] Will he rather mount guards for others than for Christ on station days?[60] And what about the Lord's Day? Will he not even then do it for Christ? Will he stand guard before temples, that he has renounced? Will he eat at pagan banquets, which the Apostle forbids? [cf. 1 Cor 8:10]. Will he protect by night those very demons whom in the daytime he has put to flight by his exorcisms, leaning on a lance such as pierced the side of Christ [on the cross]? [cf. John 19:34]. Will he bear, too, a standard that is hostile to Christ, and will he ask the watch-word from his commander-in-chief—he who has already received one from God? Moreover, after death, will he be disturbed by the horn of the trumpeter—he who expects to be aroused by the trumpet of the angel? [cf. 1 Cor 15:52; 1 Thess 4:16]. Will his corpse be cremated according to military custom—when he, a Christian, was not permitted to burn incense in sacrifice, when to him Christ remitted the eternal punishment by fire he had deserved?

[4] Yes, these and many other offenses can be observed in the discharge of military duties—offenses that must be interpreted as acts of desertion. To leave the camp of Light and enlist in the camp of Darkness means going over to the enemy. To be sure, the case is different for those who are converted after they have been bound to military service. John admitted soldiers to baptism [cf. Luke 3:14]; then were the two most faithful centurions: the one whom Christ praised [Matt 8:10; Luke 7:9], and the other whom Peter instructed [Acts 10]. But, once we have embraced the faith and have been baptized, we either must immediately leave military service (as many have done); or we must resort to all kinds of excuses in order to avoid any action which is also forbidden in civilian life, lest we offend God; or, last of all, for the sake of God we must suffer the fate which a mere citizen-faith was no less ready to accept.

In this section Tertullian also addresses the question of conscription, following the same line of argument. The Christian obligation is to civil disobedience welcoming the resultant punishment.

60. In military language, *statio* is the post or guard; Christians called the two weekly fast days (Wednesday and Friday) *stationes*.

[5] For, military service offers neither exemption from punishment of sins nor relief from martyrdom. The Gospel is one and the same for the Christian at all times whatever his occupation in life. Jesus will deny those who deny Him and confess those who confess Him [Matt 10:32, 33; Luke 12:8–9]; He will save the life that has been lost for His Name's sake, but He will destroy the one that has been gained against His Name [cf. Matt 10:39; Mark 8:35; Luke 9:24]. With Him the faithful citizen is a soldier, just as the faithful soldier is a citizen. [6] The state of faith admits no plea of compulsion [(i.e., even conscription)]. Those are under no compulsion to sin whose sole obligation is not to sin. A Christian may be pressed to the offering of sacrifice and to the straight denial of Christ under threat of torture and punishment. Yet, the law of Christianity does not excuse even that compulsion, since there is a stronger obligation to dread the denial of the faith and to undergo martyrdom than to escape suffering and to perform the sacrificial rite required. [7] Moreover, that kind of argument destroys the very essence of our sacramental oath, since it would loosen the fetters for voluntary sins. For, it will be possible to maintain that inclination is a compulsion, too, since there is, indeed, some sort of compelling force in it. The foregoing principles I wish to have also applied to the other occasions for wearing crowns in some official capacity (it is with reference to such occasions especially that people are wont to plead compulsion), since for this very reason we must either refuse public offices lest we fall into sin, or we must endure martyrdom in order to sever our connection with them.

The Crown 12

12. [1] I will not waste any more words over the essential point of the question, namely, the unlawfulness of military life itself, but return to the secondary point of the matter. Indeed, if, employing all my efforts, I do away with military service altogether, there will be little point in issuing a challenge on the military crown. Let us assume, then, that military service is permitted up to the point of wearing a crown. Let me say, first, a word about the crown itself. We know from Claudius that the laurel crown (such as the one in question) is sacred to Apollo as the god of archery and to Bacchus as the god of triumphs. [2] He also tells us that soldiers were often garlanded with

myrtle. "For the myrtle," he writes, "belongs to Venus, the mother of the descendants of Aeneas, the mistress also of Mars, who through Ilia and her twins is Roman herself." But I myself do not believe that Venus shares in this respect the friendly feelings of Mars for Rome, in view of the god's dealing with a concubine. Moreover, when a soldier is crowned with an olive wreath, he commits idolatry to Minerva, who is also a goddess of arms, even though she crowned her head with an olive branch to celebrate her peace with Neptune. In all these relations we see the defiled and all-defiling superstitious character of the military crown. In fact, I think that the very motives for wearing it causes its defilement. [3] Take the annual public pronouncement of vows.[61] What do you think of it? The first takes place in the general's quarters; the second, in heathen temples. In addition to the places, note the words, also; "We promise to give to you, then, O Jupiter, an ox with golden horns." What is the real sense of that pronouncement? Is it not a denial of the faith? Even though the Christian says nothing on that occasion with his mouth, he makes his response by having the crown on his head. The wearing of the laurel crown is likewise enjoined at the distribution of a largess, though, plainly, you do not attend this ceremony without making a profit. [4] Idolater! Do you not see that you are selling Christ for a few pieces of gold, just as Judas sold him for silver? It is written: "You cannot serve God and mammon" [Matt 6:24; Luke 16:13]. Does this perhaps mean that you can do both things: reach out your hand to mammon and stand on the side of God? And what about "Render to Caesar the things that are Caesar's and to God the things that are God's" [Matt 22:21; Mark 12:17; Luke 20:25]? Does this perhaps mean that you can withhold the man from God and take the denarius from Caesar? Is the laurel of triumph made of leaves, or of corpses? Is it adorned with ribbons, or with tombs? Is it anointed with perfumes, or with the tears of wives and mothers, some of them, perhaps, Christian women, for we know that Christianity has also spread among the barbarians. [5] Has the man who wears a crown as a symbol of glory not actually fought in battle? There is yet another kind of military service that of the bodyguard in the imperial household. For these men, too, are called

---

61. Tertullian refers to the vows offered for the well-being of the emperor on New Year's Day. Cf. Tacitus, *Ann.* 4.17; 16.22; Pliny, *Ep.* 10.35.

"soldiers of the camp," and they perform services in connection with the ceremonial observed in the imperial court. But, even then you are still the soldier and servant of another, and if of two masters God and Caesar then, certainly, not of Caesar, when you owe yourself to God, who, I am inclined to believe, has a higher claim even in matters in which both have an interest.[62]

The Crown 15

15. [1] Keep for God untainted what is his [viz. your head]. He will crown it if so he chose. And, he will; in fact, he invites us [to be crowned]. To him who conquers He says: "I will give the crown of life" [cf. Rev 2:10; Jas 1:12]. You, too, be faithful unto death; you, too, fight the good fight whose crown the Apostle is so justly confident has been laid up for him [cf. 1 Tim 6:12; 2 Tim 4:8]. The angel of victory, also, who, riding a white horse, goes forth to conquer, receives a crown, and another is adorned with a rainbow which [in its fair colors] is like a celestial meadow. The elders, too, sit crowned with golden crowns and the Son of Man himself, wearing a golden crown, shines forth above the clouds. . . . [2b] [You too are destined for a crown, made of flowers] from the root of Jesse, upon which the grace of the divine Spirit has rested in all its fullness, an incorruptible flower, unfading, and everlasting. [3] By choosing this flower, the good soldier has advanced in the ranks of the heavenly army. Be ashamed, fellow soldiers of Christ, if you are condemned not by Christ, but by some soldier of Mithras who, at his initiation, deep in a cavern, in the very camp of darkness, was presented with a crown at the point of a sword as if in mimicry of martyrdom.

Flight in Persecution 13.5b; 14.1, 3

Tertullian wrote the *De fuga in persecutione* sometime after 208 CE in an attempt to encourage Christians to stay firm in the face of impending persecution. In the treatise he addresses a number of important issues, including the problem of evil and pain, which, he concludes, have educative purpose in the life of a Christian. Tertullian suggests that a

---

62. Adapted from Tertullian, *Disciplinary, Moral and Ascetical Work*, translated by Arbesmann, Daly, and Quain, 258–60.

number of Christians faced a situation similar to that in Bithynia where, as Pliny informs us, their names were circulated in anonymous lists and they were often blackmailed by informants, soldiers, or low-level officials (*Fug.* 12.3). It appears that some Christians (even priests and bishops) resorted to bribery in return for their safety, and this is the situation Tertullian needed to address (*Fug.* 13). Tertullian then makess a case for the sovereignty of God, reminding Christians that, regardless of the trust they may place on their own ingenuity, strength, or political connections, at the end, it is their Christian duty of be found faithful to their calling, which may include even martyrdom.

Flight in Persecution 13.5b

13. [5b] I do not know if it is more a case for grief or shame, when Christians are added to the tax rolls of privileged soldiers and spies, among shopkeepers, and pickpockets, bath-thieves, gamblers, and pimps!

Flight in Persecution 14.1, 3

14. [1] "But how, then, shall we gather together?" you say [i.e., how will our churches be safe from persecution if we do not bribe the authorities], "How shall we celebrate the solemn rites of the Lord?" To be sure, just as the apostles also did, who were protected by faith, not by money; for if this faith can remove mountains [cf. Matt 17:20; Mark 11:22–23; 1 Cor 13:2], it can much more remove a soldier. Let your protection be your wisdom, not a bribe. For even if you buy off the interference of the soldiers, you will not then, at once, also have security from the people [viz., mob]. Therefore, all you need for your protection is to have both faith and wisdom: for if you do not make use of these, you may even lose the redemption you have purchased for yourselves, but if you use [faith and wisdom] you will not be in need of any [other kind of] ransoming.[63]

[3] The one who is afraid to suffer cannot belong to him who suffered [for us]; but the one who is not afraid to suffer, this one will be perfect in love, [in the love,] that is, of God: "For perfect love cast

---

63. Tertullian plays here with the double meaning of the word *redemptionem* to indicate the redemption of the Christian in salvation, on the one hand, and the ransoming of one's life through a bribe, on the other.

out fear" [1 John 4:18]. And so, "many are called but few are chosen" [Matt 22:14]. It is not asked who is ready to follow the broad road, but who the narrow path [Matt 7:13–14]. And, therefore, the Paraclete is needed, who guides to all truth [John 16:13], the source of all endurance. Those who have received him will neither seek to flee from persecution nor to ransom [their lives], for they have the One who will be at our side, ready to speak for us when we are interrogated an to assist us when we suffer.

To Scapula 1.1–4; 2.5–10

Towards the end of this literary career (212–213 CE), Tertullian, wrote to the proconsul of African prefect Scapula Tertullus to argue for a change in provincial policy and to bring an end to the persecution of Christians. *Ad Scapulam* is an "impeccably orthodox exposition of Romans 13."[64] To be sure, Tertullian threatens the magistrates with divine vengeance (*Scap.* 3.4–5), but on the whole, he advocates for religious freedom (*Scap.* 2.1–2) in much softer tones than in many of his other letters and treatises. Tertullian's primary argument to Scapula is that, unlike their pagan counterparts, Christians do not rebel against the emperor (*Scap.* 2.3–5) and, in fact, restrain the anger of God even against those who persecuted them (*Scap.* 2.10). Tertullian notes for Scapula examples of other governors who persecuted Christians and were punished by God, while a number of his colleagues had actively protected Christians from injustice (*Scap.* 4.2–3). Tertullian closes the letter with an invitation to consider becoming a Christian and thus escape the wrath of God (*Scap.* 5.4). In this section, Tertullian presents the Christian distinctive of love of enemy and persecutor as unique among peoples and as quite different from ordinary goodness: indeed, a sign of divine grace.

To Scapula 1.1–4[65]

1. [1] For us, the things we suffer at the hands of ignorant men are not a source of great fear or dread. When we joined this sect we plainly undertook to accept the conditions this involved. So we come to these contests as men who have already hired themselves out for them.

---

64. Gero, "*Miles Gloriosus*," 293.
65. Wiles and Santer (eds.), *Documents in Early Christian Thought*, 226–27.

Our hope is to attain the promises of God; our fear is lest we should have to undergo the punishments with which he threatens whose who live otherwise. [2] When you turn on us with your utmost ferocity we are quite ready to do battle with you; indeed we enter the fray of our own accord. We find more cause for joy in condemnation than in acquittal. So it is not fear for ourselves that makes us send you this pamphlet, but fear for you and for all your enemies, or I should rather say, our friends, [3] since it is the teaching of our faith that we are to love even our enemies and pray for those who persecute us [see Matt 5:44]. Here lies the perfection and distinctiveness of Christian goodness. Ordinary goodness is different; for all men love their friends but only Christians love their enemies. [4] We are moved with sorrow at your ignorance and with pity for the errors of men's ways, and, as we look to the future, we see signs of impending distress every day. In such circumstances we have no choice but to take the initiative and lay before you those things which you refuse to listen to openly and publicly.

To Scapula 2.5–10[66]

2. [5] Another charge against us concerns treason with respect to the person of the Emperor. Yet Christians have never been found among the followers of Albinus or Niger or Cassius.[67] Those who have actually been found in practice to be enemies of the Emperor are the very same people who only a day before had been swearing by his genius [i.e., an oath of allegiance], had been solemnly offering sacrifices for his safety, and not infrequently had been condemning as well. [6] A Christian is an enemy of no man—certainly not to the Emperor, for he knows that it is by his God that the Emperor has been appointed. He is bound therefore to love him, to revere him, to honour him and to desire the safety not only of the Emperor but of the whole Roman empire as long as the world endures—for as long as the world endures, so also will the Roman empire. [7] So then we do "worship"

---

66. Ibid., 227–28.

67. Clodius Albinus and Pescennius Niger were Septemius Severus's unsuccessful rivals for power in the period of civil war which followed the death of Pertinax in 193. Avidius Cassius was an unsuccessful claimant to the throne in 175, during the reign of Marcus Aurelius (Ibid., 227).

the Emperor in such manner as is both permissible to us and beneficial to him, namely as a man second only to God. All that he is he has
received from God, and it is God alone whom he ranks below. This
surely is what the Emperor himself will desire. He ranks above all
else; it is the true God alone whom he ranks below. This means that
he is above even the gods themselves and they come within his sovereignty. [8] So also we "offer sacrifices" for the safety of the Emperor,
but we do so to our God—and his—and we do it in the way that God
has ordained, namely by the offering simply of prayers. (For God,
being the creator of the whole Universe, is in no need of smells or of
blood. [9] That is the fodder of petty demons. We do not merely despise these demons; we subdue them; we put them to daily disgrace;
we drive them out of people, as multitudes can testify.) So then our
prayers for the safety of the Emperor are all the more real as we offer
them to the one who is able to grant them.

[10] Our religion teaches a divine patience and it is on this basis that we conduct our lives. You can see this clearly enough from
the fact that although we are such a large company of men (almost
a majority in fact of every city) yet we live out our lives quietly and
temperately; we are probably better known individually than as a
corporate entity, since the only way we can be distinguished is by
the way we get rid of our former vices. Far be it from us to react with
indignation when we suffer things which in fact we welcome or in
any way plot the vengeance at our own hands which we confidently
await from God.

SEVEN

Origen of Alexandria
(ca. 184/5–ca. 253/4 CE)

Origen was no ordinary Christian. One of the most brilliant and prolific writers of early Christianity, Origen's theology and biblical interpretation influenced Christian thought for centuries. His six-column edition of parallel texts of the Hebrew Scriptures (the *Hexapla*) was considered the standard in biblical studies for over a thousand years, while his biblical commentaries and his three-tiered method of interpretation of Scripture became the basis of most Christian exegesis for many centuries.[1] On the issue at hand, Origen was not simply a theoretician but on the contrary, as Louis Swift noted, he "wrestled with the real issues, and he fashioned a kind of ideal that would live long after him. He was, in fact, the most articulate and eloquent pacifist in the early Christian Church."[2]

Origen's own life was bracketed by persecution and martyrdom. The oldest of seven children born to a devout Christian family in Alexandria, one of the principle intellectual centers of the ancient world, Origen received a splendid education under Clement of Alexandria and the famous philosopher, Ammonius Saccas. Eusebius tells us that Origen's brilliant mind and inquisitive spirit were also nurtured at home, where his father, Leonides, "drilled him in sacred studies," requiring him "to learn and recite every day Divine Scriptures from childhood."[3] Origen

---

1. Most of the biographical information comes from Eusebius of Caesarea who devoted almost the entire sixth book of his *Ecclesiastical History* to Origen. The best modern biography of Origen is still Nautin, *Origène*. See also, Trigg, *Origen*.

2. Swift, *Early Fathers*, 60.

3. Eusebius, *Hist. eccl.* 6.2.7–8.

was only seventeen when his father, Leonides, was arrested and imprisoned during the local but fierce persecution that erupted in the city of Alexandria in 202 CE. Prevented by his mother from rushing after his father and sharing in his fate, Origen sent to his father "an encouraging letter on martyrdom, in which he exhorted him, saying, 'Take heed not to change your mind on our account.'"[4] The execution of Leonides under the charge of sedition and impiety left the family impoverished as their property was confiscated. A wealthy Christian woman took Origen under her care and enabled him to complete his studies and begin to support his family as a *grammateus*, a teacher of Greek literature. A year later, in an effort to assist the family of the martyr and keep Origen out of the courtrooms he frequented to encourage other Christian prisoners, bishop Demetrius charged him with reviving the catechetical school at Alexandria, succeeding his teacher Clement who had been driven out of Alexandria by the same persecution.

In the years that followed, Origen's brilliance and ascetical zeal brought great numbers of men and women to the school who sought to be trained in doctrine and the Bible and established the catechetical school at Alexandria as one of the foremost centers of Christian learning. Origen turned more and more to biblical interpretation and he is one of the very few early Christian writers to have studied Hebrew. He visited Rome (211–212 CE) and Arabia (213/14 CE) before another popular uprising at Alexandria forced him to follow his friend Ambrosius (whom Origen had won away from Gnosticism) to Caesarea Maritima for a period. Here, following the local custom, bishops Alexander of Jerusalem and Theoctistus of Caesarea asked Origen to preach and interpret the Scriptures even though he was not yet ordained. This was against the custom in North Africa and, inadvertently, brought Origen in conflict with bishop Demetrius, who recalled him to Alexandria, probably in 216 CE. Of Origen's activity during the next decade only few details survive, but it was obviously devoted to teaching and writing. At the request of Ambrosius, Origen began a voluminous commentary on the Bible, an exegetical series on selected texts, two books on the resurrection, and the work *On First Principles*. His literary career flourished due, in no small part, to the generosity of Ambrosius who made seven stenographers and a number of copyists available to him on a permanent basis.

---

4. Eusebius, *Hist. eccl.* 6.2.6.

Eventually, Origen moved to Caesarea (first in 231 CE and then settled in the city in 234 CE) where he was ordained a presbyter and was charged with establishing another catechetical school and a library. It was while at Caesarea, in 231 CE, that Origen's reputation reached Julia Mammaea, the mother of the young emperor Alexander Severus, who sent a military escort to bring him to Antioch so that he might explain Christianity to her. Origen spent the last twenty-five years of his life in the city that welcomed him and provided the opportunity for him to concentrate on teaching and writing. Though little is known about the last twenty-five years of life in Caesarea, we know that he preached regularly on Wednesdays and Fridays, and later daily and that he was devoted to the work of the church. At Caesarea, Origen was deeply loved by his pupils, preached and taught dialectics, physics, ethics, and metaphysics and engaged intensely with the Greek-speaking Jewish community of the city.

Origen was sixty-five years old in 249 CE, when Decius overthrew Philip the Arab to ascend to the imperial throne. With the millennial celebrations of Rome as the backdrop, Decius inaugurated the most extensive, effective, and deadly persecutions the church had ever experienced. The Decian persecution targeted Christian leaders in particular and claimed the lives of the bishop of Rome, Fabian, as well as the bishops of Jerusalem and Antioch, Alexander and Babylas respectively. The elderly Origen was arrested and tortured, being "extended and stretched to the distance of four holes on the rack,"[5] but not killed, as the authorities deemed it would be of much greater value to break him rather than kill him. Origen did not break, but his body suffered permanent damage and even though he was still alive at the death of Decius (251 CE), he died shortly thereafter as a result of the injuries he received during the persecution.

Origen wrote his treatise *Contra Celsum* just a few years before his death (probably in 248 or 249 CE). Ambrosius sent Origen a copy of a work entitled *True Logos,* which Celsus had written some seventy years earlier. In *True Logos,* Celsus provided what Joseph Trigg has called, an "anti-apology,"[6] a pagan response to the Christian apologies in circulation at the time. Among other charges he raised, Celsus accused Christians of misusing the philosophical idea of Logos producing a "False Logos," in the person of Jesus of Nazareth. Furthermore, Celsus brought detailed

---

5. Eusebius, *Hist. eccl.* 6.39.

6. Trigg, *Origen,* 52.

accusations, charging Christians with being a novel, illegal sect, a secret society whose refusal to exhibit their loyalty by acts of worship of the person of the emperor not only manifested their seditious character, but also constituted an adequate reason for their persecution. Origen's response, as we have already seen in chapter 3, included an ardent defense of the non-violent character of the Christian faith and practice, and argued that though Christians "do not become fellow-soldiers with him [i.e., the emperor], even if he presses for this, yet we are fighting for him and composing a special army of piety through our intersessions to God" (*Cels.* 8.73). Christians, insisted Origen, are of much more use to the emperor if they provide an example to be followed by Romans and barbarians alike: "For if as Celsus has it, every one were to do the same as I, obviously the barbarians would also be converted to the word of God and would be most law-abiding and mild. And all other worship would be done away with and only that of the Christians would prevail" (8.68).[7] In spite of Celsus's inability to see how the barbarians that surrounded the Roman empire would be convinced to rejoice with a Christian empire, Origen posited that the Logos would change the hearts and attitudes of all people, including the barbarians, creating one harmonious soul in the world: "For since the Logos and the healing power within him are more powerful than any evils in the soul, he applies this power to each individual according to God's will, and the end of the treatment is the abolition of evil" (*Cels.* 8.72).

Against Celsus 2.30[8]

2. [30] Celsus also threw out this remark: But no one gives proof of a god or son of a god by such signs and false stories, nor by such disreputable evidence. He ought to have quoted the false stories and refuted them, and to have shown by argument the disreputable evidence, so that if a Christian appeared to say anything convincing, he might attempt to combat it and to overthrow the statement. Now that which he says ought to have happened to Jesus actually did happen, because Jesus was a great person; but he did not want to see that this was so, as the self-evident nature of the facts about Jesus proves.

---

7. Trigg, Review of J. Helgeland, 206.

8. The Greek text can be found the digital library, *Thesaurus Linguae Graecae*, which is based on *Contre Celse* (ed. and trans. by Borret).

For, he says, as the sun which illuminates everything else first shows itself, so ought the Son of God to have done. We would maintain that he actually did this. For "righteousness arose in his days and abundance of peace" [Ps 71:7]⁹ began with his birth; God was preparing the nations for his teaching, that they might be under one Roman emperor, so that the unfriendly attitude of the nations to one another, caused by the existence of a large number of kingdoms, might not make it more difficult for Jesus' apostles to do what he commanded them when he said, "Go and teach all nations" [Matt 28:19]. It is quite clear that Jesus was born during the reign of Augustus, the one who reduced to uniformity, so to speak, the many kingdoms on earth so that he had a single empire. It would have hindered Jesus' teaching from being spread through the whole world if there had been many kingdoms, not only for the reasons just stated, but also because men everywhere would have been compelled to do military service and to fight in defense of their own land. This used to happen before the times of Augustus and even earlier still when a war was necessary, such as between the Peloponnesians and the Athenians, and similarly in the case of the other nations which fought one another. Accordingly, how could this teaching, which preaches peace and does not even allow men to take vengeance on their enemies, have had any success unless the international situation had everywhere been changed and a milder spirit prevailed at the advent of Jesus?¹⁰

Against Celsus 3.7–8

One should note that in this section Origen highlights that the prohibition is not based on idolatry or the moral excess of military life, but simply on Jesus's prohibition against killing.

3. [7] The assertion that "certain Jews at the time of Christ revolted against the Jewish community and followed Jesus" is not less false than the claim "that the Jews had their origin in the revolt of certain

---

9. There has been a long tradition in the early Church of connecting the *pax Romana* and the spread of the gospel. See Eusebius, *Hist. eccl.* 4.26.7; Hippolytus, *Comm. in Dan.* 4.9.

10. For *Contra Celsum* I have followed Henry Chadwick's classical translation as much as possible, since it still retains the beauty of Origen's argument. Origen, *Contra Celsum* (trans. by Chadwick), 92.

Egyptians." Celsus and those who agree with him will not be able to cite a single act of rebellion on the part of the Christians. If a revolt had indeed given rise to the Christian community, if Christians took their origins from the Jews, who were allowed to take up arms in defense of their possessions and to kill their enemies, the Christian Law-giver would not have made homicide [or, the taking of human life] absolutely forbidden. He would not have taught that his disciples were never justified in taking such action against a man even if he were the greatest wrongdoer. [Jesus] considered it contrary to his divinely inspired legislation to approve any kind of homicide whatsoever. If Christians had started with a revolt, they would never have submitted to the kind of peaceful laws which permitted them to be slaughtered "like sheep" [Ps 44:11] and which made them always incapable of taking vengeance on their persecutors because they followed the law of gentleness and . . . [8] . . . Concerning the Christians, on the other hand, we say that they have been taught not to defend themselves against their enemies; and because they heave kept the laws which command gentleness and love of people, on this account they have received from God that which they could not have succeeded in doing if they had been given the right to make war, even though they may have been quite able to do so.[11]

Against Celsus 5.33

5. [33] To those who ask us where we have come from or who is out author we reply that we came in accordance with the commands of Jesus to beat the spiritual swords that fight and insult us into ploughshares, and to transform the spears that formerly fought against us into pruning-hooks. No longer do we take the sword against any nation, nor do we learn [the art of] war any more, since we have become sons of peace [cf. Luke 10:6] through Jesus who is our leader [cf. Acts 3:15, 5:31; Heb 2:10, 12:2] instead of following the traditional customs, by which we were "strangers to the covenants" [Eph 2:12]. We received a law from which we give thanks to him who delivered us from error and say: "Because our fathers have inherited lying idols, and there is none among them that sends rains" [Jer 16:19, 14:22].

11. *Contra Celsum* 3.8 is adapted from ibid., 133.

Our chorus-leader and teacher came forth from the Jews to control the whole world by the word of his teaching.[12]

Against Celsus 7.20; 7.25; 7.26

In the fourth and fifth books of the treatise, Origen also addresses Celsus's objection that Christians seem not to accept the Old Testament allowance, even mandate at times, for war and killing. He presents the twofold sense of interpretation, the literal and the spiritual, and argues that Scripture ought to be interpreted Christologically. Thus, there is no contradiction between the Jewish law and the gospel, nor did God change God's mind. Later, in book seven, he is going to show another difference between the Israel of the Old Testament and the Church of the New, namely that, while Israel was a bordered state with a national identity, Christianity is a transnational community that transcends ethnic identities and cannot, therefore, be compared to the ancient nation of Israel in any literal sense.

7. [20] We maintain that the law has a twofold interpretation, one literal and the other spiritual, as was also taught by some of our predecessors.[13] And it is not so much we as God speaking in one of the prophets, who described the law literally understood as "judgments that are not good" and "statutes that are not good"; and in the same prophet God is represented as saying that the law spiritually understood is "judgments that are good" and "statutes that are good" [Ezek 20:25]. The prophet is obviously not making contradictory statements in the same passage. It is consistent with this when Paul also says that "the letter kills," which is equivalent to the literal interpretation; whereas "the spirit gives life" [2 Cor 3:6], which means the same as the spiritual interpretation.[14]

7. [25] Celsus does not quote any passages from the law which are apparently in contradiction to what stands in the gospel, so that we might compare them. He says: And to a man who has struck one once one should offer oneself to be struck again. But we will say that

---

12. Adapted from ibid., 290.

13. Philo, *Spec.* 1.287 and passim.

14. Origen, *Contra Celsum* (trans. by Chadwick), 411.

we are aware that "it was said to them of old time, An eye for an eye and a tooth for a tooth," and that we have read also the words: "But I say unto you, to him that strikes you on one cheek offer the other one also" [Matt 5:38–39]. However, as I imagine that Celsus derived some vague notions from those who say that the God of the gospel is different from the God of the law, and do made remarks like this, I would reply to his objection that the Old Testament also knows the doctrine that to him that strikes you on the right cheek you should offer the other one also. At any rate, it is written in the Lamentations of Jeremiah: "It is good for a man when he bears a yoke in his youth, he will sit alone and in silence when he has taken it on himself. He will give a cheek to the man who smites him and shall be filled with reproaches" [Lam 3:27–9]. The gospel, then, does not lay down laws in contradiction to the God of the law, not even if we interpret literally the saying about a blow on the jaw. And neither Moses nor Jesus is wrong. Nor did the Father forget when he sent Jesus the commands which he had given to Moses [as Celsus accuses]. Nor did He condemn His own laws, and change His mind, and send His messenger for the opposite purpose.[15]

Origen, then, moves on to show Celsus's arguments to be irrational (or at least straw-man arguments) on pragmatic grounds. He argues that it is impossible for the Christians who live under Roman rule as a transnational community, to adhere to the same laws and practices of the nationed Jews of old:

> 7. [26] . . . It was not possible for the structure of life of the ancient Jews to remain without any modification if, for instance, they were to obey the form of life enjoined by the gospel. It was impossible for Christians to follow the Mosaic law in killing their enemies or those who acted illegally and were judged to be deserving of death by fire or by stoning, although, in fact, even the Jews were not able to inflict these punishments on them, as the law commanded, even if they wanted to do so. Again, if you took away from the Jews of that time, who had their own political life and country, the power to go out against their enemies and to fight for their traditional customs, and to take life, or at any time to punish adulterers or murderers or people who

15. Ibid., 415.

had committed any such crime, the inevitable consequence would have been their complete and utter destruction when their enemies attacked the nation, because by their own law they would have been deprived of strength and prevented from resisting their enemies. But the providence which long ago gave the law, but now has given the gospel of Jesus Christ, did not wish that the practices of the Jews should continue, and so destroyed their city and temple and the service to God in the temple offered by means of sacrifices and the prescribed worship. Just as providence did not want them to be performed, and destroyed them, in the same way it increased the success of the Christians added daily to the multitude, and also granted boldness in spite of the fact that there were countless hindrances to the spread of the teaching of Jesus in the world. But because it was God who wanted the Gentiles also to be helped by the teaching of Jesus Christ, every human design against the Christians has been frustrated; and the more emperors and rulers of nations and peoples in many places have humiliated them, the more they have increased in number so that "they have become exceedingly strong" [Exod 1:7].[16]

It is worth quoting Louis J. Swift at length at this point:

Here the ethical change effected by the Gospel is explained in historical and political terms. The demise of the autonomous Jewish state removed the need for physical force among God's people, who were, in any case, no longer to be identified with a particular nation. Under an interim peace established by Rome they could now work toward the goal of universal peace without the weapons of war. Whatever coercive methods were needed to keep the barbarians at bay could be entrusted to the armies of Rome, but for the Christians the New Dispensation absolutely forbade violence. When Peter cut off Malchus' ear in the Garden of Gethsemane (Matthew 26:51) he demonstrated that he had not taken the peace of the Lord to heart but was still operating within the Old Testament context.[17]

16. Ibid., 415–16.
17. Swift, *Early Fathers*, 58.

Against Celsus 8.73–75

In the last book of the treatise, 8.65–75, Origen returns to his objections to military service and Christian participation in war and frames his arguments also on moral grounds, not simply to idolatry and imperial worship.[18] He appealed to the Christians' sense of justice and to the civic obligation of all Romans, insisting that it is the Christians' patriotic duty to join the emperor in "what is right, and fight for him, and be fellow-soldiers if he presses for this, and fellow-generals with him" (8.73) because "it is unjust for people who partake of [all the good things which the Emperor offers, including security and wealth] to offer nothing in return" (8.55, 67). Contrary to Celsus's inability to see how the barbarians that surrounded the Roman empire would be convinced to rejoice with a Christian empire, Origen posited that, at the end, the Logos will change the hearts and attitudes of all people, including the barbarians, creating one harmonious soul in the world (8.68). It is important to note in this section that Origen does not grant Celsus's claim that Christians are beholden to the magistracy for what earthly possessions they have; on the contrary, rejecting the claim, he turns the question to the sovereignty and providence of God.

Against Celsus 8.55–70

8. [55] After this Celsus says: *Reason demands one of two alternatives. If [Christians] refuse to worship in the proper way the lords in charge of the following activities, then they ought neither to come to marriageable age, nor to marry a wife, nor to beget children, nor to do anything else in life. But they should depart from this world leaving of descendants at all behind them, so that such a race would entirely cease to exist on earth. But if they are going to marry wives, and beget children, and taste of the fruits, and partake of the joys of this life, and endure the appointed evils (by nature's law all men must have experience of evils; evil is necessary and has nowhere else to exist), then they ought to render the honors to the beings who have been entrusted with these things. And they ought to offer the due rites of worship in this life until they are set free from their bonds, lest they even appear ungrateful to*

---

18. See also Trigg, Review of J. Helgeland, 206. Helgeland follows Chadwick (Origen, *Contra Celsum*, pp. xxi–xxii) on this.

them. *It is wrong for people who partake of what is their property to offer them nothing in return.*

. . . These matters do not cause difficulties to us when we refuse to obey the demons who are allotted the earth. Since we have been armed with the whole armor of God [Eph 6:11, 13] as athletes of piety, we resist the race of demons which is hostile to us.

[56] Even though by his words Celsus dismisses us utterly from life in order that, as he supposes, this race of ours may entirely cease to exist on earth, yet we who are concerned with the business of our Creator will live according to the laws of God. . . . For we worship the Lord our God, and serve Him only, praying that we may become imitators of Christ. . . . That is why we do not render the customary honor to the beings to whom, Celsus says, earthly things have been entrusted, since "no one can serve two masters" [Matt 6:24]; and we cannot at the same time serve God and mammon, whether that name refers to any one particular thing or to many. Furthermore, if anyone dishonors the lawgiver "by the transgression of the law" [Rom 2:23], it appears obvious to us that, if there are two laws opposed to one another, the law of God and the law of mammon, it is preferable for us to dishonor mammon by the transgression of the law of mammon in order to pay honor to God by keeping God's law, rather than to dishonor God by the transgression of the law of God in order to pay honor to mammon by keeping mammon's law.

[65] We ought to despise the kindly disposition of men and of emperors if to propitiate them means not only that we have to commit murders and acts of licentiousness and savagery, but also that we have to blaspheme the God of the universe or make some servile and cringing utterance, alien to men of bravery and nobility who, together with the other virtues, wish to possess courage as the greatest of them.

[67] [Since we have dealt with this before (8.65)], it is unnecessary for us to reply again to this: *Even if some one tells you to take an oath by an emperor among men, that also is nothing dreadful. For earthly things have been given to him, and whatever you receive in this life you receive from him.* But in our judgment it is certainly not true that all earthly things have been given to him; nor do we receive from him whatever we receive in this life. Whatever we receive that

is right and good we have from God and His providence, such as cultivated crops and bread "that strengthens a person's heart," and the pleasant vine and "wine that gladdens the heart." From the providence of God we also have the fruits of the olive "to make the face shine with olive-oil" [Ps 103:5].

Celsus raised the objection that if everyone followed the example of the Christians and abstained from military service, the emperor would be "abandoned, alone, and deserted," and would not be able to stand against the whims of the "most lawless and savage barbarians."

[68] [On the contrary,] if, as Celsus, has it, every one were to do the same as I, obviously the barbarians would also be converted to the word of God and would be most law-abiding and mild. And all other worship would be done away and only that of the Christians would prevail. One day it will be the only one to prevail, since the word is continually gaining possession of more souls.

[70] However, if as Celsus suggests all the Romans were convinced and prayed, they would be superior to their enemies, or would not even fight wars at all, since they would be protected by divine power which is reported to have preserved five entire cities for the sake of fifty righteous men [cf. Gen 18:24–26]. For the people of God are the salt of the world, preserving the permanence of things on earth and earthly things hold together so longs as the salt does not turn bad. For if the salt has lost its savor, it is of no further use either for the earth or for the dunghill, but is cast out and trodden under people's feet. Let him who has ears to hear, understand what this means [cf. Luke 14:34–35]. We, moreover, are only persecuted when God allows the tempter and gives him authority to persecute us. And when it is not God's will that we should suffer this, even in the midst of the world that hates us by a miracle we live at peace, and are encouraged by him who said: "Be of good cheer, I have overcome the world" [John 16:33]. And he really has overcome the world, so that the world prevails only in so far as he who overcame it wills, for he received from his Father the victory over the world. And by his victory we are encouraged.[19]

---

19. Origen, *Contra Celsum* (trans. by Chadwick), 493–506.

Against Celsus 8.72

8. [72] But we believe that the Logos will overcome the entire rational nature, and will have remodeled every soul to his own perfection, when each individual simply by the exercise of his freedom will choose what the Logos wills and will be in that state which he has chosen. . . . For since the Logos and the healing power within him are more powerful than any evils in the soul, he applies this power to each individual according to God's will, and the end of the treatment is the abolition of evil.

[73] Then Celsus next exhorts us to help the emperor with all our power, and cooperate with him in what is right, and fight for him, and be fellow-soldiers if he presses for this, and fellow generals with him. We may reply to this that at appropriate times we render to the emperors divine help, if I may so say, by taking up even the whole armor of God [Eph 6:11]. And this we do in obedience to the apostolic utterance which says: "I exhort you, therefore, first to make prayers, supplications, intercessions, and thanksgivings for all men, for emperors, and all that are in authority" [1 Tim 2:1–2]. Indeed, the more pious a man is, the more effective he is in helping the emperors—more so that the soldiers who go out into the lines and kill all the enemy troops that they can.

We would also say this to those who are alien to our faith and ask us to fight for the community and to kill men: that it is also your opinion that the priests of certain images and wardens of the temples of the gods, as you think them to be, should keep their right hand undefiled for the sake of sacrifices, that they may offer the customary sacrifices to those who you say are gods with hands unstained by blood and pure from murders.[20] And in fact when war comes you do not enlist the priests. If, then, this is reasonable, how much more reasonable is it that, while others fight, Christians also should be fighting as priests and worshippers of God, keeping their right hands pure and by their prayers to God striving for those who fight in a righteous cause and for the emperor who reigns righteously, in

---

20. It is worth noting here that the *Ante-Nicene Fathers* translation misses the force of the word φόνους (murders) by translating the passage as: "keep their hands free from blood, that they may with hands unstained and free from human blood" (*ANF* 4:667–68).

order that everything which is opposed and hostile to those who act rightly may be destroyed? Moreover, we who by our prayers destroy all demons which stir up wars, violate oaths, and disturb the peace, are of more help to the emperors than those who seem to be doing the fighting. We who offer prayers with righteousness, together with ascetic practices and exercises which teach us to despise pleasures and not to be led by them, are cooperating in the tasks of the community. Even more do we fight on behalf of the emperor. And though we do not become fellow-soldiers with him, even if he presses for this, yet we are fighting for him and are composing a special army of piety through our intercessions to God.

[74] If Celsus wishes us to be generals for our country, let him realize that we do this; but we do not do so with a view to being seen by men and to being proud of it. Our prayers are made in secret in the mind itself, and are sent up as from priests on behalf of the people in our country. Christians do more good to their countries than the rest of mankind, since they educate the citizens and teach them to be devoted to God, the guardian of the city; and they take those who have lived good lives in the most insignificant cities up to a divine and heavenly city. To them it could be said: You were faithful in a very insignificant city [cf. Luke 16:10; 19:17]; come also to the great city where "God stands in the congregation of the gods and judges between gods in the midst," and numbers you even with them, if you no longer "die like men" and do not "fall like one of the princes" [Ps 81:1, 7].

[75] Celsus exhorts us also to accept public office in our country if it is necessary to do this for the sake of the preservation of the laws and of piety. But we know of the existence in each city of another sort of country, created by the Logos of God. And we call upon those who are competent to take office, who are sound in doctrine and life, to rule over the churches [instead]. We do not accept those who love power. But we put pressure on those who on account of their great humility are reluctant hastily to take upon themselves the common responsibility of the church of God. And those who rule us well are those who have to be forced to take office, being constrained by the great King who, we are convinced, is the Son of God, the divine Logos. And if those who are chosen as rulers in the church rule well

over God's country (I mean the church), or if they rule in accordance with the commands of God, they do not on this account defile any of the appointed civic laws.

If Christians do avoid these responsibilities, it is not with the motive of shrinking the public services of life. But they keep themselves for a more divine and necessary service in the church of God for the sake of the salvation of men. Here it is both necessary and right for them to be leaders and to be concerned about all men, both those who are within the Church, that they may live better ever day, and those who appear to be outside it, that they may become familiar with the sacred words and acts of worship; and that, offering a true worship to God in this way and instructing as many as possible, they may become absorbed in the word of God and the divine law, and so be united to the supreme God through the Son of God, the Logos, Wisdom, Truth, and Righteousness who unites to Him every one who has been persuaded to live according to God's will in all things.[21]

Commentary on 1 Corinthians 26.98 [22]

In his commentary on 1 Cor 5:9–11, Origen takes that occasion to expound upon Paul's admonition for the Corinthian Christians "not to associate with sexually immoral persons—not at all meaning the immoral of this world, or the greedy and robbers, or idolaters, since you would then need to go out of the world." After a long excursus on adultery and sexual immorality, he returns to idolatry and castigates those Christians who would propose that participating in pagan worship is not morally reprehensible since the Christian knows that these gods do not exist, and therefore, one is free of the moral consequence.

Commentary on 1 Corinthians 26.98

26. [98] And there are some who are [worse] idolaters than those who are in the world. I mean those who want to teach that participating in idol worship is of no consequence. And this sin is particularly found among those serving in the army. "I am forced into it," they say. "The

---

21. Origen, *Contra Celsum* (trans. by Chadwick), 509–10, also Wiles and Santer, *Documents*, 228–30.

22. The Greek text is found in Jenkins, "Documents," 366.

army demands it. I risk my life if I do not sacrifice or if I do not put on the white robe and offer incense according to the customs of the army." And yet such a person calls himself a Christian! Do not even eat with the one who says such a thing.

Homilies on Joshua 14.1; 15.1

In his voluminous *Homilies on Joshua*, Origen had to confront the biblical narratives of exodus and conquest. For Origen, the coming of Christ not only transformed God's people into a transnational, peaceful community, but also interpreted the Scriptures themselves. As such, the actions of Israel of old cannot be simply emulated by Christians, and the wars of the Old Testament must be understood as having a spiritual sense if they are to be incorporated into the Christian scheme of things. Christians have no place in war; nor do they have any use for it. In the New Economy, Christ's presence "poured the peaceful light of knowledge into human heart" (*Hom. Jos.* 14.1).

Homilies on Joshua 14.1

14. [1] When that Israel that is according to the flesh read these same Scriptures before the coming of our Lord Jesus Christ, they understood nothing in them except wars and the shedding of blood, from which their spirits, too, were incited to excessive savageries and were always fed by wars and strife. But after the presence of my Lord Jesus Christ poured the peaceful light of knowledge into human hearts, since, according tot he Apostle, he himself is "our peace" [Eph 2:14], he teaches us peace from this very reading of wars. For peace is returned to the soul if its own enemies—sins and vices—are expelled from it.

And therefore, according to the teaching of our Lord Jesus Christ, when we indeed read this things, we also equip ourselves and are roused for battle, but against those enemies that "proceed from our heart": obviously, "evil thought, thefts, false testimony, slanders" [Matt 15:19] and other similar adversaries of our soul. Following what this Scripture sets forth, we try, if it can be done, not to leave behind any "who may be saved or who may breathe" [Jos 10:40]. For if we gain possession of these enemies, we shall fittingly also take possession of "the airy authorities" [Eph 2:2] and expel them from his kingdom, as they had gathered within us upon thrones of vices.[23]

Homilies on Joshua 14.1

15. [1] Unless those physical wars [i.e., of the Old Testament] bore the figure of spiritual wars, I do not think the books of Jewish history would ever have been handed down by the apostles to the disciple of Christ, who came to teach peace, so that they could be read in the churches. For what good was that description of wars to those to whom Jesus says, "My peace I give to you; my peace I leave to you" [John 14:27], and to whom it is commanded and said through the Apostle, "Not avenging your own selves" [Rom 12:19], and "Rather, you receive injury," and, "You suffer offence" [1 Cor 6:7]?

In short, knowing that now we do not have to wage physical wars, but that the struggles of the soul have to be exerted against spiritual adversaries, the Apostle, just as a military leader, gives an order to the soldiers of Christ, saying, "Put on the armor of God, so that you may be able to stand firm against the cunning devices of the Devil" [Eph 6:11]. And in order for us to have examples of these spiritual wars from deeds of old, he wanted those narratives of exploits to be recited to us in church, so that, if we are spiritual—hearing that "the Law is spiritual" [Rom 7:14]—"we may compare spiritual things with spiritual" [Rom 7:14] in the things we hear. And we may consider, by means of those nations that fought visibly against physical Israel, how great are the swarms of opposing powers from among the spiritual races that are called "spiritual wickedness in the heavens" [Eph 6:12] and that stir up wars against the Lord's Church, which is the true Israel.[24]

---

23. Origen, *Homilies on Joshua*, 130.
24. Ibid., 138.

EIGHT

Cyprian of Carthage
(ca. 202–258 CE)

Little is known of the early life of Tertullian's younger contemporary, Cyprian. Thacius Caecilius Cyprianus was born around 202 CE to a pagan family of wealth and social status in Carthage.[1] Educated as a *rhetor*, Cyprian probably practiced law as an *aduocatus* in the courts in the Forum of Carthage and seems to have gained substantial influence and esteem in his own right. Like all Roman colonies, Carthage too, was seen as a "transplant"[2] of the city of Rome, in a way, "little copies and likenesses of the Roman People," as the emperor Hadrian famously stated.[3] *Romanitas* centered on civic obligations, and Cyprian's ideal social world was characterized by the constitutional order embodied in the *Twelve Tables of Roman Law*, bronze copies of which were prominently displayed at the Forum of Carthage (*Don.* 10). Yet, the third century was one of dramatic changes. The dream that was the *pax Romana* was dashed within Cyprian's own lifetime. "Capellianus, governor of Numidia, had marched against Carthage in support of Maximinus against Gordian I, during which campaign both he and his son died. A massacre of the inhabitants followed, and the treasury was raided."[4] By the time Decius came to power, the long period of (relative) peace that had characterized

---

1. For an excellent look into Cyprian, the Roman environment into which he was born and raised, and the controversies that surrounded his episcopacy, see Brent, *Cyprian and Roman Carthage*; and Burns, *Cyprian the Bishop*.

2. Brent, *Cyprian and Roman Carthage*, 44.

3. Aulus Gellius, *Noct. att.* 16.13.9; cf. Sherwin-White, *The Roman Citizenship*, 413.

4. Brent, *Cyprian and Roman Carthage*, 45.

the Severan years had been replaced by an almost permanent state of revolt and civil wars. Seven emperor had claimed the throne in the span of thirteen years. The Goths were a continuous threat in the West and the Persians in the East. In the midst of the civil chaos of this period, the increased importance of the armies as king-makers and protectors was underscored by a series of increases in pay and benefits. A number of reforms and an appeal to one's patriotic duty, made a military career an appealing choice for many, including Christians.

Cyprian was converted to Christianity late in life. He was baptized into the Church at the time of the Easter Vigil, around 246 CE and was ordained a priest shortly thereafter. Around 248 CE, following the death of Donatus, the bishop of Carthage, even though still a young Christian and only a priest, Cyprian was—apparently with some reluctance on his part—elected bishop of Carthage by the clergy and the people of the city. Within a year, the first empire-wide persecution under emperor Decius erupted (249–251 CE) with devastating effects on the Church.

Like most persons of his time, emperor Decius, too, was deeply influenced by a cyclic Stoic metaphysics of decline and renewal. A dominant eschatology of the third century that interpreted societal crises and anticipated material rebirth, Stoic eschatology interpreted for the emperor the events that threw the Empire into civil chaos in the decades preceding his accession as part of the narrative of decline, and provide the backdrop to his religious policy and political rhetoric.

Decius's order for a universal supplication came at the heels of the millennial celebrations of Rome (249 CE) and needs to be interpreted as apotropaic in nature, fulfilling the emperor's religious obligation as *pontifex maximus,* with the expressed aim of securing the *pax deorum* against the impending cosmic crisis, a peace whose reality he alone would have to determine as *augur.*[5] Numbers of the faithful responded to the imperial edicts and assembled as the stadia and fora of North Africa to offer sacrifices for the welfare of the emperor and receive the official *libellus,* the state-issued receipt that they had performed their duty as instructed. Others did not. They were the *stantes,* those who stood in the face of persecution; the martyrs and confessor who were now rhetorically identified in the imagination of the faithful as the *militia Christi,* the soldiers of Christ.

---

5. Ibid., 143.

The variety of Christian responses to Decius's edict manifested in a very public and disturbing way how profoundly the Roman appeals to the *mos maiorum*, the "ancestral customs," clashed with Christ's "New Law." Roman rhetoric had presented the edict within the framework of civic obligation and had persuaded a number of Christians it was their patriotic duty to conform. In horror, Cyprian interpreted such acts of conformity as apostasy and a dreadful crime. At the end of the persecution an account had to be given by lapsed and *stantes* alike; and the large number of confessors it had produced now presented a particular kind of challenge for the Church. The purity and unity of the Church, the role and authority of the episcopate, and the efficacy and reconciliation of rituals, all had to be worked out and the lull in persecution during the subsequent six years allowed the Church to begin the process. A protagonist in the efforts of the Church to reconcile and define its unity, Cyprian was executed in 248 CE under the emperor Valerian, whose edict of universal conformity seems to have been directed specifically against the presbyters and bishops of the Church.

To Donatus 6, 11

Cyprian wrote *Ad Donatum* shortly after his conversion and baptism in 246 CE. In it, Cyprian describes the corruption of the present age, the dissolution of the world, and the impending eschatological victory of Christ. Swift notes that Cyprian rejects a "double standard for private and public morality in this area, and elsewhere he suggests that there is an inherent conflict between acts of violence and the celebration of the Christian mysteries."[6]

To Donatus 6

6. Notice that the roads have been made impassable by robbers, the seas have been filled with pirates, and everywhere wars have broken out with the ghastly bloodletting of the camp. The world is drenched with mutual bloodshed. And murder, when committed by an individual, it is a crime: when it is committed on behalf of the state, it is called virtue. Crimes go unpunished not because the perpetrators are said to be guiltless but because their cruelty is so extensive. An argument for innocence secures no freedom from such punishment.[7]

6. Swift, *Early Fathers*, 48.

7. Adapted from ibid.

To Donatus 11

In this section, Cyprian warns against the vanity of the military and the corrupting influence of power.

11. So now let me show you what the present age in ignorance thinks is good. There what you will witness you ought to shun. You will now see what you think to he honors, what you think to be the ornaments of magisterial office, the extravagance in being rich, the power that lies in a military command, the purple that reflects the magistrates' splendor, the power that resides in the unrestricted freedom of being in government. Nevertheless the poison of wickedness that charms you is a concealed poison. Evil when it smiles may even appear joyful, but its deceptive appearance is in reality a hidden disease.[8]

On the Goodness of Patience 14

Addressing himself specifically to Christians, in *De Bono Patientiae* Cyprian insists in the most stark of terms that participating in the mysteries of the Church, especially the Eucharist, is incompatible with the taking of human life.

14. Patience, however, beloved brethren, not only preserves what is good, but also repels what is evil. Devoted to the Holy Spirit and cleaving to heavenly and divine things, it struggles with the bulwark of its virtues against the acts of the flesh and the body whereby the soul is stormed and captured. Accordingly, let us look at a few out of many of these acts, so that from these few, all the rest may be understood. Adultery, deceit, homicide, are mortal sins. Let patience be strong and stable in the heart, and then the sanctified body and temple of God will not be corrupted by adultery, innocence dedicated to justice will not be infected by the contagion of deceit, and the hand that has held the Eucharist is not to be stained with the sword and bloodshed.[9]

Like Tertullian and many of the Christian writers before him, Cyprian uses common military language and imagery throughout his writings. In *Epistle* 73.10, Cyprian uses the generic example of military discipline

8. Cyprian, *On the Church: Treatises*, 61 (trans. by Allen Brent).

9. The whole text of the treatise can be found at http://www.ewtn.com/library/ SOURCES/GOODPAT.TXT.

when he argues that Christian leaders ought to guard the faith from the threat of heretics: "It is the task of a good soldier to defend the camp of his commander against traitors and enemies. It is the task of a glorious leader to carry out the commissions entrusted to him."[10] And again in his letter *To Fortunatus* 13, he uses the imagery of the returning victorious armies to describe humanity's eschatological destiny: "If it is a glorious thing for soldiers in the world to return home in triumph to their native land after defeating the enemy, how much more impressive and glorious is man's triumphant return to paradise following the devil's defeat." Commonplace statements like these cannot be taken as endorsing Christian participation in military service any more than Paul's exhortation for Christians to put on the full armor of God (Eph 6:10–18) can be interpreted as an apostolic call to enlistment.

The same holds true for Cyprian's letter *To Demetrianus* 20, where he states that he prays for the safety of the empire and that her enemies would be kept at bay. Again it would be quite a stretch of the evidence to argue that commonplace sentiments like these may be taken as endorsing Christian participation in the imperial armies.[11]

To Demetrianus 20

20. Only when we go to God will we receive the promised rewards. Nevertheless, we always pray that enemies be kept at bay, that rains be granted, and that adversities either be taken away or mitigated; day and night we pour out our supplications beseeching and placating God, earnestly and continually pleading with him for your safety and peace.[12]

One of the most interesting letters is *Epistle* 39, in which Cyprian makes that comment that the martyr Celerinus, who died during the Decian persecution, came from a long line of Christian including his grandmother Celerina, who herself was martyred. Cyprian tells us that both Celerinus's paternal and maternal uncles (Laurentinus and Egnatius) were "formerly fighting in the worldly camp," but were subsequently martyred "while they cast down the devil by the confession of Christ."

10. In Cyprian, *Letters* (1–81), 274 (trans. by Rose Bernard Donna).

11. Or to interpret the language as a positive disposition towards the imperial armies and military campaigns, as in Swift, *Early Fathers*, 48–49.

12. Ibid., 49.

While at first glance it might seems that Cyprian presents the military record of Laurentinus and Egnatius in an approving manner, the context of the arguments cannot support such a conclusion. Cyprian's description does not indicate whether these two men were Christians before they joined the army or whether they were converted while in service, or even after they left the army. All Cyprian says is that at one time, they were in the service of the armies of the world, but their Christian faith moved them to join the *militia Christi*, rejecting their former way of life and dying a martyr's death—hardly an endorsement of Christians enlisting in the armies of the empire.

Epistle 39.2b-3a

39. [2b] The bright marks of [Celerinus's] wounds shine in his glorious body; they stand out and appear clear tokens in the sinews of the man and in the limbs consumed by long wasting away. They are great, they are remarkable things which the brotherhood may hear of his courage and of his praises. . . . In the servant of God, the glory of wounds made a victory; memory preserves the glory of the scars.

    [3a] Nor is this title of glories strange and new in our dearly beloved Celerinus. He is following the footprints of his kindred; he rivals his parents and relatives with a similar distinction of divine condescension. His grandmother, Celerina, was long ago crowned with martyrdom. His paternal and his maternal uncles, likewise, Laurentine and Egnatius, themselves also formerly fighting in the worldly camp, but true and spiritual soldiers of God, while they cast down the devil by the confession of Christ, deserved the palms and crowns of the Lord by their glorious passion.[13]

---

13. Cyprian, *Letters* (1–81), 100 (trans. by Rose Bernard Donna).

NINE

Acts of the Military Martyrs (ca. 260–303 CE)

Throughout the book we have seen a variety of reasons for which Christians begun joining the legions in the late-second, early-third century.[1] Even though Tertullian's rhetorical flourish that the Christians were taking over every niche of the Roman world (*Apology* 37.4) might had been a hyperbole at the end of the second century, it was certainly a conceivable future reality by the time of Diocletian, a century later. The Christian population of the empire had exploded during the troubled times of the early third century from less than one percent in the major urban centers to roughly ten percent of the population by 300 CE.[2] Christians could be found in every facet of life, including the upper echelons of the palace itself. And even though Christians could also be found dispersed among the legions, Roman discipline and army practice would not tolerate soldiers who, for whatever reason, refused to act as ordered. As we have already seen in Tertullian's *On the Crown* (pp. 121–27), when Christians were identified as such from among the ranks, the incommensurability of their faith profession with the demands of

1. See especially ch. 3.

2. Any such demographic estimates are notoriously difficult due to lack of literary evidence. However, most estimates of the Christian population in the Roman empire from Decius to Constantine agree that the proportion probably varied from about one-twentieth to one-ninth between West and East and between urban and rural areas. See McMullen, *Christianizing the Roman Empire*, 85. Stark, *The Rise of Christianity*, 7, estimates that there were some 6.3 million Christians in a population of roughly 55–50 million people. Fox, *Pagans and Christians*, 592, estimates Christians only at 4–5 percent of the total population.

the army *disciplina* resulted in the Christian's trial and, if one did not recant one's faith, summary execution.

In *The Acts of the Military Martyrs* we have a number of accounts of men in active military service, recruits, and veterans who have to face a choice between the military and Christ. All these are events that took place from the middle of the third century to the beginning of the fourth, before the rise of Constantine as the sole ruler of the Empire.

What then of those who those soldiers we know to have been Christians during at least part of their service? What were their reasons for joining or not leaving upon converting? How they did it we can only conjecture. What we do know is that both the theological and the ecclesiastical witness of the Church unanimously objected to the practice. John Helgeland has suggested that it might even be as simple as that some "probably modeled their Christianity along the lines of Roman polytheism—*Mars* is for victory, *spring nymphs* are for fresh water, *Jupiter Dolichenus* is for weapons that do not break in combat, and *Christ*, is for when your weapon does break and you die."[3]

The Martyrdom of St. Marinus (ca. 260–262 CE)

In the seventh book of his *Ecclesiastical History*, Eusebius tells the story of Marinus, a soldier with the *legio X Fretensis*, who was stationed in Caesarea in Palestine during the time of this account.[4] From the account we can gather that Marinus had had a long career in the army and had risen to the position of *optio ad spem ordinis*, the rank just before the promotion to centurion (each legion had 59 or 60 centurions). On the eve of his promotion, a rival denounced Marinus for being a Christian, "who would not offer sacrifice to the emperors" (*M. Marinus* 2). Given three hours to recant his faith and reconsider his fate, Marinus went for a walk. The bishop of Caesarea, Theotecnus, met him and brought him to the church where he revealed for him the true nature of his dilemma. Marinus was executed that same day. What remains unsaid in this account is how would have Marinus acted as a centurion if his rival had not brought forth the charge. Would he offer the requisite sacrifices? And why did it take the sharp eye—or, at least, the jealousy—of a pagan to bring Marinus to this crisis of conscience? The account does not

3. Helgeland, Daly, and Burns, *Christians and the Military*, 55; emphasis added.

4. Eusebius, *Hist.eccl.* 7.15.

address any of these questions, but what it does bear witness to is that when confronted with the antithesis between what Christians said they believed and what they practiced, when the state did not turn a coopting blind eye to Christians among its ranks, the consequences for the choices Christians were forced to make were grave.

The Martyrdom of St. Marinus[5]

[1] During time [of Pope Xystus and other bishops][6] the churches everywhere enjoyed peace. Yet at Caesarea in Palestine, a man named Marinus, who had been honored with many posts in the army and was know for his wealth and his good family, was beheaded for his witness to Christ. It came about in the following way. [2] Among the Romans the vine branch is a mark of honour; and those that obtain it, they believe, become centurions. An army post fell vacant, and according to the order of promotion it was Marinus who was entitled to fill it. But when he was on the point of receiving the office, another man came up before the magistrate and attached Marinus, saying that as a Christian Marinus would not sacrifice to the emperors, and should therefore not be allowed to share in honors that belonged to the Romans according to the ancient laws; but that instead the post should fall to himself.

[3] It is said that that the magistrate (whose name was Achaeus)[7] was moved by this, and he first asked Marinus what views he held. And then, when he saw that he persistently confessed that he was a Christian, he granted him a stay of three hours to reconsider. [4] No sooner had Marinus left the court than Theotecnus, the bishop of Caesarea, approached and drew him aside in conversation; taking him by the hand he led him to the church. Once inside, he placed Marinus right in front of the altar, and drawing aside Marinus' cloak pointed to the sword attached to his side. At the same time he brought a copy of the divine Gospels and he set it before Marinus, asking him to choose which he preferred. Without hesitation Marinus put out his right hand and took the divine writings.

---

5. In Musurillo, *Acts of the Christian Martyrs*, 241, 243.

6. Mentioned by Eusebius in a preceding paragraph, *Hist. eccl.* 7.14–15.

7. Achaeus seems to have been *legatus* of Syria and Palestine about 260/1 CE.

"So then," said Theotecnus, "hold fast, hold fast to God, and given strength by him, may you obtain what you have chosen. Now go in peace."

[5] No sooner had Marinus returned than a herald cried out to summon him before the tribunal; for the allotted time was now over. Marinus presented himself before the judge and showed even greater loyalty to the faith; and immediately, just as he was he was led off to execution, and so found his fulfillment [*or*, perfection].

The Acts of Maximilian (12 March 295 CE)

The *Acts of Maximilian* refers to an event that took place in Tebessa in Numidia, in March 295 CE. It seems that the proconsul Dion went to Tebessa with the expressed purpose of recruiting soldiers for the *legio III Augusta*. Maximilian's father, Fabius Victor, was a *temonarius*, an official in charge of receiving the tax for the outfitting of new recruits,[8] and presented his son for enlistment. The young recruit refused on the grounds that he was a Christian and service in the army would be a sin. He thus became the first recorded conscientious objector.

A number of themes are woven in this account, most interesting of which is that Maximilian's own father was a Christian himself, yet, he did not share in his son's misgiving about military service; yet, following his sons exchange with the magistrate and Maximilian's execution, Victor, too seems to have had a change of heart and even to have been empowered to defy the civil authorities himself: Victor "returned to his home in great joy, giving thanks to God that he had sent ahead such a gift to the Lord, since he himself was soon to follow" (*M. Max.* 3.5).

Also worth noting is the exchange between Dion and Maximilian in section 8. The perplexed proconsul turns to the obstinate youth and in an effort to show him an alternative view makes the remarkable statement that Christians could be found even in the sacred bodyguard of the Tetrarchs. Maximilian replied: "They know what is best for them. But I am a Christian and I cannot do wrong" (*M. Max.* 2.9). That was a refrain that was repeated in a number of accounts.

---

8. For an excellent discussion see Zuckerman, "Two Reforms," 79–139, esp. 136–39.

The Acts of Maximilian[9]

1. [1] On the twelfth day of March at Tebessa, in the consulship of Tuscus and Anullinus, Fabius Victor was summoned to the forum together with Maximillian; Pomeianus was permitted to act as their advocate.

The advocate spoke: "Fabius Victor, agent in charge of the recruiting tax [*temonarius*], is present for his hearing along with Valerian Quintianus, imperial representative, and Victor's son Maximilian, an excellent recruit. Seeing that Maximilian had good recommendations, I request that he be measured [for a uniform]."

[2] The proconsul Dion said: "What is your name?"

Maximilian replied: "But why do you wish to know my name? I cannot serve because I am a Christian."

[3] The proconsul Dion said: "Get him ready."

While he was being made ready, Maximilian replied: "I cannot serve. I cannot commit a sin. I am a Christian."

[4] "Let him be measured," said the proconsul Dion.

After he was measured, one of the staff said: "He is five foot ten."[10]

[5] Dion said to his staff: "Let him be given the military seal."

Still resisting, Maximilian replied: "I will not do it! I cannot serve!"

2. [1] "Serve, or you will die," said Dion.

"I shall not serve," said Maximilian. "You may cut off my head, I will not serve this world [*saeculo*] [I will serve] only my God."

[2] The Proconsul Dion said: "Who has turned your head?"

"My own soul," said Maximilian, "and the one who has called me."

[3] Dion said to Victor, the boy's father: "Speak to your son."

Victor said: "He is aware and can take his own counsel on what is best for him."

[4] Dion said to Maximilian: "Agree to serve and receive the military seal."

---

9. In Musurillo, *Acts of the Christian Martyrs*, 245, 247, 249.
10. That is around 5 ft. 8 in. in English measurements

"I will not accept the seal," he replied. "I already have the seal of Christ who is my God."

[5] Dion said: "I shall send you to your Christ directly."

"I only wish you would," he replied. "This would be my glory."

[6] Dion addressed his staff: "Let him be given the seal."

Maximilian resisted and said: "I will not accept the seal of this world; and if you give it to me, I shall break it, for it is worthless. I am a Christian. I cannot wear a piece of lead around my neck after I have received the saving sign of Jesus Christ my Lord, the son of the living God. You do not know him; yet he suffered for our salvation; God delivered him up for our sins. He is the one whom all we Christians serve: we follow him as the prince of life and author of salvation."

[7] "You must serve," said Dion, "and accept the seal—otherwise you will die miserably."

"I shall not perish," said Maximilian. "My name is already before my Lord. I may not serve."

[8] Dion said: "Have regard for your youth: serve. This is what a young man should do."

"My service is for my Lord," Maximilian replied. "I cannot serve the world. I have already told you: I am a Christian."

[9] The proconsul Dion said: "In the sacred bodyguard[11] of our lords Diocletian and Maximian, Constantius and Maximus, there are soldiers who are Christians, and they serve."

Maximilian replied: "They know what is best for them. But I am a Christian and I cannot do wrong."

[10] "What wrong do they commit," said Dion, "who serve in the army?"

Maximilian replied: "Why, you know what they do."

[11] The proconsul Dion said: "Serve. If you despise the military service you will perish miserably."

Maximilian replied: "I shall not perish, and if I depart from this world, my soul lives with Christ my Lord."

---

11. Or: company, *in sacro comitatu:* these were highly mobile troops under the emperor's direct command.

3. [1] "Strike out his name!" said Dion. And when his name had been struck out, Dion said: "Because you have refused military service out of disloyalty, you will receive a suitable sentence as an example to the others." Then he read the following decision from a tablet: "Whereas Maximilian had disloyally refused the military oath, he is sentenced to die by the sword."

[2] "Thanks be to God!" [*Deo gratias*] said Maximilian.

He had lived in this world twenty-one years, three months, and eighteen days. And when he was led to the spot, he said: "My dearest brothers, hasten with all eagerness, with as much courage as you can, that it may be given to you to see the Lord, and that he may reward you with a similar crown."

[3] Then with a joyous countenance he turned and said to his father: "Give this executioner my new clothes which you prepared for my military service. Then I shall receive you with my division of a hundred,¹² and we shall glory with the Lord together."

[4] Soon afterwards he died. A woman named Pompeiana obtained his body from the magistrate and, after placing it in her own chamber, later brought it to Carthage. There she buried it at the foot of a hill near the governor's palace next to the body of the martyr Cyprian. Thirteen days later the woman herself passed away and was buried in the same spot. [5] But Victor, the boy's father, returned to his home in great joy, giving thanks to God that he had sent ahead such a gift to the Lord, since he himself was soon to follow.

Thanks be to God! Amen.

The Acts of Marcellus (21 July 298 CE)

In the summer of 298 CE, in the city of Tingis (modern Morocco), the army was celebrating the birthday of the emperors Maximian and Diocletian. Roman tradition held the day of the emperor's ascension to the throne and the day of his birth as sacred and sacrifices were offered to the gods for his welfare. In a very public display of defiance, Marcellus, a centurion with the *legio II Traiana*, threw down his *balteus*, his military belt (and symbol of his authority as centurion) before the standards. To the scandal of his fellow soldiers, Marcellus denounced military service

12. That is, as though he were serving as a centurion in heaven.

both because of the pagan religious practices and because his Christian conviction would not allow him to fight any more.[13] Marcellus was executed for treason.

The Acts of Marcellus[14]

1. [1] In the city of Tigris, while Fortunatus[15] was governor, it was the celebration of the emperor's birthday. At length, when everyone was dining at the banquet table, a centurion named Marcellus[16] rejected these pagan (lat. *profana*) festivities, and after throwing down his soldier's belt[17] in front of the legionary standards which were there at the time, he bore witness in a loud voice: "I am a soldier of Jesus Christ, the eternal king. From now I cease to serve your emperors and I despise the worship of your gods of wood and stone, for they are deaf and dumb images."

[2] Now the soldiers that heard this were amazed, and arresting him, they threw him into prison and went to report the affair to the governor Fortunatus. When he had heard the story he ordered Marcellus to be kept in prison. After the banquet was over, he ordered Marcellus to be brought into the council chamber. [3] When the centurion Marcellus was brought him the prefect Anastasius Fortunatus spoke to him as follows: "What was your intention in violating military discipline by taking off your belt and throwing it down with your staff?"

---

13. *M. Marc.* (Recension M) 1.1; 4.3. I recite Recension M of this account because it is more reliable than Recension N, used in Helgeland, Daly, and Burns *Christians and the Military*, 60–61.

14. In Musurillo, *Acts of the Christian Martyrs*, 251, 253, 255.

15. Musurillo notes that Anastasius Fortunatus was *praefectus* of the *legio II Traiana* in Mauretania Tingitana under Diocletian (ibid., 251n1).

16. Marcellus was a *centurio ordinarius*, commanding one of the centuries of the lower-numbered cohorts (II-X) of the *legio VII Gemina*, in which most of the legionaries were of Spanish origin. Marcellus himself held from the town of Hasta Regia, not far from ancient Gades. Being a "centurion first class" indicates that Marcellus had a long and distinguished career with the legion. The account, however, emphasizes the voluntary aspect of Marcellus's action, indicating that he had come to a point of personal crisis of conscience.

17. This action is akin to removing his uniform in public, while still in on active duty.

2. [1] "On 21 July," Marcellus replied, "while you were celebrating the emperor's feast day, I declared clearly and publicly before the standards of this legion that I was a Christian, and said that I could not serve under this military oath, but only for Christ Jesus, the son of God the Father almighty."

[2] The prefect Fortunatus said: "I cannot conceal your rash act. And so I must report this to the emperors and to Caesar; and you will be handed over to my lord Aurelius Agricolanus, deputy for the praetorian prefects, with Caecilius Arva, staff-officer, in charge."

3. [1] On 30 October, at Tingis, when Marcellus of the rank of centurion was brought into court, one of the court secretaries announced: "The prefect Fortunatus has referred the case of the centurion Marcellus to your jurisdiction. There is a letter from him, which I shall read with your permission."

[2] Agricolanus said: "Have it read."

The secretary read: "To you, my lord, from Fortunatus . . . " (and so forth).

4. [1] After the letter was read, Agricolanus said: "Did you say the things that are recorded in the prefect's report?"

"Yes, I did," replied Marcellus. "You held the military rank of centurion, first class?"[18] asked Agricolanus.

"Yes," said Marcellus.

[2] "What madness possessed you," asked Agricolanus, "to throw down the symbols of your military oath [*sacramenta*] and to say the things you did?"

Marcellus replied: "No madness possesses those who fear [God]"

[3] "Then you did say all of those things," asked Agricolanus, "that are set down in the prefect's report?"

"Yes, I said them," answered Marcellus.

Agricolanus said: "You threw down your weapons?"

---

18. That is, a centurion in the first cohort, the most trusted and battle-ready cohort in each legion. This is the highest position to which a centurion could aspire.

Marcellus replied: "Yes, I did. For it is not fitting that a Christian, who fights for Christ his Lord, should fight for the armies of this world."

5. [1] Agricolanus said: "What Marcellus has done merits punishment according to military rules. And so, whereas Marcellus, who held the rank of centurion, first class, has confessed that he has disgraced himself by publicly renouncing his military oath [*publice sacramento pollui*],[19] and has further used expressions completely lacking in control as are recorded in the report of the prefect, I hereby sentence him to death by the sword."

[2] As Marcellus was being led out to execution he said, "Agricolanus, may God reward you." Thus was it fitting that Marcellus should depart a glorious martyr from this world.

(Recension N adds: "After these words were spoken, Marcellus was beheaded and thus won the martyr's palm that he desired, in the reign of our Lord Jesus Christ, who has received his martyr in peace: to him is honour, glory, valor, and power for ever. Amen.")

The Martyrdom of Julius the Veteran (ca. 303 CE)

The veteran Julius was probably serving with the *legio XI Claudia* in Durostorum (modern Bulgaria) when and was martyred. Though a Christian for the twenty-seven years of his military service, Julius came to a point of personal conviction deciding he needed to amend his ways and cease from military service. What brought Julius to the crisis of conscience in which he came to realize he could not be a Christian and serve in the army we do not know. What we do know is that Julius renounced his identity as a soldier and refused to sacrifice decrying: "All the twenty-seven years in which I made the mistake, so it appears, to serve foolishly in the army" (*M. Jul.* 1.3–4; 2.1).

A number of issues are important to note throughout this account. Maximus, the judge, was willing to bribe Julius and even make it appear as though the veteran soldier had been forced to sacrifice, so that his fellow Christians (and Julius's own conscience) would not judge him as lapsed, just so long as he performed the rites. It did not matter in the

---

19. That is, what Marcellus does and thinks in private is one thing, to do it publicly, that is a "pollution."

least whether Julius's heart was in what he was doing. It is also worth noting that there at least three Christian soldiers who are executed in this account, and Julius himself seems to be led to his execution under the guard of fellow-Christians (*M. Jul.* 4.1). Lastly, in the climactic scene of his execution, Julius is shown to be in absolute control of his situation: he ties the blindfold himself and he offers his head to the executioner (*M. Jul.* 4.4). In the long tradition of Christian martyrs, the *mors voluntaria*, the voluntary death, shows that the martyr is not a victim; and reversal of power is again complete.

The Martyrdom of Julius the Veteran[20]

1. [1] In the time of persecution, when the glorious ordeals which the Christians faced looked to merit the eternal promises, Julius was arrested by the prefect's staff soldiers and he was brought before the prefect Maximus.

   [2] "Who is this?" asked Maximus.

   One of the staff replied: "This is a Christian who will not obey the laws."[21]

   [3] "What is your name?" asked the prefect.

   "Julius," was the reply.

   "Well, what say you, Julius?" asked the prefect. "Are these allegations true?"

   "Yes, they are," said Julius. "I am indeed a Christian. I do not deny that I am precisely what I am."

   [4] "You are surely aware," said the prefect, "of the emperors' edicts which order you to offer sacrifice to the gods."

   "I am aware of them," answered Julius. "But I am a Christian and I cannot do what you want; for I must not lose sight of my living and true God."

2. [1] The prefect Maximus said: "What is so serious about offering some incense and going away?"

---

20. In Musurillo, *Acts of the Christian Martyrs*, 261, 263, 265.

21. Does this indicate that there were "Christians who obeyed the law" and to whom Julius is an exception? Probably. Hence the ambivalence of the prefect.

Julius replied: "I cannot despise the divine commandments or appear unfaithful to my God. In all the twenty-seven years in which I made the mistake, so it appears, to serve foolishly in the army, I was never brought before a magistrate either as a criminal or a trouble-maker. [2] I went on seven military campaigns, and never hid behind anyone nor was I the inferior of any man in battle. My chief never found me at fault. And now do you suppose that I, who was always found to be faithful in the past, should now be found unfaithful to higher orders?"

[3] "What military service did you have?" asked Maximus the prefect.

"I was in the army," answered Julius, "and when I had served my term I re-enlisted as a veteran. All of this time I worshipped in fear the God who made heaven and earth [cf. Acts 4:24], and even to this day I show him my service."

[4] "Julius," said Maximus, "I see that you are a wise and serious person. You shall receive a generous bonus if you will take my advice and sacrifice to the gods."

"I will not do what you wish," answered Julius, "lest I incur an eternal penalty."

[5] "If you think it a sin," answered the prefect Maximus, "let me take the blame. I am the one who is forcing you, so that you may not give the impression of having consented voluntarily. Afterwards you can go home in peace, you will pick up your ten-year bonus, and no one will ever trouble you again."

[6] "This is the money of Satan, and neither it nor your crafty talk can deprive me of the eternal light. I cannot deny God. So, deliver sentence against me as a Christian."

3. [1] Maximus said: "If you do not respect the imperial decrees and offer sacrifice, I am going to cut your head off."

"That is a good plan!" answered Julius. "Only I beg you, good prefect, by the welfare of your emperors, that you execute your plan and pass sentence on me, so that my prayers may be fulfilled."

[2] "If you do not change your mind and sacrifice," said Maximus the prefect, "you will be delivered to your desires."

"If I should deserve to suffer this, I shall have eternal praise," answered Julius.

[3] "You are being offered advice," said Maximus. "For if you endured this for the sake of the civil law, you would have eternal glory."

Julius replied: "I surely suffer for the law—but it is the divine law."

[4] Maximus said: "You mean the law given you by a man who was crucified and died? Look how foolish you are to fear a dead man more than living emperors!"

"It was he who died for our sins" [cf. 1 Cor 15:3], answered Julius, "in order to give us eternal life. This same man, Christ, is God and abides for ever and ever. Whoever believes in him will have eternal life [cf. John 6:47, etc.]; and whoever denies him will have eternal punishment."

[5] "I counsel you out of pity," said Maximus, "that you sacrifice and continue to live with us."

"To live with you," answered Julius, "would be death to me. But, in God's sight, if I die I shall live for ever."

[6] "Listen to me and offer the sacrifice," said Maximus, "lest I put you to death as I promised."

"I have chosen death for now," said Julius, "that I might live with the saints for ever."

[7] The prefect Maximus then delivered the sentence as follows: "Whereas Julius has refused to obey the imperial edicts, he is sentenced to death."

4. [1] When he was led off to the usual spot, everyone kissed him. The blessed Julius said to them: "Let each one consider what sort of kiss is this."[22]

[2] There was a man named Isichius, a soldier who was a Christian, who was also being kept in prison. He said to the holy martyr: "Julius, I beg you, fulfill your promise in joy. Take the crown which the Lord promised to give to those who believe in him [cf. Jas 1:12], and remember me, for I too will follow you. Give my warmest

---

22. Is he addressing fellow soldiers, asking them to consider their continued service and, therefore, offer of sacrifice? Isichius and Valentio seem to indicate so. Julius is warning his fellow soldiers that they are greeting him with the "kiss of Judas" betraying their Lord.

greetings to the servant of God, our brother Valentio,[23] who has already proceeded us to the Lord by his loyal confession of faith."

[3] Julius then kissed Isichius. "Hasten, my brother, and follow me," he said. "He whom you greeted will hear your last request."

[4] Then he took the blindfold and bound his eyes, bent his neck, and said: "Lord Jesus Christ, I suffer this for your name. I beg you, deign to receive my spirit [cf. Acts 7:59] together with your holy martyrs."

[5] And so the Devil's servant struck the blessed martyr with a sword and brought his life to an end, in Christ Jesus our Lord, to whom is honour and glory for ever. Amen.

The Martyrdom of the Saintly Dasius (ca. 303 CE)

The soldier Dasius was also serving with the *legio XI Claudia* in Durostorum (modern Bulgaria) when he, too, rejected his very identity as a soldier along with the religious practices of the Roman army (*M. Das.* 6.1). *The Martyrdom of Saintly Dasius* is a highly idealized and interpolated document, whose only copy is from the eleventh century. The first part of the account is a description of the Saturnalia, a festival of Saturn, lasting from the seventh to the twenty-fifth of December, but the account presented here is highly dramatized, especially in the breakdown of military discipline and human sacrifice, which are presented in particularly evocative way, so as to underscore the difference between pagan practices and Dasius's Christian confession. Dasius's trinitarian confession is also, most likely, a later interpolation. However, Dasius's refusal to participate in the sacrifices that became mandatory during the years of the Great Persecution (303–311 CE) is highly probable and the authentic account begins with paragraph 6, where we pick up the story:

The Martyrdom of the Saintly Dasius[24]

6. When the holy martyr Dasius had been brought by the detachment before the tribunal of the commander Bassus, Bassus looked at him and said: "What is your station and what is your name?"

---

23. Musurillo notes that his name probably ought to be Valentinus (in the Roman Martyrology for 25 May), a fellow soldier.

24. In Musurillo, *Acts of the Christian Martyrs*, 277, 279.

The blessed Dasius answered with sincerity and openness: "I am a soldier by rank. Of my name I shall tell you, that I have the excellent one of Christian; but the name given me by my parents is Dasius."

7. [1] Bassus the commander said: "Venerate the images of our lords the emperors, who give us peace, give us our rations, and every day show concern for our every advantage." [2] The blessed Dasius replied: "I have already told you and I repeat, I am a Christian, and I do not fight for any earthly king but for the king of heaven. His is the bounty I possess, I live by his favor, and I am wealthy because of his ineffable kindness."

8. [1] The commander Bassus said: "Dasius, supplicate the holy images of our emperors, which even the barbarian nations worship and revere." [2] The blessed martyr Dasius said: "I confess I am a Christian as I have confessed many times before, and I obey no one else but the one undefiled and eternal God, Father, Son, and Holy Spirit, who are three in name and person but one in substance [ἐν μιᾷ οὐσίᾳ]. So now by this triple formula I confess my faith in the holy Trinity, for strengthened by it I can quickly conquer and overthrow the Devil's madness."

9. [1] "You forget, Dasius," said the commander Bassus, "that every man is subject to the imperial decree and to the sacred laws. Since I am sparing you, you will answer me fearlessly and without anxiety." [2] But Dasius, the blessed and saintly athlete of Christ, replier and said: "Do whatever has been commanded you by the impious and evil emperors. For I guard my faith which I once pledged to God to preserve, and I believe that I shall persevere firmly and unshakably in my confession. Nor can your threats shake my resolution."

10. [1] The commander Bassus said: "Here now, you are granted a delay in case you wish to consider in your mind how you might be able to live among us in honour." [2] But the blessed Dasius said: "What need is there for a delay? I have already revealed to you my intention and my resolve when I said, 'Do what you will: I am a Christian!' For, look you, as for your emperors and their honour, I spit upon it and despise it, that after the release from this life I may be able to live in that one."

11. [1] Then the commander Bassus, after subjecting him to many torments, passed sentence that he should be beheaded. As he was going off to his glorious martyrdom, he had someone preceding him with the forbidden censer. [2] But when they tried to force Dasius to offer sacrifice to the impure demons, picking it up in his own hands he scattered all their incense about and threw down the impious and unlawful images of the sacrilegious emperors and trampled on them, whilst he fortified his forehead with the seal of the precious cross of Christ, by whose power he so mightily resisted the tyrant.

12. [1] Thus the holy martyr went to his beheading on the twentieth of November, on Friday at the fourth hour, on the twenty-fourth day of the moon. Put to death by the executioner Ioannes Anicetus, he fulfilled his martyrdom in peace. [2] The contest of the saintly Dasius took place in the city of Durostorum, under the emperors Maximian and Diocletian, and he was arraigned by the commander Bassus, while our Lord Christ Jesus was ruler in heaven, to whom is glory with the Father and the Holy Spirit, now and for all ages. Amen.

TEN

Arnobius of Sicca
(ca. 253–ca. 330 CE)

Arnobius came from Sicca Veneria (in modern Tunisia), a regional center of learning some one hundred miles southwest of Carthage. A convert to Christianity, Arnobius was a teacher of rhetoric and wrote seven books of Christian apologetic titled *Adversus nationes* (*Against the Nations*) sometime in the first decade of the fourth century, probably between the years 302–305 CE, during the early years of the devastating persecution under Diocletian.[1] In his work Arnobius addresses a number of accusations leveled against Christians by pagans. Chief among them, at the end of the third century, was the accusation that the rise of Christianity had angered the pagan gods who, in turn, had brought calamities of war and civil strife, economic depression, and a general spirit of unrest upon the Empire. Arnobius refuted the pagan call for spiritual revival and a fervent return to the worship of the gods as apotropaic, arguing that, in reality, the teaching of Christ had led to far less bloodshed and a relative prosperity in society (*Nat.* 1.6). Like Terence and Tertullian before him, Arnobius turned to the very character of the worship of war by the Romans and their thirst for conquest as the causes for the spirit of unrest, and criticized the wars by which Rome exterminated other nations, finding a natural target in the worship of Mars, the God of War (*Nat.* 3.26). At the end, even though he argued that in the years since Christ, "many victories over conquered enemies have been won, that the boundaries of the empire have been extended and nations

---

1. See Simmons, *Arnobius of Sicca*.

with names hitherto unheard-of, have been brought under your sway" (*Nat.* 1.14), such statements are scarcely an endorsement of Christian participation in war. And even though Arnobius did not wrestle specifically with the issue of Christian participation in military service, "we are left with the general impression that he could not reconcile Christian principles with participation in war."[2]

Against the Pagans 1.6.1–3[3]

6. [1] Actually, regarding the wars which you say were begun on account of hatred for our religion, it would not be difficult to prove that after Christ was heard on earth, not only did they not increase but in great measure were reduced as a result of the repression of fierce passion. [2] For when we, so large a number as we are, have learned from His teachings and His laws that *it is not right to repay evil for evil*; that it is better to suffer wrong than be its cause, to pour forth one's own blood rather than to stain our hands and conscience with the blood of another: the world, ungrateful as it is, has long had this benefit from Christ by whom the rage of madness has been softened and has begun to withhold hostile hands from the blood of fellow beings.

   [3] And if all without exception who understand that [they] are human beings, not through the form of their bodies but through the power of reason, would for a little while be willing to lend an ear to His wholesome and peaceful commandments, and would believe not in their own arrogance and swollen conceit but rather in His admonitions, the whole world, long since having diverted the use of iron to more gentle pursuits, would be passing its days in the most placid tranquility and would come together in wholesome harmony, having kept the terms of treaties unbroken.

---

2. Swift, *Early Fathers*, 61.

3. Arnobius of Sicca, *The Case Against the Pagans*, 1:64–65. The Latin text of Arnobius's *Adversus nationes* can be found online at *The Latin Library* (http://www.thelatin-library.com/arnobius.html).

Against the Pagans 1.13–14[4]

13. [1] "Because of the Christians," they say, "the gods contrive all these evils and destruction of crops is produced by the heavenly deities." I ask, do you fail to see that when you say this you are slandering us wickedly with open-faced and demonstrable lies? [2] It is almost three hundred years, more or less, since we began to be Christians and to be known on the earth: in all these years have wars been without interruption? . . . 14. [1] Do we not see that in the intervening years and intervening seasons many victories over conquered enemies have been won, that the boundaries of the empire have been extended and nations with names hitherto unheard-of, have been brought under your sway.

Against the Pagans 2.1.3–4[5]

Arnobius decried the wars and military expansionism of Rome and juxtaposed the example of Christ as the founding principle for the peaceful character of the Christian community.

2.1 [3] Did [Christ] ever, as he claimed royal power for himself infest the whole world with the fiercest legions, and of nations at peace from the beginning did he destroy and exterminate some and force others with necks bent under the yoke to be obedient to him? [4] Did he ever, inflamed with greedy avarice, claim by right of his own possession all the abundance with which the human race strives eagerly to enrich itself?

Against the Pagans 3.26.2b–3[6]

To show the absurdity of pagan worship, Arnobius singles out the worship of Mars, the God of War, who had lent Rome its militaristic character.

26. [2b] "Mars," he says, "has power over wars." To cause those in progress to cease, or to stir them up when things are quiet and peaceful?

4. Ibid., 1:68–69.
5. Adapted from ibid., 1:114.
6. Adapted from ibid., 1:212–213.

... [3] [Mars] sows the seeds of discords and strife among far-separated nations of the earth; brings together from different places so many thousands of mortals and, before you can say a single word, piles the fields with corpses; causes bloody torrents to flow; destroys the most firmly established empires; levels cities to the ground, takes away freedom from the freeborn and places on them the condition of slavery, rejoices in civil strife, in the fratricidal slaughter of brothers dying together, and, finally, in the horror of murderous conflict between sons and fathers.

ELEVEN

Lactantius (ca. 240–ca. 320 CE)

A pupil of Arnobius, L. Caecilius Firmianus Lactantius was a famous teacher of Latin rhetoric who converted to Christianity in the late middle age. St. Jerome called Lactantius "the most eloquent man of his time"[1] and even a thousand years later, the Renaissance philosopher, Pico de la Mirandola referred to Lactantius as *Cicero Christianus*.[2] Lactantius's reputation as a teacher and a rhetorician attracted a number of pupils to him from famous and influential families. Even though newly a Christian convert, Lactantius was appointed to the chair of Latin rhetoric in Nicomedia in Asia Minor (modern Turkey), the seat of the emperor Diocletian, early in the fourth century. He served in that capacity until 305 CE when he moved West, as the fierce Great Persecution was raging in the East. Around the year 310 CE, Constantine brought Lactantius to Trier to tutor his son Crispus.[3] Lactantius wrote his most famous surviving work, *Divine Institutes*, while still in Nicomedia in response to the outbreak of the persecution. In this work Lactantius attempted to provide nothing less than the first summary of Christian thought that appealed exclusively to the Roman educated class (the *docti*), arguing that it is a fundamental fact that "*sapientia* and *religio* are inseparable, and neither can be true independently of the other."[4] In do-

---

1. Jerome, *Epist.* 58.10; *Chron. ad annum* 317 p.Chr.n (see Eusebius, *Die Chronik des Hieronymous*, 230).

2. *De Studio Divinae atque humanae philosophiae*, ch. 7.

3. For a fuller description of the life and work of Lactantius see Bowan's and Garnsey's introduction in Lactantius, *Divine Institutes*, 1–54. See also Meinking, "Anger Matters."

4. Bowman and Garnsey in Lactantius, *Divine Institutes*, 7.

ing so, Lactantius sought to provide a positive and comprehensive statement about doctrine, "the nature of god and man, the beginning and
end of the world, the life and mission of Christ, and Christian ethics." [5]
As Bowman and Garnsey suggest, it would be quite appropriate to claim
the *Divine Institutes* as a forerunner of the *City of God* by Augustine, or
the *Summa Theologiae*, by Thomas Aquinas.[6] While under the protection and patronage of Constantine, Lactantius wrote the triumphalist
treatise *On the Death of the Persecutors* (ca. 313–315 CE), and *On Anger*
(ca. 316 CE), as well as an *Epitome of the Divine Institutes* (ca. 320 CE).

Because of the transitional times during which Lactantius lived and
wrote, and because of the two cataclysmic event that bracketed his literary career: the Great Persecution (303–311/313 CE) on the one hand,
and the rise of Constantine to uncontested power (defeating Maxentius
in 312 CE in the West and Licinius in 324 CE to become the sole emperor
of the Roman empire), on the other, the chronology and circumstances
of the writing of Lactantius must be kept in mind as one examines what
he says about the state, war, and military service.

By the time Lactantius became a Christian in the late middle age,
the Decian persecutions of the mid-third century that claimed the lives
of Cyprian, Origen, and countless others, had become the somewhat
distant memory of two generations past, and the Church had enjoyed a
lengthy period of relative peace and prosperity within the Roman empire. Peaceful—or at least unmolested—coexistence within the Empire
was quickly becoming the expected norm. When the Great Persecution
erupted in February 303 CE, Christians were caught by surprise. The
ferocity and duration of the persecution (especially in the East) fed the
eschatological expectations of Christian writers who saw clear signs
of the end and Christ's return as imminent. Lactantius composed the
Divine Institutes during this time at the imperial capital of Nicomedia,
and in this work he has nothing but harsh words for any form of bloodshed. From defense of self (*Inst.* 6.18.17; cf. 6.18.25, 29–32) to capital
punishment (*Inst.* 6.20.15) and the bloodthirsty spectacles of the gladiatorial combats (*Inst.* 5.17.13), Lactantius is adamant that bloodshed is
not permissible for the Christian, for "killing a human being whom God
willed to be a sacred being, is always wrong": to this there are no exception (*Inst.* 6.20.17). Lactantius also criticized the bloody wars of Rome

5. Ibid., 14.
6. Ibid.

and rejected military service on the same grounds, arguing that that a "righteous person cannot engage in war" (*Inst.* 6.20.16). It is important to note that, as Swift shows, Lactantius makes no distinction between military service during times of peace and times of war.[7] Contrary to the Roman claims of piety and religiosity, Lactantius argues that the true spirit of *pietas* is found "among those who have nothing to do with war, who preserve a spirit of peace with everyone, who are friendly even with their enemies, who love all men as their brothers, and who know how to control their anger and to temper their wrath with a tranquil spirit" (*Inst.* 5.10.10).[8] The only piety, the only justice, the only peace can be found in the worship of the one true God (*Inst.* 5.8.6) whose millennial reign was about to begin.

Lactantius and his generation lived through the twin revolutions of the Great Persecution and the rise of Constantine to the throne. In the span of one generation the world changed in unimaginable ways. At the beginning of the fourth century it was inconceivable that the Roman empire would be anything but pagan and that the *signa* of the gods of Rome would lead her legions into battle. By the time Constantine entered Rome in triumph, the Augustus of the West was at least protective of the Church, if not a professing Christian.[9] In 299 CE, Diocletian instituted an empire-wide purge of Christians from the Roman armies; on 28 October 312, Constantine's armies marched against Maxentius at the Battle of the Milvian Bridge, on the northern side of Rome, with the Christogram[10] on their shields.[11] The world was changing at a bewildering pace. Was Christ coming to claim his kingdom?

---

7. Swift, Early Fathers, 63.

8. Ibid.

9. Whether Constantine was a Christian by the time he defeated Maxentius, in 312 CE, is highly debated (see Barnes, *Constantine and Eusebius*, for an excellent discussion). What cannot be disputed is that just a year after defeating Licinius and becoming the sole emperor, Constantine called the First Ecumenical Council of the Christian Church (in 325 CE) and participated in its proceedings with enthusiasm and theological intelligence. Though not baptized into the Church until his deathbed, Constantine claimed the Christian faith unapologetically.

10. The famous XP, symbolizing the first letters of Christ's name, Χριστός, in Greek.

11. It is also worth noting that in 416 CE Theodosius II purged the Roman armies of all pagans, and while in 303 CE, co-emperors Diocletian and Galerius vowed to uproot Christianity from the empire once and for all, in 380 CE emperor Theodosius I made Christianity the official religion of the Roman empire.

Christ, however, did not return. Unlike the East, the persecution quickly subsided in the West and by the time Lactantius was summoned to the imperial court in Trier, Constantine was becoming the uncontested ruler of the occidental part of the empire. Lactantius wrote the triumphalist tract *On the Death of the Persecutors* following Constantine's victory over Maxentius, his last rival in the West, and the official end of the persecution in 312 CE. In Roman tradition, it was the Senate that declared an emperor as good or bad; in this work, Lactantius transposes that traditional role to the divine Judge, as he sets out "to explain from the beginning, since the Church's foundation, who were its persecutors and with what penalties the severity of the heavenly Judge punished them" (*Mort.* 1.7). Lactantius's argument is quite simple: if emperors were good, it is because they did not persecute Christians, not because the Senate claimed them to be so. At the end, *On the Death of the Persecutors* is a "bare-bones panegyric [of Constantine]: you are special, Constantine, you are the first emperor, the only emperor, to acknowledge the true God (thereby showing your superiority over 'good' emperors of the past). God is behind your success; with divine aid you have brought justice back to the world. May God continue to support you, as you protect the realm and punish the remaining enemies of [true] religion."[12]

As we read the writings of Lactantius and his contemporaries, then, we have to keep in mind not so much the so-called (anachronistically) "Constantinianism" of the fourth century, as the profound eschatological and millennialist expectations of the decades that framed the Great Persecution, and recognize the gravity of the events that transformed a persecuted minority facing the wrath of the empire into a triumphalist—though still minority—political reality unimaginable by the writers of the earlier centuries.

Divine Institutes 1.18.8–16[13]

1.18. [8] [Romans] despise athletic excellence because it doesn't impinge anyway, but a king's power, because of its tendency to cut a broad swathe, they so admire that they think bold and belligerent leaders belong in the company of the gods, and the only path to immortality is leading armies, ravaging other people's land, wiping out cities,

---

12. Lactantius, *Divine Institutes*, 50.

13. Ibid., 101.

destroying towns and either slaughtering free people or forcing them into slavery. [9] Presumably the more people they have oppressed, robbed and killed, the more famous and glorious they think they are: they are deceived by a sort of sham glory and label their wicked deeds with a tag saying virtue. [10] I would rather people made gods for themselves from the slaughter of animals than have them endorse an immortality as bloodily got as that. If you cut the throat of one man, you are treated as contagiously evil, and no one thinks it right for you to be admitted into a god's house here on earth; but the man who has slain his tens of thousands, soaking the fields in gore and fouling rivers, is let into heaven, not just into temples. [11] Ennius Africanus speaks as follows: "If it is right for any man to climb to the tracts of the heavenly ones, then the great gate of heaven lies open for me alone"—because, of course, he had wiped out a large fraction of humanity. [12] O what darkness for you to work in, Africanus—or rather, for you the poet! For it was the poet who thought that ascent into heaven lay open to men by way of blood and slaughter. [13] Even Cicero allied himself to such nonsense . . . [14] I cannot make up my mind whether I think it lamentable or ludicrous to see serious, educated men, men wise in their own eyes, bobbling up and down in a sorry storm of error. [15] If this is virtue that makes us immortal, I'd rather die than cause of death to as may as possible. [16] If immortality can only be delivered through blood, what will happen in a universal concord? That will certainly be a possibility if people are willing to abandon their destructive and wicked passions and become innocent and just.

Divine Institutes 5.8.6, 8b[14]

5.8. [6] If one God were worshipped, there would be no discord and no war; people would know that they were children of the one God and so were bound together by a holy, inviolable chain of divine kinship; there would be no secret plots, since they would know what sort of penalties God had ready for those who kill the soul: he perceives their covert wickedness, and even their very thinking; there would be no treachery and theft if they had learnt from God's advice and

14. Ibid., 296.

were "content with what they had, however small," [Cic. *Off*. 1.70], so that things solid and permanent had preference over things fragile and fleeting; . . . [8b] How blessed and how golden the state of humanity would be if all the world were civilized, pious, peaceful, innocent, self-controlled, fair and faithful!

Divine Institutes 5.10, 15a[15]

Lactantius argues that the true Roman spirit of reverence (*pietas*) is found only among the Christians:

5.10. [10] What then is piety? Where is it? What is it like? It exists where people know nothing of wars, live in concord with all, are friendly even to enemies, love all men like brothers, know how to curb their anger and how to soothe all strong emotions with a tranquillising control . . . [15a] It is difficult to explain why worshippers of gods cannot be good and just. When they worship gods of blood like Mars and Bellona, how will they keep from blood themselves?

Divine Institutes 5.17.10, 12[16]

5.17. [10] Let us see then whether justice can have any bond with folly. . . . [12] Why would [a just man] go to sea, or what would he want from other people's lands when his own sufficed? Why go to war and tangle himself in other people's lunacies when his heart was full of peace with everyone eternally?

Divine Institutes 5.18.1–3, 12–14[17]

In chapter 18, Lactantius addresses presents the certainly of eternal life as the reason why Christians neither rise in self defense nor participate in war but rather live in peace with their neighbors, secure in their fate.

5.18. [1] The apparent folly of a man who prefers to be in need or to die rather than cause hurt or seize another man's property is caused no doubt by the fact that people think death destroys a man. That belief

---

15. Ibid., 301–2.

16. Ibid., 314. There is a parallel here with Tertullian, *Idol.* 11 and 19.

17. Lactantius, *Divine Institutes*, 317–19.

is the source of all the confusion, on the part of philosophers as much as of ordinary people. [2] If we are nothing after death, then certainly it is the mark of a very great fool not to consider how this life may last as long as possible and be full of every advantage. [3] Anyone so doing is bound to depart from the rule of justice. But if a longer and better life awaits us, which is what we learn from the arguments of great philosophers, from the response of the poets and from the divine utterance of prophets, then it is the mark of the wise to despise this temporal life with its goods; every loss of this life is repaid with immortality . . . [12] I have explained, I think, why our people are thought fools by fools. To prefer to be tortured and killed, rather that pick three fingers of incense and cast it on a fire, does seem as foolish as caring more at a moment of peril for someone else's soul than one's own. [13] They don't know how wicked a thing it is to worship anything besides God "who founded earth and heaven," who created the human race, and gave it breath and light. [14] But if the wickedest of servants is the one who runs away from his master and is judged to deserve beating, and if in the same way a son is considered depraved and impious who deserts his own father in order not to obey him, and for that reason is thought to be disinherited and to have his name deleted from the family for ever, how much more so the man who deserts God, in whom two titles of equal worth and honor combine, master and father?

Divine Institutes 6.6.18–24; 6.9.4–7[18]

In this book of the *Divine Institutes*, Lactantius delivers one of the most poignant critiques of the Roman concept of just war, showing the arbitrary use of both religious and civil order to justify a thirst for power and conquest. Both the concept of justice and that of benefit have been corrupted by those who do not know God.

6.6. [18] Virtue is not a matter of being enemy of the bad or defender of the good, because virtue cannot be subject to uncertainty. "Virtue: to believe your country's needs come first" is, in the absence of human discord, utterly without substance. [19] What are a country's interests other than the disadvantage of some other community or

18. Ibid., 343, 347.

people? Working land stolen from others by violence, for instance, expanding one's own power and levying heavier taxes: none of those is a virtue; they are the overthrow of virtue [20] First of all, the ties of human society are removed, and so is innocence, and abstention from the property of others, and justice itself: justice cannot endure division in the human race.

[22] How can a man be just who does harm, who hates, who ravages, who kills? And all those are actions of people striving to do their country good. People who think that the only useful or advantageous thing is something you can grasp simply do not know what doing good is. But what you can grasp, another can grab. [23] So anyone who goes for these "goods of his country," as they themselves call them—anyone, that is, who destroys communities, wipes out nations, fills the treasury with money, grabs land and makes his fellow citizens richer—is lauded to heaven, and people think he is the embodiment of perfect virtue. This is a mistake made not only by the ignorant mob but also by philosophers; they also give their advice on injustice, in case folly and malice should lack the authority of discipline. [24] So when they debate the duties relevant to time of war, nothing they have to say is aimed at justice and true virtue: it is all aimed at the life and behavior of citizens present, which is not justice at all.

6.9. [4] The gap between justice and expediency is well demonstrated by the people of Rome, who got themselves control of the whole world by using Fetials[19] to declare wars and by using forms of law to cover their wrongdoings and to seize and to take other people's property. . . . [6b] Does obedience to human institutions make them just, when human beings themselves have been quite capable of error or injustice, like the authors of the Twelve Tables, or have certainly bowed to public convenience to suit the situation? [7] Civil law, which varies everywhere according to custom, is quite different from true justice, which is uniform and simple, being God's provision for us all; and anyone ignorant of God is bound to be ignorant of true justice also.

---

19. Ibid., 347n32, "in theory, the Romans did not wage war without an ultimatum, delivered by the priesthood of the Fetiales, demanding of the enemy restoration or compensation . . . It is clear that the fetial procedure was manipulated in the cause of Roman expansionism."

Divine Institutes 6.20.9–12; 6.20.15–17[20]

Along with Rome's wars, Lactantius criticized all forms of killing, including military service, the gladiatorial games, and capital punishment. Lactantius insists that for Christians it is unthinkable even to be present in such events, let alone take a human life.

6.20. [9] We must avoid [the shows] because they are a strong enticement to vice, and they have an immense capacity for corrupting souls. Rather than contributing something to a happy life they are, in fact, exceedingly harmful. [10] For anybody who finds it pleasurable to watch a man being slain (however justly the person was condemned) has violated his own conscience as much as if he had been a spectator and participant in a clandestine murder. [11] The actual term used by the pagans for these events in which human bleed is spilled is "games." They are so alienated from their own humanity that they believe they are playing when they take human lives. In fact, however, the perpetrators are more harmful than all those people whose blood is a source of delight to them. [12] I ask, then, whether anyone can be just and reverent if he not only permits men who are facing imminent death and are pleading for mercy to be slain but also flogs his victims and brings death through cruel and inhuman punishments whenever he finds himself unsated by the wounds already inflicted or by the blood already spilled.

[15] It is not right for those who are striving to stay on the path of virtue to become associated with this kind of wholesale slaughter [i.e. of the gladiatorial combats] or to take part in it. For when God forbids killing, he is not only ordering us to avoid armed robbery, which is contrary even to public law, but he is forbidding what men regard as ethical [16] Thus, it is not right for a just man to serve in the army since justice itself is his form of service. Nor is it right for a just man to charge someone with a capital crime. It does not matter whether you kill a man with the sword or with a word since it is killing itself that is prohibited. [17] And so there must be no exception to this command of God. Killing a human being whom God willed to be a sacred creature, is always wrong.

20. Adapted from Swift, *Early Fathers*, 62–63.

It is important to note here that in the *Epitome,* Lactantius's summary of the *Divine Institutes* composed ca. 320 CE, military service has been dropped from the catalogue of examples he presents. Instead, suicide—which is condemned as murder elsewhere—is now included in the list of acts forbidden by the sixth commandment (*Epit.* 59.5).

Divine Institutes 1.1.13–16[21]

Almost a decade after he composed the *Divine Institutes,* Lactantius, now in Trier at the court of Constantine, added an inscription to the work that identified the emperor of the West as God's viceroy whom God had entrusted with the restoration of justice and the protection of the Church. The laudatory character of the additions have to be read within the light of that realized eschatology, as well as a not-so-veiled warning to the regent that the true sovereign is the God of Heaven who raises rulers and destroys kingdoms for his purposes; a theme Lactantius repeats in *On the Death of the Persecutors* (18.10).

1.1.   [13] Now we take up our task under your auspices, O Constantine, greatest of emperors, the first of Roman princes to cast aside error and to acknowledge and honor the majesty of the one true God. For when that most happy day dawned all over the world, when the all high God raised you to the heights of power, you inaugurated your rule—desirable and beneficial as it is to all people—with a noble beginning. You brought back justice, which had been overturned and blotted out, and you expiated the horrible crimes of other rulers. [14] For this accomplishment God will grant you success, courage and length of days so that even when you are advanced in years, you may continue to direct the helm of state with the same justice with which you commenced your rule as a young man, and you may pass on to your children that responsibility for protecting Rome's name which you received from your Father. [15] On those who continue to afflict the just in other parts of the world[22] that same omnipotent Father will wreak vengeance for their wrong doing. The more delayed that vengeance is the more severe it will be, for just as he is a most indulgent Father toward good men, so, too, is he a very strict judge toward the wicked.

21. Adapted from Swift, *Early Fathers,* 67–68.

22. This is a reference to Licinius, the emperor of the eastern part of the Empire, who turned against the Church around the time Lactantius added the dedication to his work.

[16] In my desire to see to it that God be revered and worshipped, whom should I call upon, whom should I speak to but the man who has restored justice and wisdom to human affairs?

On the Death of the Persecutors 44.1–10; 46.1–6; 47.1–3; 48.1–3; 52.4

In this section, Lactantius describes two pivotal recent battles. The first one was between Constantine and Maxentius, for control of the Western part of the empire. Here, Lactantius lauds Constantine's obedience to the divine vision which instructed him to inscribe the shields of his soldiers with the Christogram (XP). 28 October 312 CE marked the first time in history Roman soldiers marched into battle with Christian insignia leading the way. The second description is of the battle of Tzirallum (in modern Turkey) between Licinius and Maximinus Daia, on 30 April 313 CE, for control of the East. In both cases, Lactantius attributes the victory to the emperor's obedience to the divine vision. In these accounts it becomes immediately obvious that the divine Judge has deemed Constantine and Licinius as "good" emperors; a fact that is underscored by the issuing of what has come to be considered a joint decree known as the "Edict of Milan," on the ides of June of that same year. The Edict of Milan recognized Christianity as a licit religion, making it possible for persons to be identified as Christians openly and without the threat of persecution.

On the Death of the Persecutors 44.1–10; 46.1–6; 47.1–3

44. [1] Civil war had already started between [Constantine and Maxentius].... [2] Maxentius had the larger forces ... [3] Fighting took place in which Maxentius' troops held the advantage until Constantine at a later stage, his courage renewed and "ready for either success or death," moved all his forces nearer to the city of Rome and based himself in the region of the Milvian bridge.... [5] Constantine was advised in a dream to mark the heavenly sign of God on the shields of his soldiers and then engage in battle. He did as he was commanded and by means of a slanted letter X with the top of its head bent round, he marked Christ on their shields. [6] Armed with this sign, the army took up its weapons. The enemy came to meet them without their emperor and crossed the bridge. The lines clashed, their

fronts of equal length, and both sides fought with the most extreme ferocity; . . . [7–8] [A riot ensued within the walls of the city of Rome and Maxentius asked for an omen from the oracle of Sibyl who uttered the famous words: "On this day the enemy of the Romans will perish."] [9] Led by the reply to hope for victory, Maxentius marched out to battle. The bridge was cut down behind him. As the sight of this, the fighting became harder, and the Hand of God was over the battle-line. The army of Maxentius was seized with terror, an he himself fled in hast to the bridge which had been broken down; pressed by the mass of [retreating soldiers], he was hurled in to the Tiber.

[10] With this bitterest of wars at last finished, Constantine was received as emperor with great joy by the senate and people of Rome.[23]

46. [1] With the armies approaching one another, it became evident that an engagement would take place shortly. [2] At this juncture Maximinus [Daia] made a vow to Jupiter that if he won he would blot out and utterly destroy the name of Christians. [3] On the next night an angel of God appeared to Licinius in his sleep telling him to get up right away and with his entire army to offer prayers to the all high God. If he did that, the victory would be his. [4] Licinius dreamed that when he got up in response to these words, the angel stood at his side and told him how to pray and what words to use. [5] When he woke up, Licinius called for his secretary and dictated to him the words he had heard: [6] "All High God, we beseech you; Holy God, we beseech you. To you we completely entrust our just cause; to you we entrust our safety; to you we entrust our empire. Through you we have life; through you we are victorious and blessed. All High and Holy God, hear our prayers; we stretch forth our arms to you. Hear us, O Holy, All High God."[24]

47. [1] The armies drew nearer, the trumpets sounded, the standards [*signa*] advanced. The Licinians launched an attack and penetrated the lines of their opponents, who in their terror could neither draw their swords nor hurl their missiles . . . [2] [Maximinus's] army was cut to pieces without resistance, his large and powerful legionary

---

23. Lactantius, *De Mortibus Persecutorum*, 63, 65.

24. Swift, *Early Fathers*, 66.

force mown down by a handful of men. [3] None of them called to mind his renown, his valour, or the reward he had received in the past; as if they had come not to fight, but as victims destined for slaughter, the supreme God delivered them to their enemies to be butchered. [25]

On the Death of the Persecutors 48.1–3

48. [1] After taking over part of Maximinus's army and distributing it among his troops,[26] Licinius brought his forces over into Bithynia within a few days of the battle. On entering Nicomedia, he gave thanks to God, by Whose help he had been victorious, and on 13 June in Constantine's and his own third consulships [in 313 CE], he ordered the letter which had been sent to the governor about the restoration of the Church to be publicly displayed. This is what it said:

[2] "When I, Constantine Augustus, and I, Licinius Augustus, happily met at Milan and had under consideration all matters which concerned the public advantage and safety, we thought that, among all the other things that we saw would benefit the majority of people, the arrangements which above all needed to be made were those which ensured reverence for the Divinity [*divinitatis*], so that we might grant both to Christians and to all people freedom to follow whatever religion each one wished, in order that whatever divinity there is in the seat of heaven may be appeased and made propitious towards us and towards all who have been set under our power."[27]

On the Death of the Persecutors 52.4

52. [4] With great rejoicing, then, let us celebrate the triumph of God; let us extol the victory of the Lord; day and night let us pour out our prayers in rejoicing; let us pray that he establish forever the peace that has been granted to his people after ten years [of persecution].[28]

---

25. Lactantius, *De Mortibus Persecutorum*, 69.

26. A standard practice aimed at realigning the loyalty of the soldiers and making it possible for former enemy units from forming cohesive units that could turn against the victor.

27. Adapted from, Lactantius, *De Mortibus Persecutorum*, 71.

28. Swift, *Early Fathers*, 67.

Lactantius's rejoicing for the victories of Constantine and Licinius is unquestionably at odds with his earlier attitudes towards war and military service, from a time when it was not imaginable that the commander-in-chief could be obedient to the true God. Yet, as the last statement reveals, this rejoicing in the defeat of enemies was also the expression of jubilation by a generation that had lived through one of the most brutal and far reaching persecutions. The enemies of God seemed to have been defeated, if only for a moment, and the promise of a new era appeared to dawn.

Licinius, however, did not remain faithful to the "divine call" and turned against the Church. As we saw in the inscription to the *Divine Institutes* Lactantius added a few years later, his fate was to be counted with the "bad" emperors, and God's judgment eventually removed him from his throne as Constantine became the sole emperor in 324 CE.

TWELVE

Church Order Documents
and Conciliar Canons

*The Synod of Arles, Canon 3 (314 CE) and The Council of Nicaea,
Canon 12 (325 CE)*

With the end of the Great Persecution and the ascent of Constantine
as the undisputed sole ruler of the West, Christians were facing a dra-
matically new experience. In October 312, when Constantine faced
Maxentius on the Northern approach to Rome, his soldiers carried the
Christogram on their shields. When Constantine entered victorious the
Eternal City two days later, he was greeted as a liberator by the populous
and honored by the Senate. In Constantine the Church, too, was quickly
finding a proponent—even a friend.

Just two years later, in 314, the Donatist churches of North Africa
appealed to Constantine to adjudicate their dispute with the church of
Rome. For the first time the emperor summoned the bishops of the Church
to an ecclesiastical council, this one at Arles, in southern Gaul (modern
France). The third canon of the Synod of Arles said the following:

> **Canon 3.** Those who threw down their arms in time of peace are
> to be excluded from communion[1]

The exact Latin wording of the canon has been significantly debated
among scholars, especially on the placement and exact meaning of the

---

1. De his qui arma *proiciunt in pace,* placuit abstineri eos a communione (italics
added).

phrase "in time of peace." Did the bishops at Arles intend to reverse the long-standing tradition of conscientious objection among Christians in the legions? Did they acquiesce to the changing demands of a powerful new emperor? Or did they make a distinction—for the first time—between the work of the army as police force during the periods of peace versus the objectionable practice of killing during wartime? If it is the latter, then there is an apparent continuity with the practices of the late third century, as Christians could remain in their military posts unencumbered by pagan oaths or necessity for battle.

My reading of Canon 3 of the Synod of Arles, however, is in substantial agreement with Louis Swift who does not see a compelling distinction between police work and military campaign in the function of the legions. To be sure, during peacetime, the legions were also responsible for preserving civic order in the provinces where they were stationed, the *sacramentum* and rituals of the army were exactly the same, and the violence involved in the Roman understanding of "police work" was equally notorious. The idea that Christians would be invited by the bishops to serve under these conditions in times of peace and then desert in times of war is simply not credible. Furthermore, as Swift notes, "no emperor, either Christian or pagan, could endorse or tolerate an arrangement of that kind."[2] Rather, it seems that Arles recognizes the changing character of the empire—at least in the West at this time—and the removal of some of the more prominent and offensive pagan aspects of military service. This reading of Canon 3 runs counter to the literary evidence of the first three centuries and indicates a clear shift in the relationship between Church and State. It this, Canon 3 foreshadows the revolution of the end of the century, when emperor Theodosius I declared Christianity not only as *religio licita* but also as *religio regalis*, the official religion of the Roman empire (30 February 380 CE) and the exclusion of pagans from the Roman army in 416 CE, under Theodosius II.

Eleven years after Arles, in 325 CE, Constantine called what has come to be recognized as the first ecumenical council of the Church at Nicaea. Among the twenty canons produced by the Council, Canon 12 reads as follows:

> Canon 12. Those who responded to the call of grace and initially expressed their faith by putting off the military belt, but who

2. Swift, *Early Fathers*, 91.

subsequently acted like dogs returning to their vomit when they offered money and gifts in order to get back into the army must remain among the hearers for three years and then among the supplicants for ten years.[3]

Notwithstanding the graphic and harsh language, Canon 12 is not as sharp of a return to the pacifist stance as it may first appear. If one keeps in mind the history immediately preceding the Council of Nicaea, one recognizes that Canon 12 applies to a very specific case and is not a universal prescription. Even though in 313 CE the eastern emperor Licinius joined Constantine in issuing the Edict of Milan recognizing Christianity as a *religio licita*, in the decade that followed Licinius drifted from toleration of Christianity to implicit disapproval and eventual intolerance.[4] As a series of wars with Constantine for control of the empire ensued, Licinius expelled Christians from the imperial palace purged his bodyguard of Christians, and later ordered all those in the imperial administration and the armies to either sacrifice to the gods or forfeit their rank and be discharged. This, Licinius demanded annually of all troops. By the time Constantine defeated Licinius in 324 CE, the emperor of the East has inflicted a number of new (some even bloody) persecutions upon the Christians under his rule. Canon 12 of Nicaea was intended to address those soldiers in the armies of Licinius who first left the army because they were unwilling to offer sacrifices and then sought to return to their former careers.

The Apostolic Tradition (ca. 380 CE); Canons of Hippolytus (ca. 336–340 CE); Apostolic Constitutions (ca. 375–380 CE); and Testamentum Domini (5th century CE)[5]

The situations faced by Arles and Nicaea were not limited in one locale or a period of time. Since the middle of the third century, the numerical growth of Christianity meant that a number of practical issues that were not imaginable before had to be addressed.[6] The church order document known as *The Apostolic Tradition* bears witness to the complexities facing

---

3. Swift, *Early Fathers*, 92.

4. Barnes, *Constantine and Eusebius*, 70.

5. For the most recent work on these church order documents, see Bradshaw, Johnson, and Phillips, *Apostolic Tradition*.

6. The best treatment of the variant views on military service in the church order documents is still Kreider, "Military Service."

the growing Christian movement. As we have already seen, (pp. 63–64) the *Apostolic Tradition* went through various editions and is sometimes attributed to Hippolytus of Rome. The document contains instructions for ordination, ministry, catechesis, baptism, etc., and versions of it were widely used for many centuries. Like Tertullian, the *Apostolic Tradition* recognizes the realities of life and the practical issues facing women and men who want to join the Church. It recognizes that people come to Christ from all walks of life, women and men with established professions and lucrative careers; those who are poor needing to find jobs; rich who became such by keeping brothels and selling slaves; slaves who had no control over their bodies and free citizens who did; those who were raised as pagans, and those who grew up in Christian families. The Church had to account for all these and many more; and it seems that the instructions found in the church order documents are substantially at odds with the Synod of Arles.

The church order documents address the trades and professions that are permissible for Christians and the ones that are forbidden. In the section *Concerning Crafts and Professions*, section 16 speaks to the catechumens and lists the alternatives: pimps and brothel keepers, prostitutes, magicians, makers of spells and pagan priests, astrologers and soothsayers, they should desist immediately or be rejected from baptism and the Church. So should gladiators, who were most often slaves, or public officials of gladiatorial games, who were free citizens.

The Church recognized that among those who wanted to join the Church and participate in the mysteries were also soldiers who had been converted while in service. The instructions for them were very clear: soldiers who became Christians while in service had to refuse to kill, under any circumstances, "even if they receive the order to kill." On the other hand, a Christian or a catechumen who considered joining the army was to be excommunicated, "For he has despised God by this his thought . . . and has treated the faith with contempt."

Along with the *Apostolic Tradition*, the *Apostolic Constitutions*, the *Canons of Hippolytus*, and the *Testamentum Domini*, survived in Greek, Latin, Sahidic, Arabic, Ethiopic, and Bohairic (a dialect of Coptic). The breadth of geographical acceptance and longevity of these documents attests to their importance as catechetical and community formative instructions.

Since the versions and derivative documents show variation in language, it seems pertinent to include the parallels as they appear in the critical edition by Bradshaw, Johnson, and Phillips.

Apostolic Constitutions 8.83.7–13[7]

If anyone is a brothel keeper, either let him stop his pimping or be rejected. Let a prostitute who comes either stop or be rejected. Let an idol maker who comes either stop or be rejected. If any of them belong to the theater, whether man, woman, charioteer, gladiator, stadium runner, trainer of athletes, one who participates in the Olympic Games, or one who accompanies the chorus on flute, lute, or lyre, or who puts on a display of dancing or is a fraudulent trader, let them either stop or be rejected.

Let a soldier who comes [viz. one converted while in service] be taught to do no injustice or to extort money, but to be content with his given wages. Let the one who objects be rejected. A doer of unmentionable things, a lustful person, a lascivious person, a magician, a mob leader, a charmer, an astrologer, a diviner, a charmer of wild beasts, a pimp, a maker of charms, one who purifies by applying objects, a fortune-teller, an interpreter of oracles, an interpreter of bodily vibrations, one who upon encountering them, observes defects of eyes, or feet, or birds, or cats, or loud noises, or significant chance remarks—let them be examined for a time, for the evil is hard to wash out. Then, let those who stop be received, but let those not persuaded be rejected.

Canons of Hippolytus 13–14[8]

13. Whoever has received the authority to kill, or else a soldier, they are not to kill in any case, even if they receive the order to kill. They are not to pronounce a bad word. Those who have received an honor are not to wear wreaths on their hands (i.e., reject the honor). Whosoever is raised to the authority of prefect or the magistracy and does not put on the righteousness of the gospel is to be excluded from the flock and the bishop is not to pray with him.

7. Bradshaw, Johnson, and Phillips, *Apostolic Tradition*, 89.
8. Ibid., 91.

14. A Christian must not become a soldier, unless he is compelled by a chief bearing the sword [i.e., conscription]. He is not to burden himself with the sin of blood. But if he has shed blood, he is not to partake of the mysteries, unless he is purified by a punishment, tears, and wailing. He is not to come forward deceitfully but in the fear of God.

Apostolic Tradition 16.1–11 (Sahidic)

[The teachers of those who seek to join the Church and are, there-fore, entering catechesis] [1] shall inquire about the crafts and work of those who will be brought in to be catechized as to what they are. [2] If one is a brothel keeper, who is a caretaker of prostitutes, either let him cease or be cast out. [3] If he is a maker of idols or painter, let them [sic] be taught not to make idols; either let them cease or be cast out. [4] If one is an actor or he does performances in the theater, either let them cease or be cast out. [5] If he teaches young children, it is good indeed for him to cease. If he has no trade, then let him be forgiven.

[6] Likewise, a charioteer who contends and who goes to the games, either let him cease or be cast out. [7] One who is a gladiator or who teaches gladiators to fight, or a hunter who performs hunts [i.e. the shows of wild beasts at the gladiatorial games] or an official who regulates the gladiatorial contests either let them cease or be cast out. [8] One who is a priest of the idols, or who is a watchman or the idols, either let him cease of be cast out.[9]

The parallel Sahidic, Arabic, and Ethiopic versions of paragraphs 16.9–11, as found in Bradshaw, Johnson, and Phillips, *Apostolic Tradition* are as follows:[10]

---

9. Ibid., 88.

10. Alistair Stewart-Sykes, translates sections 16.9–11 this way: "[9] A soldier in command must be told not to kill people; if he is ordered so to do, he shall not carry it out. Nor should he take the oath [the *sacramentum*]. If he will not agree, let him cease of be cast out. [10] Anyone who has the power of the sword, or who is a civil magistrate wearing the purple either let him cease or be cast out. [11] If a catechumen or a believer wishes to become a soldier let them [sic] be cast out, for they have despised God" (Hippolytus, *On the Apostolic Tradition*, 100).

Sahidic	Arabic	Ethiopic
[9] A soldier who has authority,	A soldier in the sovereign's army	They are not to accept soldiers of an official,
let him not kill a man. If he is ordered,	should not kill, or if he is ordered to kill	
let him not go to the task nor let him swear.	he should refuse.	and if he is given an order to kill he is not to do it; if he does not stop, he is to be expelled.
But if he is not willing, let him be cast out.	If he stops, so be it; otherwise, he should be excluded.	
	Concerning those who wear red or believers who become soldiers or astrologers or magicians or such like: let them be excluded.	Concerning other people, either a believer who becomes a soldier or an astrologer or magician or the like.
[10] One who has authority of the sword, or a ruler of a city who wears the purple, let him cease or be cast out.	One who has the power of the sword or the head of a city and wears red, let him stop or be excluded.	An official who has a sword or a chief of appointed people and who wears purple is to stop or be expelled.
[11] A catechumen or faithful [person] if he wishes to become a soldier, let them [sic] be cast out, because they despised God	A catechumen or a believer, if they want to be soldiers, let them be excluded because they distance themselves from God.	A catechumen or believer, if they wish to become a soldier, are to be expelled because they are far from God.

Testamentum Domini 2.2[11]

If anyone be a soldier or in authority, let him be taught not to oppress or to kill or to rob, or to be angry or to rage and afflict anyone. But let those rations suffice to him that are given to him. But if they wish to be baptized in the Lord, let them cease from military service or from the [post of] authority, and if not let them not be received.

Let a catechumen or a believer of the people, if he desires to be a

11. Bradshaw, Johnson, and Phillips, *Apostolic Tradition*, 89.

soldier, either cease from his intention, or if not let him be rejected. For he has despised God by this his thought, and leaving the things of the Spirit, he has perfected himself in the flesh, and has treated the faith with contempt.

THIRTEEN

Epilogue

A New Vocabulary of Gods and Men

"History does not belong to us; we belong to it."
—Hans-Georg Gadamer, *Truth and Method*

Four centuries before Constantine, the Roman rhetor and political theorist, Cicero, spoke of language and practice as interdependent realities interpreting each other and each to the other. Cicero understood that language is character formative. We experience the world in and through language, through signs, speech acts, and practices. Language provides the structure of our experience, understanding, and perspectives. Cicero recognized that as the language of the Romans changed, so did their understanding, first of themselves and then of those around them. Cicero spoke of the transformation of the meaning and, therefore, the concept of *hostis*, from its earlier understanding as "guest" and "stranger" to "enemy." Instead of welcoming a stranger, instead of hosting a *hostis*, in their very use of language the Romans of his time revealed the fact that they now saw the stranger—primarily—as *hostile*. He wrote: "'Enemy' (*hostis*) meant to our ancestors what we now call 'stranger' (*peregrinus*) . . . Long lapse of time has given that word (*hostis*) a harsher meaning: for it has lost its significance of 'stranger' and has taken on the technical connotation of 'an enemy under arms'" (*De officiis* I, 122.12).

The fourth century was such a time of change for the Christian vocabulary as well. At the dawn of the century, especially during the period of the Great Persecution (303–311 CE), no Christian could have imagined the events that took place in the beginning of June[1] 325 in the small town of Nicaea in Bithynia, near the imperial residence of Nicomedia. It was here that the emperor Constantine convened the bishops of the Church to what has become known as the First Ecumenical Council:

> The opening ceremony was held in the judgment hall of the imperial palace. The bishops took their places on benches arranged in rows along the length of the hall. In silence, Constantine's attendants entered—not the usual soldiers of the bodyguard, but friends of the emperor who were Christians—all unarmed. At a sign, all stood. Constantine entered, clad in the imperial purple, with a diadem and insignia of gold and diamonds. He advanced as far as the first seat in each row. A small stool of wood encrusted with gold was produced. After requesting permission from the bishops, Constantine sat down; the rest followed suit. The bishop immediately to his left, Eusebius of Nicomedia, rose and delivered a panegyrical address of welcome. After Eusebius resumed his seat, Constantine replied briefly and formally in Latin. . . . An interpreter translated the speech into Greek. . . . The debates then begun.[2]

From among those present, preeminent place was reserved for confessors, "especially those whose missing eyes and maimed ankles manifested proof of their steadfastness during the persecution."[3] These confessors were a constant reminder of the collision of these two worlds: one that had come to an end, and another now inaugurated: Christ's promised millennial kingdom was at hand—or so Eusebius and those around him thought.

By the end of the century, Tertullian's rhetorical enthusiasm in claiming the *oikoumenē* for the Church (*Apol.* 37.4) seemed simultaneously prophetic and strangely out of place. Prophetic because, with the exception of Julian's short interlude (361–363 CE), all who ascended to the Roman throne from the reign of Constantine onward were Christians.

---

1. The traditional date of May 20 had been greatly debated in recent years. A good analysis is found in Barnes, "Constantinian Settlement," 648.

2. Barnes, *Constantine and Eusebius*, 215

3. Ibid., 214.

"Eusebius' dreams of one God, one emperor, one empire, one church and his celebration of Constantine as a 'mighty victor beloved of God'"[4] might have seemed possible. It was out of place because, even as the Empire divided into its Western (Latin) and Eastern (Greek) parts, the language of "resident aliens" almost disappeared into the new vocabulary of "we" and "you" in which "we" did not indicate the Church simply as the body of Christ anymore, and the "you" was not addressing Romans as those in authority. The *locutions* remained the same, but the *signs* changed as radically as the concept of *hostis* did in Cicero's time.

The fourth century was a time of conceptual changes. In 380 CE, Emperor Theodosius I (379–395 CE), issued the "Edict of Thessalonica" (the decree known as *Cunctos Populos*) establishing Nicene Christianity as *the* faith of his subjects.[5] Between 389–391 CE the "Theodosian decrees" banned pagan sacrifices[6] and closed pagan temples, practically outlawing traditional Roman religion. In 313 CE, the Edict of Milan declared Christianity a *religio licita* within the Roman Empire. By the turn of the century, the worship of the ancient gods who had superintended Rome's rise to power was declared a *religio illicita*. At the beginning of the fourth century Romans were persecuting Christians with passion. At the end of the century, Christians were returning the favor with equal fervor. The eternal fire in the Temple of Vesta in Rome was extinguished in 391 CE, and public funds were forever withheld from pagan civic rites. The last Olympic Games were held in 393 CE, and in 416 CE Theodosius II purged the Roman armies of all pagans. The gods of Rome were no more. The Olympians had been defeated.

Cicero understood the power of language, for language is character formative. The language of Diognetus, Tertullian, Origen, and even (early) Lactantius had been transformed. The broad categories of "barbarian" and "heretic" had become the new threats replacing the earlier binaries of "Christian" and "pagan," allowing for a linguistic shift where "we" now enjoy the undeniable protection *of* the State and are, thus, responsible *for* the protection of the State. The decades that followed the first council at Nicea are replete with appeals to the State to resolve ecclesiastical matters and enforce conciliar decrees. The language of excommunication was no longer restricted to ecclesial isolation but carried with it the imperial

---

4. Wilken, "Jews and Christian Apologetics," 452.

5. The decree was issued on 27 February 389. *Codex Theodosianus* 1.16.2.

6. Decree *Nemo se hostiis polluat, Codex Theodosianus* 16.10.10.

threat (and not only) of *confiscatio* and exile—a traditional Roman, political, penalty.

By the end of the fourth century, what were interpreted to be the primary stumbling blocks for Christian enlistment, namely the idolatry of the Roman army and loyalty to the *divine* Caesar, seemed to have been removed. Beginning with Constantine, the very rhetoric of imperial sovereignty had changed from its Republican antecedents to clear claims of divinely anointed authority exercising God's rule over the Realm. Nowhere was this re-conceptualization of hierarchies between State and Church more publicly manifested than in Theodosius I's excommunication by Ambrose, the bishop of Milan, in the year 390 CE, following the emperor's massacre of 7,000 persons in Thessalonica as reprisal for the mob killing of the military magistrate, Buthericus. A baptized Christian, the Emperor accepted the excommunication and was received back into Eucharistic communion only after a public penance of several months. The example of Ambrose and Theodosius stands as a sticking exception in the renegotiation of the balance of power and the rhetoric of hierarchy between State and Church over the next centuries.

By the time of the Crusades, the Western and Eastern parts of the now permanently fractured empire had developed rather different ideologies and theologies of war and military service. The West had developed an ideology of holy war that allowed, even fostered, Christian participation in the armies, encouraging soldiers to "consider themselves to be the army of God, carrying out the highest duty of a Christian, fighting for the Christian religion."[7] This was particularly true for the crusaders who saw themselves as "*pugnatores Dei*, the *milites Christi* fighting under Jesus Christ." The advancing crusaders "expected and almost demanded that other Christians share this view and give them every assistance, with enthusiasm."[8] It was on this basis that Pope Urban II charged the Frankish knights at Clermont in 1095 CE, and initiated the First Crusade: "If in olden times the Maccabees attained to the highest praise of piety because they fought for the ceremonies and the Temple, it is also justly granted you, Christian soldiers, to defend the liberty of your country by armed endeavor. . . . We now hold out to you wars which contain the glorious reward of martyrdom, which will retain

---

7. Laiou, "Just War of Eastern Christians," 30.

8. Ibid.

that title of praise now and forever."[9] By this very *religious* act of military service in a war that is holy because God mandates it and the Church has declared it, the warriors for the faith find salvation through the very act of war. By its very nature, "holy war is a justifying war."[10]

Angeliki Laoiou has argued that unlike their Western counterparts, the Christians of the Byzantine East did not share the Latin enthusiasm or ideology of holy war. In the long tradition of the Christian East, the *milites Christi* were the monks and ascetics, the true army of God, not the soldiers of the State. Though in an almost constant state of war, against Persians, Arabs, or Seljuk Turks, the Byzantines refused to acquiesce to the concept of holy war and retained a much more robust—and Roman—understanding of just war. In this secular concept of war, the first principle was that war had to be defensive and its aim the restoration of peace. Not only did the war have to be just, it also had to be seen to be just.[11] Moreover, even well into the late medieval period, the Christian East would not accept soldiers who died in battle as martyrs, and in the early thirteenth century, "Byzantine theologians still argued against the concept of the remission of the sins of the crusaders dying in war."[12]

As influential as St. Augustine was for the West, so St. Basil of Caesarea was for the East. In Canon 13, Basil insisted that for the spiritual benefit and restoration to ritual purity of both the soldiers and the communities who received them, those who returned from military campaigns having killed were to be excluded from Eucharistic communion for the period of three years: "Our fathers have not included the murders committed in time of war in the category of murder, pardoning, I think, those who defend prudence and piety. But it seems to me that it is proper to advise them to abstain from communion for three years, for their hands are unclean"[13]

John McGuckin has argued,

> [B]y his regulation and by the ritual exclusion of the illumined
> warrior from the sacrament . . . Basil is making sure at least one
> public sign is given to the entire community that the Gospel

9. Pope Urban II's speech can be found at the *Internet Medieval Source Book* (http://www.fordham.edu/halsall/source/urban2-5vers.html).

10. Laiou, "Just War of Eastern Christians," 30.

11. Ibid., 34–35.

12. Ibid., 36. See also Harakas, "No Just War in the Fathers."

13. Laiou, "Just War of Eastern Christians," 34

standard has no place for war, violence and organized death. He is trying to sustain an eschatological balance: that war is not part of the Kingdom of God (signified in the Eucharistic ritual as arriving in the present) but is part of the bloody and greed-driven reality of world affairs which is the Kingdom-Not-Arrived. . . . By moving in and out of Eucharistic reception Basil's faithful Christian (returning from his duty with blood on his hands) is now in the modality of expressing his dedication to the values of peace and innocence, by means of the lamentation and repentance for life that has been taken, albeit the blood of the violent. Basil's arrangement that the returning warrior may stand in the Church (rather than in the narthex, where the other public sinners were allocated spaces) but refrain from communion makes the statement that a truly honorable termination of war, for a Christian, has to be an honorable repentance.[14]

Basil's understanding that "all violence, local, individual, or nationally-sanctioned, is . . . an expression of hubris that is inconsistent with the values of the Kingdom of God, and while in many circumstances that violence may be necessary or unavoidable (Basil states the only legitimate reasons as the defense of the weak and innocent), it is never justifiable,"[15] is not so far removed from those of St. Augustine.[16] For all the abuse he has received at the hands of those who use him to justify state-sanctioned violence in its pluriform manifestations, the greatest

14. McGuckin, "St. Basil's Guidance."

15. Ibid.

16. For an exceptional treatment of how Augustine has been misread at this point, see O'Donovan, "Political Thought"; also Lee, "Republics and Their Loves." As Lee so pointedly notes,

> For about a decade beginning in the 390s, Augustine joined his contemporaries in identifying the Christianization of the Roman Empire with the culmination of redemptive history, but he gradually came to abandon this view, both before and especially after the sack of Rome in 410. By the time he began *City of God* in 413, Augustine had developed a more established position on the ambiguity of history before the return of Christ that rejected efforts to mine contemporary events for their significance in God's plan for salvation. Rome was neither God's instrument of salvation nor a satanic manifestation of the earthly city; she rather embodied the theological ambiguity of all human institutions in this the penultimate stage of redemptive history. Augustine understood the heavenly and earthly cities primarily as eschatological realities that resisted identification with actual institutions, and his political theology bore out this perspective. (553–54)

theologian of the West was very clear that "violence and idolatry are both symptoms of the same impulse: an inordinate desire for earthly goods coupled with a refusal to seek them from God."[17] In Book 19 of the *City of God*, Augustine redefines for the new Romans of the early fifth century the very concept of State. "Rome is indeed a *res publica*, but her history of violence and idolatry . . . reveals what she loved: dominion, glory, earthy things, and ultimately self."[18] This City of Man stands in radical opposition to the City of God "whose end or supreme good may be called 'peace in life everlasting' or 'life everlasting in peace' (*Civ.* 19.11). Augustine returned to the language of Diognetus and Tertullian, describing the just person as one who "lives by faith as a 'resident alien' from the city of heaven" (*Civ.* 19.14).

Basil and Augustine, Ambrose, Justinian, and Grotius, the fourth century, as well as the developments of the medieval period do deserve a much more thorough and detailed treatment than the present study allows. The nuances of this "linguistic turn" and the resultant ideologies of statehood and Church will need to be the focus of a future study in which we will also engage much more fully the development of the often misunderstood concept of Christian Pacifism.

What has emerged from our present study is a clearer picture of the earliest Christians and their world. Why they understood themselves as resident aliens whose charge was to be εἰρηνοποιοί, peacemakers and how that understanding reoriented the axes of their existence. This ecclesially mediated *eirenopoietic* articulation of the kingdom on earth has its roots in the understanding of the imminence of the eschaton, on the one hand, and the very character of Jesus, on the other. Christian concepts of peacemaking were never meant to be—or to be seen as—static and inert, but an active engagements with the structures of fear and death that dictate the "Roman" *summum bonum*, from their time to our own.[19]

The study of the earliest Christian writers on war and the role of Christians in its instrumentalities shows clearly that, to borrow from Tertullian, "Christians are, *precisely because they are Christians*, factors of resistance in society (*Apology* 37). They resist injustice, driven by an aggressively missionary love that impels them by nonviolent yet active

17. Lee, "Republics and Their Loves," 560.

18. Ibid., 573.

19. See Dodaro, *Christ and the Just Society*.

means to try to bring all, including the persecuting enemy, into the fold of Christ."[20]

As one reads and listens to the earliest Christian, how they understood themselves as a new race, resident aliens, a new society of the baptized, one cannot but realize that something fundamentally changed in the move from a bordered national identity with a religion to defend and a people and lineage to protect, to a universal call to discipleship and a new family of God through Jesus. This is a new kinship that transgresses national identities and gender and societal constructs through the realigning effects of baptism (Gal 3:28; Eph 2:14), a family that brings all into a new kingdom (Rom 6:1-3; Gal 3:27) whose only defense is the empty tomb (1 Cor 15)—the proof that all violence has been subsumed and conquered on the Cross. The result is a resounding alienation from the structures of loyalty and ownership that orient this world because of the new Lord, Jesus.

---

20. Helgeland, Daly, and Burns, *Christians and the Military*, 15, emphasis added.

Select Bibliography

Adamantius, Alexandrinus. *Dialogue on the True Faith in God*. Translated by Robert A. Pretty. Edited by Garry W. Trompf. Gnostica 1. Leuven: Peeters, 1997.

Adler, William. "Sextus Julius Africanus and the Roman Near East in the Third Century." *Journal of Theological Studies*, n.s., 55.2 (2004) 520–50.

Aland, Kurt. "The Relation between Church and State in Early Times: A Reinterpretation." *Journal of Theological Studies* 19 (1968) 15–27.

Allen, Sister Prudence. *The Concept of Woman: The Aristotelian Revolution, 750 B.C.– A.D. 1250*. Grand Rapids: Eerdmans, 1985.

Alonso, Victor. "War, Peace, and International Law in Ancient Greece." In *War and Peace in the Ancient World*, edited by Kurt A. Raaflaub, 206–25. Oxford: Blackwell, 2007.

Ante-Nicene Fathers: The Writings of the Fathers down to A.D. 325. 10 vols. Edited by Alexander Roberts et al. Buffalo: Christian Literature, 1885–96. Reprint, Peabody, MA: Hendrickson, 1994.

The Apostolic Fathers. Translated by Francis X. Glimm et al. Fathers of the Church 1. Washington, DC: Catholic University of America Press, 1969.

The Apostolic Fathers. 2 vols. Edited and translated by Bart Ehrman. LCL 24–25. Cambridge, MA: Harvard University Press, 2003.

The Apostolic Fathers. 2 vols. Translated by Kirsopp Lake. LCL 24–25. Cambridge, MA: Harvard University Press, 1912–13.

Arnobius of Sicca. *The Case against the Pagans*. 2 vols. Translated by George E. McCracken. Ancient Christian Writers 7–8. New York: Newman, 1949.

Athenagoras. *Embassy for the Christians. The Resurrection of the Dead*. Edited and translated by Joseph Hugh Crehan. Ancient Christian Writers 23. New York: Newman, 1955.

———. *Legatio and De resurrectione*. Edited by W. R. Schoedel. Oxford: Clarendon, 1972.

———. *Legatio Pro Christianis*. Edited by Miroslav Marcovich. Patristische Texte und Studien 31. New York: de Gruyter, 1990.

Atkinson, Clarissa W., Constance H. Buchanan, and Margaret Miles. *Immaculate and Powerful: The Female in Sacred Image and Social Reality*. Boston: Beacon, 1985.

Averbeck, Richard E. "Sacrifices and Offerings." In *Dictionary of the Old Testament: Pentateuch*, edited by T. Desmond Alexander and David W. Baker, 706–33. Downers Grove, IL: InterVarsity.

Aymer, Margaret P. "Hailstorms and Fireballs: Redaction, World Creation, and Resistance in the Acts of Paul and Thecla." *Semeia* 79 (1997) 45–62.

Bainton, Roland H. *Christian Attitudes Toward War and Peace*. Knoxville, TN: Abingdon, 1960.

———. *Early Christianity*. New York: Van Nostrand, 1960.

———. "The Early Church and War." *Harvard Theological Review* 39 (1946) 189–213.

Balch, David, and Carolyn Osiek, editors. *Early Christian Families in Context: An Interdisciplinary Dialogue*. Grand Rapids: Eerdmans, 2003.

Baldovin, John F. "Hippolytus and the Apostolic Tradition: Recent Research and Commentary." *Theological Studies* 64.3 (2003) 520–42.

Barnard, Leslie W. *Athenagoras: A Study in Second Century Christian Apologetic*. Paris: Beauchesne, 1972.

Barnes, Timothy D. *Constantine and Eusebius*. Cambridge, MA: Harvard University Press, 1981.

———. "The Constantinian Settlement." In *Eusebius, Christianity and Judaism*, edited by Harold W. Attridge and Gohei Hata, 635–57. Detroit: Wayne State University Press, 1992.

———. *Tertullian: A Historical and Literary Study*. Rev. ed. Oxford: Clarendon, 1985.

Barton, Carlin A. "The Price of Peace in Ancient Rome." In *War and Peace in the Ancient World*, edited by Kurt A. Raaflaub, 245–55. Oxford: Blackwell, 2007.

Baumeister, Theofrid. *Die Anfänge der Theologie des Martyriums*. Münster: Aschendorf, 1980.

Baynes, Norman H. *The Early Church and Social Life: The First Three Centuries*. London: Bell, 1927.

Beard, Mary, John North, and Simon Price. *Religions of Rome. Vol. 1: A History*. Cambridge: Cambridge University Press, 1998.

Bell, Catherine. *Ritual Theory, Ritual Practice*. Oxford: Oxford University Press, 1992.

Bell, Sinclair, and Inge Lyse Hansen, editors. *Role Models in the Roman World: Identity and Assimilation*. Ann Arbor: University of Michigan Press, 2008.

Berchem, Andreas. *Le martyre de la Légion Thébaine*. Basel: Schweizerische Beitrage zur Altertumswissenschaft 8, 1968.

Bobertz, Charles Arnold. "Cyprian of Carthage as a Patron: A Social Historical Study of the Role of Bishop in the Ancient Christian Community of North Africa." PhD diss., Yale University, 1988.

Boda, Mark J. *A Severe Mercy: Sin and Its Remedy in the Old Testament*. Winona Lake, IN: Eisenbrauns, 2009.

Bond, Sarah E. Review of *Children in the Roman Empire: Outsiders Within*, by Christian Laes. *Bryn Mawr Classical Review* 46 (Oct 2011) http://bmcr.brynmawr.edu/2011/2011-10-46.html.

Boughton, Lynne C. "From Pious Legend to Feminist Fantasy: Distinguishing Hagiographical License from Practice in the 'Acts of Paul/Acts of Thecla.'" *The Journal of Religion* 71.3 (1991) 363–83.

Bowman, Alan K., Peter Garnsey, and Averil Cameron, editors. *The Crisis of Empire, A.D. 193–337*. 2nd ed. Cambridge Ancient History 12. Cambridge: Cambridge University Press, 2005.

Boyarin, Daniel. *Dying For God: Martyrdom and the Making of Christianity and Judaism*. Stanford: Stanford University Press, 1999.

———. "Martyrdom and the Making of Christianity and Judaism." *Journal of Early Christian Studies* 6.4 (1998) 577–627.

Bradshaw, Paul F. *The Search for the Origins of Christian Worship*. 2nd ed. New York: Oxford University Press, 2002.

Bradshaw, Paul F., editor. *The Canons of Hippolytus*. Nottingham: Grove, 1987.

Bradshaw, Paul F., Maxwell E. Johnson, and L. Edward Phillips. *The Apostolic Tradition: A Commentary*. Hermeneia. Minneapolis: Fortress, 2002.

Bremmer, Jan N., and Istvan Czachesz, editors. *The Apocalypse of Peter*. Leuven: Peeters, 2003.

Brennecke, Hanns Christof. "Kriegsdienst und Soldatenberuf für Christen und die Rolle des römischen Heeres für die Mission." In *Krieg und Christentum: Religiöse Gewalttheorien in der Kriegserfahrung des Westens*, edited by Andreas Holzem, 180–210. Krieg in der Geschichte 50. Paderborn: Ferdinand Schöningh, 2009.

Brent, Allen. *Cyprian and Roman Carthage*. Cambridge: Cambridge University Press, 2010.

———. *Hippolytus and the Roman Church in the Third Century: Communities in Tension before the Emergence of a Monarch-Bishop*. Leiden: Brill, 1995.

Brock, Peter. *The Military Question in the Early Church: A Selected Bibliography of a Century's Scholarship (1888–1987)*. Toronto, 1988.

———. *The Roots of War Resistance. Pacifism from the Early Church to Tolstoy*. Nyack, NY: Fellowship of Reconciliation, 1981.

———. "Why Did St Maximilian Refuse to Serve the Roman Army?" *Journal of Ecclesiastical History* 45.2 (1994) 195–209.

Brock, Sebastian. "Eusebius and Syriac Christianity." In *Eusebius, Christianity and Judaism*, edited by Harold W. Attridge and Gohei Hata, 212–34. Detroit: Wayne State University Press, 1992.

Brock, Sebastian P., and Susan Ashbrook Harvey, translators. *Holy Women of the Syrian Orient*. Berkeley: University of California Press, 1987.

Brown, Peter R. L. "The Attitude of St. Augustine to Religious Coercion." *Journal of Roman Studies*, 54 (1964) 107–16.

Brown, Peter R. L. *The Body and Society: Men, Women, and Sexual Renunciation in Early Christianity*. New York: Columbia University Press, 2008.

———. *The Cult of the Saints: Its Rise and Function in Latin Christianity*. Chicago: University of Chicago Press, 1981.

———. *The Making of Late Antiquity*. Cambridge, MA: Harvard University Press, 1978.

———. *The World of Late Antiquity*. New York: Harcourt Brace, 1971.

Budde, Gerard J. "Christian Charity: Now and Always." *The Ecclesiastical Review* 85 (1931) 571–73.

Buell, Denise Kimber. "Producing Descent/Dissent: Clement of Alexandria's Use of Filial Metaphors as Intra-Christian Polemic." *Harvard Theological Review* 90 (1997) 89–104.

Burckhardt, Jacob. *The Age of Constantine the Great*. Translated by Moses Hadas. Berkley: University of California Press, 1983.

Burns, J. Patout. *Cyprian the Bishop*. Routledge Early Church Monographs. New York: Routledge, 2002.

Burrus, Virginia. *"Begotten Not Made": Conceiving Manhood in Late Antiquity*. Stanford, CA: Stanford University Press, 2000.

Cadoux, C. John. *Early Christian Attitudes to War: A Contribution to the History of Christian Ethics*. London: Headley, 1919; reprint, New York: Seabury, 1982.

Cadoux, Cecil John. *The Early Christian Attitude to Pagan Society and the State down to the Time of Constantinus*. Edinburgh: T. & T. Clark, 1925.

———. *The Early Church and the World*. Edinburgh: T. & T. Clark, 1925.

Cahill, Lisa Sowle. "Nonresistance, Defense, Violence, and the Kingdom in Christian Tradition." *Interpretation* 38.4 (1984) 380–97.

Calder, W. M. "A Fourth-Century Lycaonian Bishop." *Expositor* 6 (1908) 385–408.

———. "Studies in Early Christian Epigraphy." *Journal of Religious Studies* 10 (1920) 42–59.

Cameron, Averil. *Christianity and the Rhetoric of Empire: The Development of Christian Discourse.* Berkeley: University of California Press, 1991.

Campenhausen, Hans van. "Christians and Military Service in the Early Church." In *Tradition and Life in the Church: Essays and Lectures in Church History*, translated by A. V. Littledale, 160–70. Philadelphia: Fortress, 1968.

———. *Die Idee des Martyriums in der alten Kirche.* Göttingen: Vandenhoeck and Ruprecht, 1964.

———. "Der Kriegsdienst der Christen in der Kirche des Altertums." In *Offener Horizont. Festschrift für Karl Jaspers*, edited by Klaus Piper, 255–64. München: R. Piper, 1953.

———. *Tradition and Life in the Church: Essays and Lectures in Church History.* Philadelphia: Fortress, 1968.

Cantarella, Eva. *Pandora's Daughters: The Role and Status of Women in Greek and Roman Antiquity.* Translated by Maureen B. Fant. Baltimore: John Hopkins University Press, 1987.

Carter, Michael. "*Archiereis* and Asiarchs: A Gladiatorial Perspective." *Greek, Roman, and Byzantine Studies* 44 (2004) 41–68.

Casiday, Augustine, and Frederick W. Norris, editors. *The Cambridge History of Christianity: Constantine to c. 600.* Vol. 2. Cambridge: Cambridge University Press, 2007.

Caspary, Gerard E. *Politics and Exegesis: Origen and the Two Swords.* Berkley: University of California Press, 1979.

Castelli, Elizabeth A. *Martyrdom and Memory: Early Christian Culture Making.* New York: Columbia University Press, 2004.

Castelli, Elizabeth A., and Hal Taussig, editors. *Reimagining Christian Origins.* Valley Forge, PA: Trinity, 1996.

Cerrato, J. A. *Hippolytus between East and West: The Commentaries and the Provenance of the Corpus.* Oxford: Oxford University Press, 2002.

Chadwick, Henry. *Early Christian Thought and the Classical Tradition: Studies on Justin, Clement, and Origen.* New York: Oxford University Press, 1966.

Charles, J. Daryl. *Between Pacifism and Jihad: Just War and Christian Tradition.* Downers Grove, IL: InterVarsity, 2005.

Clark, Elizabeth A. *Ascetic Piety and Women's Faith: Essays on Late Ancient Christianity.* Lewiston, NY: Mellen, 1986.

———. *Jerome, Chrysostom, and Friends: Essays and Translations.* Studies in Women and Religion 2. New York: Mellen, 1979.

———. "The Lady Vanishes: Dilemmas of a Feminist Historian after the 'Linguistic Turn.'" *Church History* 67.1 (1998) 1–31.

Clark, Elizabeth A., editor. *Women in the Early Church.* Message of the Fathers of the Church 13. Wilmington, DE: Glazier, 1983.

Clark, Elizabeth, and Herbert Richardson. *Women and Religion: A Feminist Sourcebook of Christian Thought.* New York: Harper & Row, 1977.

Clarkson, Thomas. *An Essay on the Doctrines and Practice of the Early Christians, as They Relate to War: Addressed to Those Who Profess to Have a Regard for the Christian Name.* 3rd ed. London: Hamilton, Adams, 1832.

Clausewitz, Carl von. *On War.* Edited and translated by Michael Howard and Peter Paret. Princeton, NJ: Princeton University Press, 1976.

Clement of Alexandria. *Christ the Educator*. Edited and translated by Simon P. Wood. Fathers of the Church 23. New York: Fathers of the Church, 1954.

———. *Exhortation to the Greeks. The Rich Man's Salvation. To the Newly Baptized*. Translated by G. W. Butterworth. LCL 92. Cambridge, MA: Harvard, 1919.

———. *Le Pédagogue*. Vol. 1. Introduction and notes by Henri-Irenee Marrou. Translation by Marguerite Harl. Sources Chrétiennes 70. Paris: Cerf, 1960.

———. *Le Pédagogue*. Vol. 2. Introduction and notes by Henri-Irenee Marrou. Translation by Claude Mondésert. Sources Chrétiennes 108. Paris: Cerf, 1965.

———. *Le Pédagogue*. Vol. 3. Introduction and notes by Henri-Irenee Marrou. Translation by Claude Mondésert and C. Matray. Sources Chrétiennes 158. Paris: Cerf, 1970.

———. *Le protreptique*. Introduction, translation and notes by Claude Mondésert. 2nd ed. Sources Chrétiennes 2. Paris: Cerf, 1949.

———. *Quis dives salvetur?* In *Die griechischen Christlichen Schriftsteller*, edited by O. Stählin, 17:157–91. Leipzig, 1909.

———. *Stromateis: Books One to Three*. Edited and translated by John Ferguson. Fathers of the Church 85. Washington, DC: Catholic University of America Press, 1991.

Cloke, Gillian. *"This Female Man of God": Women and Spiritual Power in the Patristic Age, AD 350–450*. London: Routledge, 1995.

Cobb, L. Stephanie. *Dying to be Men: Gender and Language in Early Christian Martyr Texts*. New York: Columbia University Press, 2008.

Cochrane, Charles N. *Christianity and Classical Culture. A Study of Thought and Action from Augustus to Augustine*. New York: Oxford University Press, 1957.

Collins, Adela Yarbo, editor. *Feminist Prespectives on Biblical Scholarship*. Chico, CA: Scholars, 1985.

Conway, Colleen M. *Behold the Man: Jesus and Greco-Roman Masculinity*. Oxford: Oxford University Press, 2008.

Coon, Lynda L. *Sacred Fictions: Holy Women and Hagiography in Late Antiquity*. Philadelphia: University of Pennsylvania Press, 1997.

Coon, Lynda L., Katherine J. Haldane, and Elisabeth W. Sommer, editors. *That Gentle Strength: Historical Perspectives on Women in Christianity*. Charlottesville: University Press of Virginia, 1990.

Crouzel, Henri. *Origen*. Translated by A. S. Worrall. San Francisco: Harper, 1989.

Cunningham, Agnes. *The Early Church and the State*. Sources of Early Christian Thought 4. Philadelphia: Fortress, 1982.

Cyprian of Carthage. *The Letters of St. Cyprian*. 4 vols. Translated by G. W. Clarke. Ancient Christian Writers 43–44, 46–47. New York: Newman, 1984–89.

———. *Letters (1–81)*. Translated by Rose Bernard Donna. Fathers of the Church 51. Washington, DC: Catholic University of America Press, 1964.

———. *On the Church: Select Letters*. Translated by Allen Brent. Popular Patristics Series 33. Crestwood, NY: St. Vladimir's Seminary Press, 2006.

———. *On the Church: Select Treatises*. Translated by Allen Brent. Popular Patristics Series 32. Crestwood, NY: St. Vladimir's Seminary Press, 2006.

———. *De opere et eleemosynis*. In Corpus Scriptorum Ecclesiasticorum Latinorum 3/1:371–94. Vienna, 1868.

———. *Treatises*. Translated and edited by Roy J. Deferrari et al. Fathers of the Church 36. Washington, DC: Catholic University of America Press, 1958.

Daly, Mary. *The Church and the Second Sex*. New York: Harper & Row, 1975.

Daly, Robert J. "Military Force and the Christian Conscience in the Early Church: A Methodological Approach." *Proceedings of the Thirty-Seventh Annual Convention, The Catholic Theological Society of America* 37 (1982) 178–81.

———. "Military Service and Early Christianity: A Methodological Approach." *Studia Patristica* 18.1 (1985) 1–8.

———. "The New Testament: Pacifism and Non-Violence." *American Ecclesiastical Review* (1974) 544–62.

Daube, David. *Civil Disobedience in Antiquity*. Edinburgh: University Press, 1972.

Davies, R. W. "Police Work in Roman Times." *History Today* (October 1968) 700–707.

Davis, Stephen J. "Crossed Texts, Crossed Sex: Intertextuality and Gender in Early Christian Legends of Holy Women Disguised as Men." *Journal of Early Christian Studies* 10.1 (2002) 1–36.

Deane, H. A. *The Political and Social Ideas of St. Augustine*. New York: Columbia University Press, 1963.

Decret, François. *Le Christianisme en Afrique du Nord ancienne*. Paris: Editions de Seuil, 1996.

Deiver, John. *How Christians Made Peace with War: Early Christian Understandings of War*. Scottdale, PA: Herald, 1988.

DeSoucey, Michaela, Jo-Ellen Pozner, Corey Fields, Kerry Dobransky, and Gary Alan Fine. "Memory and Sacrifice: An Embodied Theory of Martyrdom." *Cultural Sociology* 2.1 (2008) 99–121.

La Didachè: Instructions des Apôtres. Edited by Jean Paul Audet. Etudes bibliques. Paris: J. Lecoffre, 1958.

Didascalia Apostolorum: The Syriac Version Translated and Accompanied by the Verona Latin Fragments. Translated by R. Hugh Connolly. London: Oxford University Press, 1929.

Dio Cassius. *Roman History*. 9 vols. Translated by Earnest Cary and Herbert B. Foster. LCL 32, 37, 53, 66, 82–83, 175–77. Cambridge, MA: Harvard University Press, 1914–1927.

Dix, Gregory, and Henry Chadwick. *The Treatise on the Apostolic Tradition of St. Hippolytus of Rome*. 1937; repr., London: Alban, 1992.

Dodaro, Robert. *Christ and the Just Society in the Thought of Augustine*. Cambridge: Cambridge University Press, 2004.

Dodds, E. R. *Pagan and Christian in an Age of Anxiety*. Cambridge: Cambridge University Press, 1968.

———. *Letters (1–81)*. Translated by Rose Bernard Donna. Fathers of the Church 51. Washington, DC: Catholic University of America Press, 1964.

Doran, Robert. *Stewards of the Poor: The Man of God, Rabbula, and Hiba in Fifth-Century Edessa*. CSS 208. Kalamazoo, MI: Cistercian, 2006.

Dörries, Hermann. *Constantine the Great*. Translated by Roland H. Bainton. New York: Harper Torchbooks, 1972.

Douglas, Mary. *Purity and Danger: An Analysis of Concepts of Pollution and Taboo*. New York: Routledge, 1966.

Droge, Arthur J., and James D. Tabor. *A Noble Death: Suicide and Martyrdom Among Christians and Jews in Antiquity*. San Francisco: Harper, 1991.

Dronke, Peter. *Women Writers of the Middle Ages: A Critical Study of Texts from Perpetua to Marguerite Porete*. Cambridge: Cambridge University Press, 1984.

Drosdek, Adam. *Greek Philosophers as Theologians: The Divine Arche*. Aldershot: Ashgate, 2007.

duBois, Page. *Sowing the Body: Psychoanalysis and Ancient Representations of Women.* Chicago: University of Chicago Press, 1988.

Dunn, Geoffrey D. *Tertullian.* The Early Church Fathers. New York: Routledge, 2004.

Early Christian Biographies. Edited and Translated by Roy J. Deferrari. Apostolic Fathers (Early Christian Collection) 15. Washington, DC: Catholic University of America Press, 1952.

Eder, Walter. "Augustus and the Power of Tradition." In *The Cambridge Companion to the Age of Augustus,* edited by Karl Galinsky, 13–32. Cambridge: Cambridge University Press, 2005.

Elliott, J. K. *The Apocryphal New Testament: A Collection of Apocryphal Christian Literature in an English Translation.* Oxford: Clarendon, 1993.

Eppstein, John. *The Catholic Tradition of the Law of Nations.* London: Burns, Oates and Washbourne, 1936.

Epstein, Julia, and Kristina Straub, editors. *Body Guards: The Cultural Politics of Gender Ambiguity.* New York: Routledge, 1991.

Eric Osborn, *Tertullian: First Theologian of the West.* Cambridge: Cambridge University Press, 1997.

Eusebius. *The Church History of Eusebius.* Translated with prolegomena and notes by Arthur Cushman McGiffert. *Nicene and Post-Nicene Father of the Christian Church,* Series 2, vol. 1, edited by Phillip Schaff and Henry Wace. Grand Rapids, MI: Eerdmans, 1972.

———. *Die Chronik des Hieronymous.* Eusebius Werke 7. Die Griechischen christlichen Schriftstellar der ersten drei Jahrhunderte 47. Translated and edited by Rudolf Helm. Berlin: Akademie-Verlag, 1956.

———. *Ecclesiastical History.* Vol. 1: Books 1–5. Translated by Kirsopp Lake. LCL 153. Cambridge, MA: Harvard University Press, 1926.

———. *Ecclesiastical History.* Vol. 2: Books 6–10. Translated by J. E. L. Oulton. LCL 265. Cambridge, MA: Harvard University Press, 1932.

Evans, R. F. "On the Problem of Church and Empire in Tertullian's *Apologeticum.*" *Studia Patristica* 14 (1976) 21–36.

Ferguson, Everett. "Early Christian Martyrdom and Civil Disobedience." *Journal of Early Christian Studies* 1.1 (1993) 73–83.

———. "Love of Enemies and Nonretaliation in the Second Century." In *The Contentious Triangle: Church, State and University: A Festschrift in Honor of Professor George Huntson Williams,* edited by Rodney L. Petersen and Calvin Augustine Pater, 81–96. Kirksville, MO: Thomas Jefferson University Press, 1999.

———. "Spiritual Sacrifice in Early Christianity and its Environment." *Aufstieg und Niedergang der römischen Welt* 2.23.1, 1169–70, 1180, 1186. New York: de Gruyter, 1980.

Ferguson, John. *The Religions of the Roman Empire.* Aspects of Greek and Roman Life. Ithaca, NY: Cornell University Press, 1970.

Fields, Rona M. *Martyrdom: The Psychology, Theology, and Politics of Self-Sacrifice.* Westport, CT: Praeger, 2004.

Forell, George W. *History of Christian Ethics.* Vol 1. Minneapolis: Augsburg, 1979.

Fox, Robin Lane. *Pagans and Christians.* New York: Knopf, 1989.

Fredoille, Jean-Claude. *Tertullien et la conversion de la culture antique.* Collection des Études Augustiniennes, Série Antiquité 47. Paris: Institut des Études Augustiniennes, 1972.

Frend, W.H.C. *The Early Church*. Philadelphia: Fortress, 1982.

———. *Martyrdom and Persecution in the Early Church: A Study of a Conflict from the Maccabees to Donatus*. New York: New York University Press, 1967.

———. *The Rise of Christianity*. Philadelphia: Fortress, 1984.

Friesen, John. "War and Peace in the Patristic Age." In *Essays on War and Peace: Bible and Early Church*, edited by Willard M. Swartley, 130–54. Occasional Papers 9. Elkhart, IN: Institute of Mennonite Studies, 1986.

Gager, John G. *Kingdom and Community: The Social World of Early Christianity*. Upper Saddle River, NJ: Prentice Hall, 1976.

Galinsky, Karl, editor. *The Cambridge Companion to the Age of Augustus*. Cambridge: Cambridge University Press, 2005.

Gero, Stephen. "*Miles Gloriosus*: The Christian and Military Service According to Tertullian." *Church History* 39 (1970) 285–98.

Gilliver, Kate. "The Augustan Reform and the Structure of the Imperial Army." In *A Companion to the Roman Army*, edited by Paul Erdkamp, 183–200. Oxford: Blackwell, 2007.

Giordani, Igino. *The Social Message of the Early Church Fathers*. East Rutherford, NJ: St. Anthony Guild, 1944.

Girard, René. *Violence and the Sacred*. London: Continuum, 2005.

Gleason, Maud W. *Making Men: Sophists and Self-Presentation in Ancient Rome*. Princeton: Princeton University Press, 1995.

González, Justo L. "Athens and Jerusalem Revisited: Reason and Authority in Tertullian." *Church History* 43 (1974) 22

———. *Mañana: Christian Theology from a Hispanic Perspective*. Nashville: Abingdon, 1990.

Goodine, Elizabeth A., and Matthew W. Mitchell. "The Persuasiveness of a Woman: The Mistranslation and Misinterpretation of Eusebius' Historia Ecclesiastica 5.1.41." *Journal of Early Christian Studies* 13.1 (2005) 1–19.

Goodspeed, Edgar J. *A History of Early Christian Literature*. Chicago: University of Chicago Press, 1966.

———, editor. *Die ältesten Apologeten*. Göttingen: Vandenhoeck & Ruprecht, 1915.

Grant, Robert M. *The Apostolic Fathers: A New Translation and Commentary*. Vol. 1: *An Introduction*. Apostolic Fathers (Early Christian Collection) 1. New York: Nelson, 1964.

———. *Augustus to Constantine. The Thrust of the Christian Movement into the Roman World*. New York: Harper & Row, 1970.

———. *Early Christianity and Society. Seven Studies*. San Francisco: Harper & Row, 1977.

———. "Sacrifices and Oaths as Required of Early Christians." *Kyriakon: Festschrift Johannes Quasten*, edited by P. Granfield and J. Jungmann, 1:12–17. Münster: Aschendorff, 1970.

———. "War—Just, Holy, Unjust—in Hellenistic and Early Christian Thought." *Augustinianum* 20 (1980) 173–89.

Green, Joel B., editor. *Methods for Luke*. Cambridge: Cambridge University Press, 2010.

Greenslade, S. L. *Schism in the Early Church*. London: SCM, 1964.

Gruen, Erich S. "Augustus and the Making of the Principate." In *The Cambridge Companion to the Age of Augustus*, edited by Karl Galinsky, 33–51. Cambridge: Cambridge University Press, 2005.

Harakas, Stanley. "The N.C.C.B. Pastoral Letter, *The Challenge of Peace*: An Eastern Orthodox Response." In *Peace in a Nuclear Age: The Bishops' Pastoral Letter in Perspective*, edited by Charles J. Reid Jr., 251–72. Washington, DC: Catholic University of America Press, 1986.

———. "No Just War in the Fathers." In *Communion: Website of the Orthodox Peace Fellowship* (http://www.incommunion.org/2005/08/02/no-just-war-in-the-fathers/).

Harnack, Adolf von. *Die Mission und Ausbreitung des Christentums in den ersten drei Jahrhunderten.* 4 vols. Leipzig: Hinrichs, 1924.

———. *Geschichte der altchristlichen Literatur bis Eusebius.* 2nd ed. Vol. 2.2. Leipzig: J. C. Hinrichs, 1958.

———. *Militia Christi. The Christian Religion and the Military in the First Three Centuries.* Translated by David M. Gracie. Philadelphia: Fortress, 1981.

———. "Die Quellen der Berichte über das Regenwunder im Feldzuge Marc Aurel's gegen die Quaden." *Sitzungsberichte der Königlich Preussischen Akademie der Wissenschaften zu Berlin* 36 (1894) 835–82.

Hart, David Bentley. "The Mirror of the Infinite: Gregory of Nyssa on the *Vestigia Trinitatis.*" *Modern Theology* 18.4 (2002) 541–62.

Haughey, John H., SJ, editor. *The Faith that Does Justice.* New York: Paulist, 1977.

Hawley, Richard, and Barbara Levick, editors. *Women in Antiquity: New Assessments.* London: Routledge, 1995.

Heather, Peter, and John Matthews. *The Goths in the Fourth Century.* Translated Texts for Historians 11. Liverpool: Liverpool University Press, 1991.

Hedley, Douglas. *Sacrifice Imagined: Violence, Atonement, and the Sacred.* New York: Continuum, 2011.

Heine, Ronald E. *Origen: Commentary on the Gospel according to John, Books 13–32.* The Fathers of the Church 89. Washington, DC: Catholic University of America Press, 1993.

Heine, Susanne, and John Bowden, translators. *Women and Early Christianity: A Reappraisal.* Minneapolis: Augsburg, 1988.

Helgeland, John. "Christians and the Roman Army A.D. 173–337." *Church History* 43.2 (1974) 149–63, 200.

———. "Christians and the Roman Army from Marcus Aurelius to Constantine." In *Aufstieg und Niedergang der römischen Welt*, 2.23.1, 724–834. New York: de Gruyter, 1979.

———. "The Early Church and War: The Sociology of Idolatry." In *Peace in a Nuclear Age: The Bishops' Pastoral Letters in Perspective*, edited by Charles J. Reid Jr., 34–47. Washington: Catholic University of America Press, 1986.

———. "Roman Army Religion." In *Aufstieg und Niedergang der römischen Welt*, 2.16.2, 1470–1505. New York: de Gruyter, 1978.

Helgeland, John, Robert J. Daly, and J. Patout Burns. *Christians and the Military.* Philadelphia: Fortress, 1985.

Hengel, Martin. *Property and Riches in the Early Church.* Philadelphia: Fortress, 1974.

Hennecke, Edgar. *New Testament Apocrypha.* Edited by Wilhelm Schneemelcher. Translated by A. J. B. Higgins et al. Translation edited by R. M. Wilson. Philadelphia: Westminster, 1965.

Heyman, George. *The Power of Sacrifice: Roman and Christian Discourses in Conflict.* Washington, DC: Catholic University of America Press, 2007.

Hippolytus, Antipope. *On the Apostolic Tradition*. Edited and translated by Alistair Stewart-Sykes. Popular Patristics Series. Crestwood, NY: St. Vladimir's Seminary Press, 2001.

Historia Augusta. Translated by David Magie. 3 vols. LCL 139–40, 263. Cambridge, MA: Harvard University Press, 1921–1932.

Holmes, Michael W. *The Apostolic Fathers: Greek Texts and English Translations*. 3rd ed. Grand Rapids: Baker Academic, 2007.

Hornus, Jean-Michel. "L'Excommunication des militaires dans la discipline chrétienne." *Communio Viatorum* 3 (1961) 41–60.

———. *It Is Not Lawful for Me to Fight. Early Christian Attitudes Toward War Violence and the State*. Rev. ed. Translated by Alan Kreider and Oliver Coburn. Scottsdale, PA: Herald, 1980. First published as *Evangile et Labarum: Etude sur l'attitude du Christianisme primitif devant les problèmes de l'Etat, de la guerre et de la violence*. Geneva: Labor et Fides, nouvelle série théologique IX, 1960.

Huik, František M., *The Philanthropic Motive in Christianity. An Analysis of the Relation Between Theology and Social Service*. Oxford: Blackwell, 1938.

Hunter, David G. "The Christian Church and the Roman Army in the First Three Centuries." In *The Church's Peace Witness*, edited by Marlin E. Miller and Barbara Nelson Gingerich, 161–81. Grand Rapids: Eerdmans, 1994.

———. "A Decade of Research on Early Christians and Military Service." *Religious Studies Review* 18 (1992) 87–94.

Ingremeau, Christiane. *Lactance: Institutions Divines. Sources Chrétiennes* 509. Paris: Cerf, 2007.

Irenaeus. *Against the Heresies*. Edited and translated by Dominic J. Unger. Ancient Christian Writers 55. New York: Paulist, 1978.

———. *Proof of the Apostolic Preaching*. Edited and translated by Jospeh P. Smith. Ancient Christian Writers 16. New York: Paulist, 1952.

Jacob, R. "Le Martyre, épanouissement du sacerdoce des Chréiens, dans la littérature patristique jusqu' en 258." *Mélange de science religieuse* 24 (1967) 57–83, 153–72, 177–209.

Jefford, Clayton N. *The Apostolic Fathers and the New Testament*. Peabody, MA: Hendrickson, 2006.

Jenkins, Claude. "Documents: Origen on I Corinthians. II." *Journal of Theological Studies* 9 (1907–8) 366–69.

Johnson, James Turner. *The Quest for Peace: Three Moral Traditions in Western Culture and History*. Princeton: Princeton University Press, 1987.

Jones, Beth Felker. *Mark of His Wounds: Gender Politics and Bodily Resurrection*. Oxford: Oxford University Press, 2007.

Julius Africanus. *Les "Cestes" de Julius Africanus*. Edited and translated by Jean-René Vieillefond. Collection d'études d'histoire, de critique et de philologie 20. Paris: Didier, 1970.

Justin Martyr. *Dialogue with Trypho*. Translated by Thomas B. Falls. Revised and with a new introduction by Thomas P. Halton. Edited by Michael Slusser. Fathers of the Church 3. Washington, DC: Catholic University of America Press, 2003.

———. *The First and Second Apologies*. Edited and translated by Leslie W. Barnard. Ancient Christian Writers 56. New York: Paulist, 1997.

———. *Writings of Saint Justin Martyr*. Edited and translated by Thomas B. Falls. Fathers of the Church 6. Washington, DC: Catholic University of America Press, 1948.

Kaizer, Ted. "Religion in the Roman East." In *A Companion to Roman Religion*, edited by Jörg Rüpke, 446–56. Oxford: Blackwell, 2011.

Karpp, Heinrich. "Die Stellung der Alten Kirche zu Kriegsdienst und Krieg." *Evangelische Theologie* 17 (1957) 496–515.

Klingshirn, William E., and Mark Vessey. *The Limits of Ancient Christianity.* Ann Arbor: University of Michigan Press, 1999.

Kreider, Alan. "Military Service in the Church Orders." *Journal of Religious Ethics* 31 (2003) 415–42.

Krüger, Thomas. "'They Shall Beat Their Swords into Plowshares': A Vision of Peace Through Justice and Its Background in the Hebrew Bible." In *War and Peace in the Ancient World*, edited by Kurt A. Raaflaub, 161–71. Oxford: Blackwell, 2007.

Kyle, Donald G. *Spectacles of Death in Ancient Rome.* London: Routledge, 1998.

Lactantius. *De Mortibus Persecutorum.* Edited and translated by J. L. Creed. New York: Oxford University Press, 1984.

———. *Divine Institutes.* Translated with introduction and notes by Anthony Bowan and Peter Garnsey. Translated Texts for Historians 40. Liverpool: Liverpool University Press, 2003.

———. *The Divine Institutes, Books I–VII.* Translated by Mary Francis McDonald. Fathers of the Church 49. Washington, DC: Catholic University of America Press, 1964.

Laeuchli, Samuel. *Power and Sexuality: The Emergence of Canon Law at the Synod of Elvira.* Philadelphia: Temple University Press, 1972.

Laes, Christian. *Children in the Roman Empire: Outsiders Within.* Cambridge: Cambridge University Press, 2011.

Laiou, Angeliki. "The Just War of Eastern Christians and the Holy War of the Crusaders." In *The Ethics of War: Shared Problems in Different Traditions*, edited by Richard Sorabji and David Rodin, 30–43. Burlington, VT: Ashgate, 2006.

Leclercq, Henri. "Militarisme." In *Dictionnaire d'archéologie chrétienne et de liturgie*, vol. XI/1, edited by Fernand Cabrol and Henri Leclercq, 1107–81. Paris: Letouzey et Ané, 1933.

Lee, Gregory W. "Republics and Their Loves: Rereading *City of God* 19." *Modern Theology* 27:4 (2011) 553–81.

Lee, Umphrey. *The Historic Church and Modern Pacifism.* Nashville: Abingdon, 1993.

Leemans, Johan, Wendy Mayer, Pauline Allen, and Boudewijn Dehandschutter. *"Let us Die That we May Live": Greek Homilies on Christian Martyrs from Asia Minor, Palestine and Syria (c. AD 350—AD 450).* New York: Routledge, 2003.

Leemans, Johan, editor. *More than a Memory: The Discourse of Martyrdom and the Construction of Christian Identity in the History of Christianity.* Paris: Peeters, 2005.

Leithart, Peter J. *Defending Constantine: The Twilight of an Empire and the Dawn of Christendom.* Downers Grove, IL: InterVarsity, 2010.

Levene, David S. *Religion in Livy.* Leiden: Brill, 1993.

Levi, Primo. *Survival in Auschwitz: The Nazi Assault on Humanity.* New York: Touchstone, 1986.

Levine, Amy-Jill, and Maria Mayo Robbins, editors. *A Feminist Companion to Patristic Literature.* New York: T. & T. Clark, 2008.

Lieu, Judith M. "The 'Attraction of Women' in/to Early Judaism and Christianity: Gender and the Politics of Conversion." *Journal for the Study of the New Testament* 21.5 (1999) 5–22.

MacGregor, G. H. C. *The New Testament Basis of Pacifism*. London: J. Clarke, 1936.

Macquarrie, J., editor. *A Dictionary of Ethics*. London: SCM, 1967.

Maier, Paul L. *Eusebius: The Church History*. Grand Rapids: Kregel, 1999.

Markus, Robert. *The End of Ancient Christianity*. Cambridge: Cambridge University Press, 1990.

Marlantes, Karl. *What It Is Like to Go To War*. New York: Atlantic Monthly, 2011.

Marrin, Albert, editor. *War and the Christian Conscience: from Augustine to Martin Luther King, Jr.* Chicago: Regnery, 1971.

Marucchi, Orazio. *Christian Epigraphy: An Elementary Treatise*. Chicago: Ares, 1974.

McGuckin, John. "St. Basil's Guidance on War and Repentance." In *Communion: Website of the Orthodox Peace Fellowship* (http://www.incommunion.org/2006/02/19/st-basil-on-war-and-repentance/).

McMullen, Ramsay. *Christianizing the Roman Empire*. New Haven: Yale University Press, 1984.

Meeks, Wayne A. *The First Urban Christians. The Social World of the Apostle Paul*. New Haven: Yale University Press, 1983.

Meinking, Kristina Ann. "Anger Matters: Politics and Theology in the Fourth Century." PhD diss., University of Southern California, 2010.

Miles, Margaret R. *Carnal Knowing: Female Nakedness and Religious Meaning in the Christian West*. Eugene, OR: Wipf and Stock Publishers, 1989.

Millar, Fergus. "Paul of Samosata, Zenobia and Aurelian: The Church, Local Culture and Political Allegiances in Third-Century Syria." *Journal of Religious Studies* 61 (1971) 1–17.

———. *The Roman Near East, 31 BC–AD 336*. Cambridge, MA: Harvard University Press, 1993.

Miller, Marlin E., and Barbara Nelson Gingerich, editors. *The Church's Peace Witness*. Grand Rapids: Eerdmans, 1994.

Miller, Patricia Cox, editor. *Women in Early Christianity: Translations from Greek Texts*. Washington, DC: Catholic University of America Press, 2005.

Minn, H. R. "Tertullian and War—Voices from the Early Church." *Evangelical Quarterly* (1941) 202–213.

Minucius Felix. *Octavius*. Translated by Gerald H. Rendall. In *Apology; De Spectaculis; Octavius*, by Tertullian and Minucius Felix, translated by T. R. Glover and Gerald H. Rendall, 304–438. LCL 250. Cambridge, MA: Harvard University Press, 1931.

———. *Octavius*. In *Tertullian Apologetical Works and Minucius Felix Octavius*. Translated by Rudolph Arbesmann et al., 3–312. Fathers of the Church 10. Washington, DC: Catholic University of America Press, 1950.

Moffatt, James. "Aristotle and Tertullian." *Journal of Theological Studies* 17 (1916) 170–71.

———. "War." In *Dictionary of the Apostolic Church*, edited by J. Hastings, 2:646–73. Edinburgh: T. & T. Clark, 1915.

Musto, Ronald G. *The Catholic Peace Tradition*. Maryknoll, NY: Orbis, 1986.

Musurillo, Herbert, translator. *The Acts of the Christian Martyrs*. Oxford Early Christian Texts. Oxford: Clarendon, 1972.

Nabulsi, Karma. "Conceptions of Justice in War: From Grotius to Modern Times." In *The Ethics of War: Shared Problems in Different Traditions*, edited by Richard Sorabji and David Rodin, 44–60. Burlington, VT: Ashgate, 2006.

Nautin, Pierre. *Origène: sa vie et son oeuvre*. Paris: Beauchesne, 1977.

Nock, Arthur D. *Conversion: The Old and the New in Religion from Alexander the Great to Augustine of Hippo.* New York: Oxford University Press, 1965.

———. "The Roman Army and the Roman Religious Year." *Harvard Theological Review* 45 (1952) 187–252.

Norris, Frederick W. "Paul of Samosata: Procurator Decenarius." *Journal of Theological Studies* 35 (1984) 50–70.

Oden, Amy, editor. *In Her Words: Women's Writings in the History of Christian Thought.* Nashville: Abingdon, 1994.

O'Donovan, Oliver. "The Political Thought of *City of God* 19." In *Bonds of Imperfection: Christian Politics, Past and Present,* edited by Oliver O'Donovan and Joan Lockwood O'Donovan 48–72. Grand Rapids: Eerdmans, 2004.

O'Donovan, Oliver, and Joan Lockwood O'Donovan, editors. *From Irenaeus to Grotius: A Sourcebook in Christian Political Thought.* Grand Rapids: Eerdmans, 1999.

Oliver, James H. *Morals and Law in Ancient Greece.* Baltimore: John Hopkins Press, 1960.

Origen. *Contra Celsum.* Translated by Henry Chadwick. Cambridge: Cambridge University Press, 1953.

———. *Contre Celse.* 5 vols. Edited and translated by Marcel Borret. Sources chrétiennes 227. Paris: Cerf, 1967–1976.

———. *Homilies on Joshua.* Translated by Barbara J. Bruce. Edited by Cynthia White. Fathers of the Church 105. Washington, DC: Catholic University of America Press, 2002.

———. *Homilies on Leviticus: 1–16.* Translated by Gary Wayne Barkley. Fathers of the Church 83. Washington, DC: Catholic University of America Press, 1990.

Orton, David E., and R. Dean Anderson, editors. *Handbook of Literary Rhetoric: A Foundation for Literary Study.* Leiden: Brill, 1998.

Osborn, Eric. *Tertullian: First Theologian of the West.* Cambridge: Cambridge University, 1997.

Osiek, Carolyn, and Margaret Y. MacDonald, with Janet H Tulloch. *A Women's Place: House Churches in Earliest Christianity.* Minneapolis: Fortress, 2006.

Oulton, John Ernest Leonard, and Henry Chadwick, editors and translators. *Alexandrian Christianity: Selected Translations of Clement and Origen.* Library of Christian Classics 2. Philadelphia: Westminster, 1954.

Parvis, Sara. "Perpetua." *Expository Times* 120.8 (2009) 365–72.

Patterson, L. G. *Methodius of Olympus: Divine Sovereignty, Human Freedom, and Life in Christ.* Washington, DC: Catholic University of America Press, 1997.

Payne, Keith B., and Karl I. Payne. *A Just Defense: The Use of Force, Nuclear Weapons, and Our Conscience.* Portland: Multnomah, 1987.

Pellegrino, M. "L'Imitation du Christ dans les Acts des martyrs." *La Vie spirituelle* 98 (1958) 38–54.

Penner, Todd, and Caroline Vander Stichele. *Mapping Gender in Ancient Religious Discourses.* Boston: Brill, 2007.

Perkins, Judith. *The Suffering Self: Pain and Narrative Representation in the Early Christian Era.* London: Routledge, 1995.

Pettersen, Alvyn. "Perpetua: Prisoner of Conscience." *Vigiliae Christianae* 41.2 (1987) 139–53.

Pirri-Simonian, Teny. "Prophetesses, Martyrs, Saints—Roles of Women in the Church Through the Ages." *The Ecumenical Review* 60 (2008) 59–70.

Potter, David S. *The Roman Empire at Bay: AD 180–395.* London and New York: Routledge, 2004.

Quasten, Johannes. *Patrology*. Vol. 2: *The Ante-Nicene Literature after Irenaeus*. Utrecht: Spectrum, 1953.

Raaflaub, Kurt A., editor. *War and Peace in the Ancient World*. Oxford: Blackwell, 2007.

Rahner, Hugo. *Church and State in Early Christianity*. Translated by Leo Donald Davis, SJ. San Francisco: Ignatius, 1992.

Rankin, David. *Athenagoras: Philosopher and Theologian*. Burlington, VT: Ashgate, 2009.

———. *Tertullian and the Church*. Cambridge: Cambridge University Press, 1995.

Reid Jr., Charles J., editor. *Peace in a Nuclear Age: The Bishops' Pastoral Letter in Perspective*. Washington, DC: The Catholic University of America Press, 1986.

Riddle, Donald W. *The Martyrs: A Study in Social Control*. Chicago: University of Chicago Press, 1931

Robinson, Thomas A. *Ignatius of Antioch and the Parting of the Ways: Early Jewish-Christian Relations*. Peabody, MA: Hendrickson, 2009.

Rosenstein, Nathan. "War and Peace, Fear and Reconciliation at Rome." In *War and Peace in the Ancient World*, edited by Kurt A. Raaflaub, 226–44. Oxford: Blackwell, 2007.

Rousseau, Jean-Jacques. *Principes du Droit de la Guerre*. Oeuvres Complètes 3. Paris: Gallimard, Bibliothèque de la Pléiade, 1964 and 1985.

Ruether, Rosemary Radford, editor. *Religion and Sexism: Images of Women in the Jewish and Christian Traditions*. New York: Simon and Schuster, 1974.

Ruether, Rosemary Radford, and Eleanor McLaughlin. *Women of Spirit: Female Leadership in the Jewish and Christian Traditions*. New York: Simon and Shuster, 1979.

Russell, Frederick H. *The Just War in the Middle Ages*. Cambridge: Cambridge University Press, 1975.

Ruyter, Knut Willem. "Pacifism and Military Service in the Early Church." *Cross Currents* 32 (1982) 54–70.

Ryan, Edward A., SJ. "The Rejection of Military Service by the Early Christians." *Theological Studies* 13.1 (1952) 1–32.

Salisbury, Joyce E. *Perpetua's Passion: The Death and Memory of a Young Roman Woman*. New York: Routledge, 1997.

Sawyer, Deborah F. "Gender Strategies in Antiquity: Judith's Performance." *Feminist Theology* 28 (2001) 9–26.

Scarry, Elaine. *The Body in Pain: The Making and Unmaking of the World*. Oxford: Oxford University Press, 1985.

Scheid, John. "Augustus and Roman Religion: Continuity, Conservatism, and Innovation." In *The Cambridge Companion to the Age of Augustus*, edited by Karl Galinsky, 175–93. Cambridge: Cambridge University Press, 2005.

Schmidt, Thomas E., and Moises Silva, editors. *To Tell the Mystery: Essays on New Testament Eschatology in Honor of Robert H. Gundry*. Journal for the Study of the New Testament Supplement Series 100. Sheffield: JSOT Press, 1994.

Schott, Jeremy M. *Christianity, Empire, and the Making of Religion in Late Antiquity*. Philadelphia, University of Pennsylvania Press, 2008.

Schüssler Fiorenza, Elisabeth. *In Memory of Her: A Feminist Theological Reconstruction of Christian Origins*. New York: Crossroad, 1990.

Scott, James C. *Domination and the Arts of Resistance: Hidden Transcripts*. New Haven: Yale University Press, 1990.

Scott, Joan Wallach. *Gender and the Politics of History*. New York: Columbia University Press, 1999.

Scullard, H. H. *Festivals and Ceremonies of the Roman Republic*. Aspects of Greek and Roman Life. Ithaca, NY: Cornell University Press, 1981.

Secrétan, H. F. "Le Christianisme des premiers siècles et le service militaire." *Revue de Théologie et de Philosophie* 2 (1914) 345–65.

Segal, J. B. *Edessa: "The Blessed City."* Oxford: Clarendon, 1970.

Seston, W. "Constantine as 'Bishop." *Journal of Roman Studies* 37 (1947) 127–31.

Shaw, Brent D. "Body/Power/Identity: Passions of the Martyrs." *Journal of Early Christian Studies* 4.3 (1996) 269–312.

———. "The Passion of Perpetua." *Past & Present* 139 (1993) 3–45.

Sheils, W.J. and Diana Wood, eds. *Women in the Church: Papers Read at the 1989 Summer Meeting and the 1990 Winter meeting of the Ecclesiastical History Society.* Oxford: Blackwell, 1990.

Shelton, Jo-Ann. *As the Romans Did: A Sourcebook in Roman Social History.* Oxford: Oxford University Press, 1998.

Shelton, W. Brian. *Martyrdom from Exegesis in Hippolytus: An Early Church Presbyter's Commentary on Daniel. Studies in Christian History and Thought.* Milton Keynes: Paternoster, 2008.

Sherwin-White, A. N. *The Roman Citizenship.* Oxford: Clarendon, 1973.

Shewring, Walter. *Rich and Poor in Christian Tradition.* London: Burnes, Oates & Washbourne, 1948.

Sider, Robert D. *Ancient Rhetoric and the Art of Tertullian.* Oxford: Oxford University Press, 1971.

———. "Credo Quia Absurdum?" *Classical Studies* 73 (1980) 417–19.

Simmons, Michael Bland. *Arnobius of Sicca: Religious Conflict and Competition in the Age of Diocletian.* Oxford Early Christian Studies. Oxford: Clarendon, 1995.

Soskice, Janet Martin. *The Kindness of God.* Oxford: Oxford University Press, 2007.

———. *Metaphor and Religious Language.* Oxford: Clarendon, 1985.

Spanneut, Michel. "La non-violence chez les Pères africains avant Constantin." In *Kyriakon: Festschrift Johannes Quasten,* edited by P. Granfield and J. A. Jungmann, 1:36–39. Münster: Aschendorff, 1970

Stark, Rodney. *The Rise of Christianity.* Princeton, NJ: Princeton University Press, 1996.

Stoll, Oliver. "The Religion of the Armies." In *A Companion to the Roman Army,* edited by Paul Erdkamp, 451–76. Oxford: Blackwell, 2007.

Streete, Gail P. C. *Redeemed Bodies: Women Martyrs in Early Christianity.* Louisville, KY: Westminster John Knox, 2009.

Suetonius. *Lives of the Twelve Caesars.* Online: http://ancienthistory.about.com/od/emperors/ig/12-Caesars/.

Sullivan, Lisa M. "'I Responded. "I Will Not…"': Christianity as Catalyst for Resistance in the *Passio Perpetuae et Felicitatis.*" *Semeia* 79 (1997) 63–74.

Swartley, Willard M., editor. *Essays on War and Peace: Bible and Early Church.* Occasional Papers 9. Elkhart: Institute of Mennonite Studies, 1986.

Swift, Louis J. "Augustine on War and Killing: Another View." *Harvard Theological Review* 66 (1973) 339–83.

———. "Early Christian Views on Violence, War, and Peace." In *War and Peace in the Ancient World,* edited by Kurt A. Raaflaub, 279–98. Oxford: Blackwell, 2007.

———. *The Early Fathers on War and Military Service.* Message of the Fathers of the Church 19. Wilmington, DE: Michael Glazier, 1983.

———. "Search the Scriptures: Patristic Exegesis and the *Ius Belli.*" In *Peace in a Nuclear Age: The Bishops' Pastoral Letter in Perspective,* edited by Charles J. Reid Jr., 48–68. Washington, DC: Catholic University of America Press, 1986.

————. "St. Ambrose on Violence and War." *Transactions and Proceedings of the American Philological Association* 101 (1970) 533–43.

————. "War and the Christian Conscience I: The Early Years." *Aufstieg und Niedergang der römischen Welt* 2.23.1, 835–68. New York: de Gruyter, 1979.

Tabbernee, William. *Montanist Inscriptions and Testimonia: Epigraphic Sources Illustrating the History of Montanism.* North American Patristic Society Monograph Series 16. Macon, GA: Mercer University Press, 1997.

————. *Prophets and Gravestones: An Imaginative History of Montanists and Other Early Christians.* Grand Rapids: Baker Academic, 2009

Tatian. *Oratio ad Graecos and Fragments.* Edited and translated by Molly Whittaker. Oxford: Clarendon, 1982.

Tertullian. *Adversus Marcionem.* Edited and translated by Ernest Evans. Oxford Early Christian Texts. Oxford: Clarendon, 1972.

————. *Apologetical Works.* In *Tertullian Apologetical Works and Minucius Felix Octavius.* Translated by Rudolph Arbesmann, Sister Emily Joseph Daly, and Edwin A. Quain, 3–312. Fathers of the Church 10. Washington, DC: Catholic University of America Press, 1950.

————. *Apologeticum.* In *Corpus Christianorum*, series Latina, 1:77–171. Turnholt, 1954.

————. *Apology.* Translated by T. R. Glover. In *Apology; De Spectaculis; Octavius,* by Tertullian and Minucius Felix, translated by T. R. Glover and Gerald H. Rendall, 2–229. LCL 250. Cambridge, MA: Harvard University Press, 1931.

————. *Christian and Pagan in the Roman Empire: The Witness of Tertullian.* Edited and translated by Robert D. Sider. Selections from Fathers of the Church 2. Washington, DC: Catholic University of America Press, 2001.

————. *De Idololatria.* In *Corpus Christianorum*, series Latina, 2:1101–24. Turnholt, 1954.

————. *De Idololatria.* Edited and translated by J. H. Waszink and J. C. M. van Winden. Supplements to Vigiliae Christianae 1. Leiden: Brill, 1987.

————. *De Spectaculis.* Translated by T. R. Glover. In *Apology; De Spectaculis; Octavius,* by Tertullian and Minucius Felix, translated by T. R. Glover and Gerald H. Rendall, 230–302. LCL 250. Cambridge, MA: Harvard University Press, 1931.

————. *Disciplinary, Moral and Ascetical Works.* Translated by Rudolph Arbesmann et al. Fathers of the Church 40. Washington, DC: Catholic University of America Press, 1959.

Thee, Francis C. R. *Julius Africanus and the Early Christian View of Magic.* Tübingen: Mohr, 1984.

Theodoret of Cyrrhus. *Thérapeutique des maladies helléniques.* Edited and translated by R. P. Canivet. Sources chrétiennes 57. Paris: Cerf, 1958

Trevett, Christine. *Christian Women and the Time of the Apostolic Fathers (AD c. 80–160) Corinth, Rome and Asia Minor.* Cardiff: University of Wales Press, 2006.

Trigg, Joseph W. *Origen.* The Early Church Fathers. London: Routledge, 1998.

————. Review of J. Helgeland, *Christians and the Roman Army from Marcus Aurelius to Constantine. Church History* 50.2 (1981) 205–6.

Tripolitis, Antonia. *Origen: A Critical Reading.* New York: Lang, 1985.

Tritle, Lawrence A. "'Laughing for Joy': War and Peace Among the Greeks." In *War and Peace in the Ancient World,* edited by Kurt A. Raaflaub, 172–90. Oxford: Blackwell, 2007.

Troeltsch, E. *The Social Teaching of the Christian Churches.* Vol. 1. Chicago: University of Chicago Press, 1981.

Van Henten, Jan Willem, and Friedrich Avemarie. *Martyrdom and Noble Death: Selected Texts from Graeco-Roman, Jewish, and Christian Antiquity.* New York: Routledge, 2002.

Volk, Katharina. *Manilius and His Intellectual Background.* Oxford: Oxford University Press, 2009.

Vööbus, Arthur. *The Didascalia apostolorum in Syriac.* 2 vols. Louvain: Secrétariat du Corpus SCO, 1979.

Walker, Andrew, Luke Bretherton, and Richard Chartres. *Remembering Our Future: Explorations in Deep Church Deep Church.* London: Paternoster, 2007.

Walsh, W. J., and Langan, J. P. "Patristic Social Consciousness—The Church and the Poor." In *The Faith That Does Justice: Examining the Christian Sources for Social Change,* edited by John C. Haughey, 113–51. New York: Paulist, 1977.

Watson, G. R. *The Roman Soldier.* Ithaca, NY: Cornell University Press, 1969.

Weigel, George. *Tranquilitas Ordinis: The Present Failure and Future Promise of American Catholic Thought on War and Peace.* Oxford: Oxford University Press, 1987.

Weinrich, J. C. *Spirit and Martyrdom: A Study of the Work of the Holy Spirit in Contexts of Persecution and Martyrdom in the New Testament and Early Christian Literature.* Washington, DC: University Press of America, 1981.

Wilcox, Amanda. "Exemplary Grief: Gender and Virtue in Seneca's Consolations to Women." *Helios* 33.1 (2006) 73–100.

Wiles, Maurice, and Mark Santer, editors. *Documents in Early Christian Thought.* Cambridge: Cambridge University Press, 1975.

Wilken, Robert Louis. *The Christians as the Romans Saw Them.* 2nd ed. New York: Yale University Press, 2003.

———. "The Jews and Christian Apologetics After Theodosius I *Cunctos Populos.*" *Harvard Theological Review* 73, no. 3/4 (1980), 451–71.

———. *The Spirit of Early Christian Thought: Seeking the Face of God.* New York: Yale University Press, 2005.

Williams, Rowan. *Why Study the Past? The Quest for the Historical Church.* Grand Rapids: Eerdmans, 2005.

Wimbush, Vincent L., and Richard Valantasis, editors. *Asceticism.* Oxford: Oxford University Press, 1995.

Windass, G. S. "The Early Christian Attitude Toward War." *Irish Theological Quarterly* 24.3 (1962) 235–48.

Wright, Donald F. "War in a Church-Historical Perspective." *Ecangelical Quarterly* 57.2 (1985) 133–61.

Yoder, John Howard. "*The Challenge of Peace:* A Historic Peace Church Perspective." In *Peace in a Nuclear Age: The Bishops' Pastoral Letter in Pespective,* edited by Charles J. Reid Jr., 273–90. Washington, DC: The Catholic University of America Press, 1986.

———. *Christian Attitudes to War, Peace, and Revolution.* Edited by Theodore J. Koontz and Andy Alexis-Baker. Grand Rapids: Brazos, 2009.

———. *The Politics of Jesus.* Grand Rapids: Eerdmans, 1972.

———. *The War of the Lamb.* Grand Rapids: Brazos, 2009;

Young, Frances. "The Early Church: Military Service, War and Peace." *Theology* 92 (1989) 491–503.

Zuckerman, Constantine. "Two Reforms of the 370s: Recruiting Soldiers and Senators in the Divided Empire." *Revue des Études Byzantines* 56 (1998) 79–139.

Subject Index

Scripture Index